STRUGGLES AND SUCCESSES IN THE PURSUIT OF SUSTAINABLE DEVELOPMENT

The challenges associated with the struggles for attaining the Sustainable Development Goals (SDGs) and objectives are as diverse and complex as the variety of human societies, national conditions and natural ecosystems worldwide. Despite decades of economic growth and technological advances, our world is plagued by poverty, hunger, disease, conflicts and inequality, and many societies are under the strain of environmental changes and governance failure.

Such global-scale challenges call for the SDGs to be translated beyond bold concepts and aspirational targets into concrete programs and feasible plans that are substantively valuable, locally acceptable, pragmatic and operationally implementable. In the pursuit of the SDGs, positive results are far from guaranteed. Success is uncertain. Instead, the path forward requires difficult learning, experimentation and adaptation by multiple stakeholders. Loss and sacrifice are foreseeable and often inevitable.

This important book captures the lessons from ongoing struggles and the early successes. Productive failures and emerging practices are identified, analyzed and promulgated for interdisciplinary learning by, and for the inspiration of, like-minded individuals, organizations, communities and nations worldwide. They can also inform and enrich the curricula in universities, training institutions and schools to prepare future generations of citizens, leaders and activists with the ethos and values of sustainability and social responsibility. The book offers a platform for academics, practitioners and concerned global citizens to identify pathways forward on the immense challenges of sustainability.

Tay Keong Tan is Director of International Studies and Leadership Studies and an associate professor in the Department of Political Science at Radford University, Virginia, USA.

Milenko Gudić is Founding Director of Refoment Consulting and Coaching, Belgrade, Serbia, and a visiting lecturer at University of Donja Gorica, Montenegro.

Patricia M. Flynn is Trustee Professor of Economics and Management at Bentley University, Massachusetts, USA, where she served as Dean of the McCallum Graduate School of Business for ten years.

Principles for Responsible Management series

Editors:
Milenko Gudić, Carole Parkes, Patricia Flynn,
Kemi Ogunyemi, Amy Verbos

Since the inception of the UN-supported Principles for Responsible Management Education (PRME) in 2007, there has been increased debate over how to adapt management education to best meet the demands of the 21st-century business environment. While consensus has been reached by the majority of globally focused management education institutions that sustainability must be incorporated into management education curricula, the relevant question is no longer why management education should change, but how.

Volumes within the Routledge/PRME book series aim to cultivate and inspire actively engaged participants by offering practical examples and case studies to support the implementation of the Six Principles of Responsible Management Education. Books in the series aim to enable participants to transition from a global learning community to an action community.

Books in the series:

Inspirational Guide for the Implementation of PRME
Learning to Go Beyond, 2nd Edition
Edited by Alan Murray, Denise Baden, Paul Cashian, Alec Wersun and Kathryn Haynes

Learning to Read the Signs
Reclaiming Pragmatism for the Practice of Sustainable Management, 2nd Edition
F. Byron (Ron) Nahser

Inspirational Guide for the Implementation of PRME
Placing Sustainability at the Heart of Management Education
Edited by the Principles for Responsible Management Education

Global Champions of Sustainable Development
Edited by Patricia M. Flynn, Milenko Gudić and Tay Keong Tan

Unmasking Irresponsible Leadership
Curriculum Development in 21st Century Management Education
Lola-Peach Martins and Maria Lazzarin

Struggles and Successes in the Pursuit of Sustainable Development
Edited by Tay Keong Tan, Milenko Gudić and Patricia M. Flynn

For more information about this series, please visit: https://www.routledge.com/ The-Principles-for-Responsible-Management-Education-Series/book-series/PRME

STRUGGLES AND SUCCESSES IN THE PURSUIT OF SUSTAINABLE DEVELOPMENT

Edited by
Tay Keong Tan, Milenko Gudić
and Patricia M. Flynn

Routledge
Taylor & Francis Group

LONDON AND NEW YORK

First published 2020
by Routledge
2 Park Square, Milton Park, Abingdon, Oxon OX14 4RN

and by Routledge
52 Vanderbilt Avenue, New York, NY 10017

Routledge is an imprint of the Taylor & Francis Group, an informa business

British Library Cataloguing-in-Publication Data
A catalogue record for this book is available from the British Library

Library of Congress Cataloging-in-Publication Data
Names: Tan, Tay Keong, editor. | Gudić, Milenko, editor. | Flynn, Patricia
   M., editor.
Title: Struggles and successes in the pursuit of sustainable development /
   edited by Tay Keong Tan, Milenko Gúdić, and Patricia M. Flynn.
Description: First Edition. | New York : Routledge, 2020. | Series:
   The principles for responsible management education series |
   Includes bibliographical references and index.
Identifiers: LCCN 2020001159 (print) | LCCN 2020001160 (ebook) |
   ISBN 9780815351764 (hardback) | ISBN 9780815351757 (paperback) |
   ISBN 9781351140560 (ebook)
Subjects: LCSH: Sustainable development. | Economic policy—Social aspects. |
   Women—Employment. | Equality. | Environmental sciences.
Classification: LCC HC79.E5 S777 2020 (print) | LCC HC79.E5 (ebook) |
   DDC 338.9/27—dc23
LC record available at https://lccn.loc.gov/2020001159
LC ebook record available at https://lccn.loc.gov/2020001160

ISBN: 978-0-8153-5176-4 (hbk)
ISBN: 978-0-8153-5175-7 (pbk)
ISBN: 978-1-351-14056-0 (ebk)

Typeset in Bembo
by Apex CoVantage, LLC

CONTENTS

CONTRIBUTORS

Editors' bios

Tay Keong Tan is Director of International Studies and Leadership Studies and an associate professor in the Department of Political Science at Radford University, Virginia, USA. His research interests are on sustainable development and anti-corruption. He headed public and nonprofit organizations in Singapore, Israel and the United States and has worked in development projects in more than 15 countries for the United Nations, United States Agency for International Development, World Bank and Asian Development Bank. He is a member of the PRME Working Groups on Sustainable Mindset, Anti-Poverty and Anti-Corruption. He has a master's degree and a doctoral degree in public policy from Harvard University. ttan2@radford.edu

Milenko Gudić is Founding Director of Refoment Consulting and Coaching, Belgrade, Serbia, and visiting lecturer at University of Donja Gorica, Montenegro. He has worked as a consultant, researcher and lecturer at the Economics Institute, Belgrade, as a visiting lecturer in several countries and as a speaker in over 30 countries. He has been engaged as a consultant to OECD, UNDP, and UNIDO on various entrepreneurship, regional, rural and public management development projects. Milenko was Founding and Managing Director (2000–2014) of the International Management Teachers Academy (IMTA) while also leading CEEMAN's major international research and educational leadership capacity building projects. He was program chair of EURAM 2008. Since 2008 he has been coordinating the UN Global Compact Working Group on Poverty: A Challenge for Management Education. In 2017, he received a PRME Pioneer Award for "Thought Leadership – Translating PRME into Action". milenko.gudic@gmail.com

Patricia M. Flynn, PhD, is Trustee Professor of Economics and Management at Bentley University, Massachusetts, USA, where she served as Dean of the McCallum Graduate School of Business for ten years. She has served on numerous corporate, mutual fund and nonprofit boards and testified before the US Congress on the impacts of technological change on jobs and workers. Since 2011, Pat has served as co-facilitator of the UN Global Compact PRME Working Group on Gender Equality and has written extensively on gender issues in business schools, corporate boardrooms and executive suites. In 2016, she became the inaugural recipient of the Patricia M. Flynn Distinguished Women Leader in Business Education Award, now given annually by the Women Administrators in Management Education at AACSB-International. In 2017, Pat received a PRME Pioneer Award for "Thought Leadership – Translating PRME into Action".
pflynn@bentley.edu

Contributors' bios

Brahim Allali holds a PhD in administration from HEC Montréal where he taught from 2004 to 2015. He also worked in manufacturing, banking and service businesses and taught in many institutions in Morocco and abroad. Allali is a recognized international business consultant and international development trainer with many national and international organizations. He is the author of five books and dozens of reports and scientific and professional articles on topics related to international development, entrepreneurship and strategic management.
ballali@esca.ma

Sonia Arsi is an assistant professor in finance at Carthage Business School at the University Tunis Carthage, Tunisia. She holds a PhD from the Institute of Higher Business Studies of Carthage (IHEC Carthage). She has been teaching topics of treasury management, international finance, derivative securities, asset pricing and corporate finance. Her current research activities comprise behavioral finance, international finance, commodities and derivatives.
sonia.arsi@msn.com

Brooke Blanks is an associate professor of special education in the School of Teacher Education and Leadership at Radford University. She teaches assessment and literacy methods courses in the Special Education Program Area and provides field-based coaching and supervision in collaborative teaching for pre-service and in-service teachers. Dr. Blanks' current work focuses on technology-enhanced professional development to address the needs of rural K–12 teachers. Dr. Blanks works as a consultant for rural school districts in Appalachia and across the United States to support teacher development for inclusive practices.
brooke.blanks@gmail.com

Jan Brace-Govan is an associate professor in the Monash Business School at Monash University, Melbourne, Australia. Drawing on critical marketing analyses, her research focuses on social justice, gender and alternatives to consumerism. Her research has appeared in journals such as the *Journal of Public Policy & Marketing*, *European Journal of Marketing*, *Marketing Theory*, *Journal of Consumer Culture*, the *Sociological Review* and the *Journal of Macromarketing*.
jan.brace-govan@monash.edu

Dominik Burger-Kloser is a senior project manager at the Research Institute for International Management at the University of St. Gallen (FIM-HSG). At the Competence Centre for Diversity & Inclusion of the FIM-HSG, he is responsible for quantitative research approaches. Dominik received a doctor of philosophy (PhD) degree in management and a master's degree in accounting and finance, both from the University of St. Gallen. He conducts research on upper echelons, gender and diversity management as well as small- and medium-sized enterprises (SMEs). His work has been published in the *Journal of Business Venturing*.
Dufourstrasse 40a, CH-9000 St. Gallen
dominik.burger@unisg.ch

Gabriela Cavagliá, PhD, is Project Manager of UNESCO Chair in Sustainable Development and Territory Management of Università di Torino (UniTo), where she leads the master's program in Social and Environmental Sustainability of Agro-Food Networks and the related research and societal outreach activities.
gabrielamaria.cavaglia@unito.it

Catherine A. Coleman (PhD, Institute of Communications Research, University of Illinois, Urbana-Champaign) is Associate Professor, Department of Strategic Communication, Bob Schieffer College of Communication at Texas Christian University, where she is also an affiliate member of the Women & Gender Studies program. Her research in advertising and consumer research focuses on representation (especially of gender and race), justice, ethics and vulnerability, consumer culture and global communication. Her research is published in the *Journal of Advertising*; *Consumption, Markets & Culture*; the *Journal of Public Policy & Marketing*; the *Journal of Popular Culture* as well as in other books and journals.
c.coleman@tcu.edu

Laura Corazza, PhD, is a postdoc research fellow at the Department of Management at the Università di Torino, Italy. She is the editor of the Sustainability Report of UniTo. Her teaching and research cover topics such as social accounting, corporate social responsibility and green business strategy. She also works in sustainability consulting for several private companies and NGOs.
laura.corazza@unito.it

Dario Cottafava is a PhD candidate in "Innovation for the Circular Economy" at the Università di Torino, Italy. He has a master's degree specializing in "Materials for

Energy and the Environment" and in "The Physics of Complex Systems." Actively engaged in environmental sustainability and passionate about the digital revolution, he is the cofounder of greenTO, a local Italian NGO that promotes sustainable development.
dario.cottafava@unito.it

Majid Kaissar el Ghaib is Professor and Head of the Social Innovation & Sustainability Institute at ESCA Ecole de Management. He is also President of Enactus Morocco, a nonprofit whose mission is to promote social progress through entrepreneurial action. Dr. El Ghaib holds a PhD from MIT and engineering degrees from France. He began his professional career as a consultant for large sustainable projects in the United States and Morocco. He then served as CEO of the Moroccan National Fisheries Office, implementing sustainable projects to modernize and develop the local fishing industry.
melghaib@esca.ma

Jalila El Jadidi holds a master's in business administration (MBA) and a master of sciences in human factors in information design (MS HFID) from Bentley University. She has more than 15 years of experience in higher education and the financial industry. Currently, she is working as a consultant with clients to optimize their business processes and leverage technology to better support their operations.
JELJADIDI@bentley.edu

Hebatallah Ghoneim is an economics lecturer at the German University in Cairo (GUC), Egypt. She has publications on poverty alleviation, foreign direct investment and ethical economics. Her research interests include the fields of economic development, international economics and labor economics.
hebatallah.ghoneim@guc.edu.eg

Margaret A. Goralski, PhD, Quinnipiac University, is a member of the UN PRME Working Group on Sustainability Mindset. She is Vice President of Publications for the International Academy of Business Disciplines and Editor-in-Chief of *Quarterly Review of Business Disciplines*. She is a board member and senior fellow of the American Society for Competitiveness and Chapter Chair of the Academy of International Business US Northeast. She has recently become an Albert Schweitzer fellow. Goralski has published in numerous academic journals worldwide on a variety of topics including, but not limited to, ethics of artificial intelligence, strategy vs. ethics, mindfulness and its pedagogical applications and competitiveness and sustainability.
margaret.goralski@quinnipiac.edu

Deanna Grant-Smith is a senior lecturer in the QUT Business School, Queensland University of Technology, Australia, and Deputy Director of the QUT Work/Industry Futures Research Program. An interdisciplinary researcher, she researches stakeholder engagement within sustainability and social justice contexts, the

regulation and management of heterotopic and ludic spaces and gender-sensitive infrastructure, planning and policy in a range of contexts.
deanna.grantsmith@qut.edu.au

A. D. Nuwan Gunarathne is a senior lecturer at the University of Sri Jayewardenepura, Sri Lanka. He is an associate member of the Chartered Institute of Management Accountants, UK, and of the Institute of Certified Management Accountants, Sri Lanka. He holds a bachelor's and master's degree in business administration from the University of Sri Jayewardenepura. Nuwan is also a committee member of the Environmental and Sustainability Management Accounting Network (EMAN) Asia Pacific (AP) and country representative of the Sri Lanka chapter of EMAN-AP.
nuwan@sjp.ac.lk

Robert L. Harrison (PhD, University of Nebraska-Lincoln) is Associate Professor of Marketing at Western Michigan University. His research focuses on advertising representations and the intersection of gender and family consumer behavior and public policy issues. His work is published in the *Journal of Consumer Psychology; Journal of Business Research; Journal of Advertising; Consumption, Markets & Culture*; among others.
robert.harrison@wmich.edu

Ines Hartmann is a senior project manager at the Research Institute for International Management at the University of St. Gallen (FIM-HSG). At the Competence Centre for Diversity & Inclusion of the FIM-HSG, she is mainly responsible for the St. Gallen Diversity Benchmarking. As a senior consultant at Sander & Sander GmbH, St. Gallen, she leads projects on inclusive leadership and diversity management. She teaches at different universities on diversity and inclusion and strategic management and writes publications on diversity management and inclusive organizational culture. Her doctoral thesis is about "Cultural diversity in hospitals – inclusion of employees of different ethnic backgrounds."
Dufourstrasse 40a, CH-9000 St. Gallen
ines.hartmann@unisg.ch

Wendy Hein (PhD, University of Edinburgh) is a lecturer in marketing at Birkbeck, University of London. Her research focuses on gender in marketing and consumer research, specifically critical approaches and methodologies in the study of gender equality, feminisms and men and masculinities. She has presented her work at various international conferences, and published chapters in various edited books and journals including *Qualitative Marketing Research: An International Journal*, the *Journal of Marketing Management* and the *Journal of Public Policy & Marketing*.
w.hein@bbk.ac.uk

Judith M. Herbst is a lecturer in the QUT Business School, Queensland University of Technology, Australia. An intercultural communication educator, she promotes the

integration of inclusive and culturally diverse principles and practices within work and study environments. Her research focuses on how organizations use systems to co-create value with stakeholders for sustainable development.
judith.herbst@qut.edu.au

Peter Jones is Emeritus Professor in the School of Business and Technology at the University of Gloucestershire in the United Kingdom. He has undertaken commercial and educational consultancy work in Norway, the Netherlands, Switzerland, Greece, Spain, India, Sri Lanka, Indonesia, China and Japan. His research interests are in sustainability and corporate social responsibility within the service sector; the introduction of information and communication technologies within retailing, pop-up retailing and hospitality ventures and urban planning within the United Kingdom.
pjones@glos.ac.uk

Nora Keller, PhD, is a postdoc research fellow and project manager at the Competence Centre for Diversity & Inclusion (CCDI), which is part of the Research Institute for International Management at the University of St. Gallen (FIM-HSG), Switzerland. At CCDI, she is responsible for qualitative research design and analysis. Nora received a PhD in political science from Columbia University. In her dissertation, she used insights from business scholarship to understand organizational development and strategic innovation in non-state organizations during civil wars.
Dufourstrasse 40a, CH-9000 St. Gallen
nora.keller@unisg.ch

Maureen A. Kilgour, PhD, is a professor in the Faculty of Business and Economics at the University of Winnipeg. She is a co-founder and co-chair of the PRME Working Group on Gender Equality and was a member of the UN Women's Empowerment Principles Leadership Group from 2011 to 2018. She researches global governance, business and human rights and corruption, with a special focus on gender equality and has co-edited three books: *Integrating Gender into Business and Management Education* (2015), *Overcoming Challenges to Gender Equality in the Workplace: Leadership and Innovation* (2016) and *Gender Equality and Responsible Business: Expanding CSR Horizons* (2016).
m.kilgour@uwinnipeg.ca

Glen T. Martin, PhD, is Professor of Philosophy and Chair Emeritus of the Peace Studies Program at Radford University in Virginia. He is President of the World Constitution and Parliament Association (WCPA), a worldwide organization that sponsors the *Constitution for the Federation of Earth*. He has received several international peace awards, including the GUSI Peace Prize International in 2013. He is the author of 11 books, including *Millennium Dawn* (2005) and his latest book *Global Democracy and Human Self-Transcendence: The Power of the Future for Planetary Transformation* (2018). WCPA websites include www.earth-constitution.org

and www.worldparliament-gov.org/. Martin's blog is found at www.oneworld renaissance.com.
gmartin@radford.edu

Hristina Mikić is a head of research in the Institute for Creative Entrepreneurship and Innovation in Serbia. She graduated from the Faculty of Economics, University of Belgrade, where she received her PhD in cultural economics. She is a consultant and member of advisory bodies in numerous national and international organizations in the area of economic development policy of culture and creative industries. These include United Nations Educational, Scientific and Cultural Organization; Council of Europe; United Nations Development Programme; United Nations; World Bank; Serbian Chamber of Commerce and many others. Her research interests include cultural and creative industries, female and ethnic creative entrepreneurship, interrelation of creative industries and tourism and public policies.
hristinamikic@gmail.com

Ijeoma Nwagwu is Centre Manager, Lagos Business School, Sustainability Centre. She earned her doctorate of juridical science (SJD) and master's in law (LLM) degrees from Harvard Law School. Ijeoma is a researcher, lecturer and writer; she currently teaches corporate social responsibility, sustainability, strategy and social entrepreneurship at Lagos Business School.
inwagwu@lbs.edu.ng

Nacima Ourahmoune (Doctor IAE d'Aix and ESSEC BS) is Associate Professor of Marketing and Consumer Culture at KEDGE Business School. As a former chair of Marketing, Consumption and Society research lab, Nacima's work interrogates how power issues influence the marketplace in various sociocultural contexts, shaping notions of body, sexuality, gender, social class or ethnicity. She has published in leading journals in her field and serves on the board of various organizations to foster transformative approaches.
Nacima.Ourahmoune@kedgebs.com

Mahendra Peiris is a professional planter, an applied researcher, an inventor and a trainer in the field of tea. He holds an honors degree in plantation crop management and a master's degree in biodiversity, ecotourism and environment management, both from the University of Peradeniya, Sri Lanka. Mahendra is the winner of the Presidential Green Award 2016 for the best sustainable farming model in Sri Lanka and also the winner of twin awards at Merrill J. Fernando Eco Innovation Awards 2016 for "Climate-smart breakthrough technologies," developed for the commercial tea industry. Currently, Mahendra is the Manager, Compliance & Project Management, at Maskeliya Plantations PLC, Sri Lanka.
suradinithp@gmail.com

Gudrun Sander, PhD, is Adjunct Professor of Business Administration with a special emphasis on diversity management at the University of St. Gallen, Switzerland. She is Director of the Competence Centre for Diversity & Inclusion (www.ccdi-unisg. ch) and Director of the Executive School of Management, Technology and Law (ES-HSG), where she is responsible for the executive education program "Women Back to Business." The focus of her research is on diversity issues around strategic management, inclusive leadership and change management in organizations. Gudrun is also a member of the Principles for Responsible Management Education (PRME) Working Group on Gender Equality.
Dufourstrasse 40a, CH-9000 St. Gallen
gudrun.sander@unisg.ch

Minita Sanghvi (PhD, University of North Carolina at Greensboro (UNGC)) is an assistant professor in the management and business department at Skidmore College, USA. Her research focuses on gender and intersectionality in political marketing and "consumptionscapes". Her dissertation, "Marketing the female president: An exploration of gender, appearance and power," won the 2014 Outstanding Dissertation Award at UNCG. Her research has been published in the *Journal of Marketing Management* and *Handbook of Research in Gender and Marketing*. Her book, titled, *Gender and Political Marketing in the United States and the 2016 Presidential Election: An Analysis of Why She Lost*, was published by Palgrave MacMillan in 2018.
msanghvi@skidmore.edu

Laurel Steinfield (DPhil, University of Oxford) is an assistant professor of marketing at Bentley University. Her research focuses on social stratifications, including gender, racial and Global North-South hierarchies. As a sociologist, transformative consumer researcher and marketing professor, she studies how social stratifications interact with marketplace dynamics and how resulting injustices may be transformed. She has published in numerous journals, including *Consumption, Markets & Culture*; the *Journal of Public Policy and Marketing*, as well as in various edited books.
lsteinfield@bentley.edu

Bianca van Dellen, MSc, obtained her master's degree in entrepreneurship major finance at the University of Liechtenstein. She has more than ten years of work experience as a business client consultant in the banking and consulting sector. She is now working toward her PhD in strategy & management at the University of St. Gallen. Bianca's PhD topic focuses on diversity in business. Bianca has also studied business education and management training at the University of St. Gallen. She works as a research assistant at the Institute for International Management (FIM-HSG), providing full support to projects of the Competence Centre for Diversity & Inclusion.
Dufourstrasse 40a, CH-9000 St. Gallen
bianca.vandellen@unisg.ch

Mario Vázquez-Maguirre holds a PhD (business) from EGADE Business School, Tecnológico de Monterrey, and an MSc (economics and public policy) from EGAP, Tecnológico de Monterrey. He is currently a professor of entrepreneurship, sustainability and corporate social responsibility (CSR) at Universidad de Monterrey (UDEM). His primary research interests include social entrepreneurship, indigenous social enterprises and sustainable development, humanistic management and CSR. He has worked in corporations such as Banco Bilbao Vizcaya Argentaria (BBVA) and United Parcel Service (UPS), and he has served as consultant to small and medium enterprises and non-governmental organizations.
mariovm@gmail.com

Patricia (Trish) Winter is an associate professor of music and the Director of the Music Therapy Program in the College of Visual and Performing Arts at Radford University. Dr. Winter has been a practicing music therapist for over 20 years and has served clients across the developmental continuum in both urban and rural settings. Her current clinical practice focuses on interprofessional collaboration with speech-language pathologists to address the needs of children who are 18 months through six years of age, with speech and language disorders.
pwinter3@radford.edu

Martin Wynn is Reader in Business Information Systems at the School of Business and Technology at the University of Gloucestershire in the United Kingdom. He has 20 years of industrial experience as an IT professional, including five years at GlaxoSmithKline and ten years as IT Director at HP Bulmer, now part of Heineken UK. He has supervised over 30 doctoral students and acted as a consultant for OECD and UNESCO, running training courses in India, Africa and many parts of Europe. His research interests include information system strategy, e-business, project management, sustainability and IT, cloud computing, technology transfer and urban planning.
mwynn@glos.ac.uk

Linda Tuncay Zayer (PhD, University of Illinois at Urbana-Champaign) is Professor of Marketing in the Quinlan School of Business at Loyola University Chicago. Her research interests include gender and identity, particularly from a transformative consumer research perspective. She has published in journals such as the *Journal of Consumer Research, Journal of Retailing, Journal of Advertising, Journal of Public Policy & Marketing*, among others and co-edited a book, *Gender, Culture and Consumer Behavior*, Routledge. Her research interests include gender and identity, particularly from a transformative consumer research perspective.
Ltuncay@luc.edu

INTRODUCTION

*Tay Keong Tan, Milenko Gudić
and Patricia M. Flynn*

Despite decades of economic growth and technological advances, our world is plagued by poverty, hunger, disease, conflicts and inequality, and many societies are under the strain of adverse environmental changes and governance failures. Emerging economies and developing countries are likely to face the greatest sustainable challenges; however, problems such as inequality, climate change, pollution, lack of adequate healthcare and threats to natural ecosystems present major challenges to developed countries as well.

On September 25, 2015, 193 United Nations (UN) member countries adopted the Sustainable Development Goals (SDGs) to guide the world's nations in eliminating the "global wicked problems" and in creating thriving cities and green economies. This ambitious global development agenda, with 17 Global Goals and 169 specific and measurable objectives, has a 15-year time frame ending in 2030.

The 17 SDGs are as follows:

1 Poverty – End poverty in all its forms everywhere
2 Food – End hunger, achieve food security and improved nutrition and promote sustainable agriculture
3 Health – Ensure healthy lives and promote well-being for all at all ages
4 Education – Ensure inclusive and equitable quality education and promote lifelong learning opportunities for all
5 Women – Achieve gender equality and empower all women and girls
6 Water – Ensure availability and sustainable management of water and sanitation for all
7 Energy – Ensure access to affordable, reliable, sustainable and clean energy for all
8 Economy – Promote sustained, inclusive and sustainable economic growth, full and productive employment and decent work for all

9 Infrastructure – Build resilient infrastructure, promote inclusive and sustainable industrialization and foster innovation
10 Inequality – Reduce inequality within and among countries
11 Habitation – Make cities and human settlements inclusive, safe, resilient and sustainable
12 Consumption – Ensure sustainable consumption and production patterns
13 Climate – Take urgent action to combat climate change and its impacts
14 Marine-ecosystems – Conserve and sustainably use the oceans, seas and marine resources for sustainable development
15 Ecosystems – Protect, restore and promote sustainable use of terrestrial ecosystems; sustainably manage forests; combat desertification and halt and reverse land degradation and halt biodiversity loss
16 Institution – Promote peaceful and inclusive societies for sustainable development, provide access to justice for all and build effective, accountable and inclusive institutions at all levels
17 Sustainability – Strengthen the means of implementation, and revitalize the global partnership for sustainable development

While some may argue, and understandably so, that these goals are too absolutist and unrealistic, many individuals and organizations across the globe have taken on the challenge and are creating and instituting a variety of sustainability programs to advance the objectives of the Global Goals. Some have overcome great odds to develop and implement programs and activities that embody solutions and best practices for sustainable development. Many have faced considerable challenges and barriers to generate the desired outcomes. In the face of setbacks and failure, rather than giving up, many have chosen to rethink, refocus and reshape their actions and return to resolve the problems afresh and achieve their objectives through other ways.

Struggles and Successes in Pursuit of Sustainable Development focuses on both the struggles and the successes of sustainable development initiatives in countries across the globe, initiated in response to the SDGs. It identifies specific practices and strategies that "make sustainability work" in different contexts around the world. It asks the questions: To what extent are businesses able to contribute to the accomplishment of the SDGs? How can governments and public agencies mobilize nations and communities to participate in the action plans emanating from the SDGs? What can international organizations and development agencies do to address these complex challenges on a global scale? And what can civic society groups and ordinary citizens do to contribute to this new global agenda?

The book also targets struggles that have impeded, but often not defeated, the individuals and organizations committed to a better world. The chapters offer a platform for practitioners, academics and concerned global citizens to identify pathways forward on the immense challenges of sustainability. It provides insights and solutions to others on the front lines of promoting sustainable development. It highlights program designs and laboratories of practice on "what works" and "what does not" in advancing the SDGs. Through these, it hopes to capture the lessons learned from those who are at the forefront of advancing the Global Goals.

This edited collection looks beyond bold concepts and aspirations to demonstrate concrete programs and feasible plans that are substantively valuable, locally acceptable and operationally implementable. Hence, the lessons from productive failures and early successes are precious nuggets that can be identified, analyzed and promulgated for interdisciplinary learning by, and for the inspiration of, individuals, organizations, communities and nations. Practitioners are encouraged to bring these important sustainability issues into the practice of their professions.

Academics are urged to incorporate the assessment of these struggles and successes into their management education courses and research to prepare future generations of citizens, leaders and activists with the ethics and values of sustainability and social responsibility. The book's editors, and several of the chapter authors, are actively involved in the UN Global Compact's PRME, the Principles for Responsible Management Education. PRME was initiated in 2007 under the auspices of Secretary General Ban Ki-moon to encourage business schools and universities worldwide to adopt practices that would advance corporate social responsibility (CSR) and a sustainable global economy. The current PRME community involves more than 800 business schools in around 90 countries.

This book is written for business practitioners, educators, public policy makers and civic leaders interested in strategies, theories, case studies and innovations related to sustainability and responsible management education. The authors of the chapters are practitioners, academics and activists from a wide range of disciplinary, organizational and global perspectives. The book is written by 35 individuals from 12 different countries across the globe.

Struggles and Successes in the Pursuit of Sustainable Development is the second volume in the Routledge/PRME two-book series on how nations and communities are addressing the global development agenda promulgated by the SDGs. The first book, *Global Champions of Sustainable Development,* published in January 2020, provides inspirational stories on how individuals and organizations in diverse social, economic and cultural contexts successfully championed the advancement of the SDGs.

Organization of the book

The book consists of 15 chapters plus the introduction and concluding remarks, organized in four main sections:

- The big picture
- Addressing SDGs at industry levels
- Gender equality, women's empowerment and social inclusion
- Programs and partnerships in developing countries

Part I: The big picture

The four chapters in this section address issues of sustainable development from a global perspective, and they discuss cross-cutting issues. They include changing the mindsets of people with respect to consumption and production, reducing unconscious bias in human resource practices, educating future leaders on sustainability through transformative learning and advocating for reforms in the global economic system and the behavior of the world's nation-states. These chapters analyze the struggles to win the hearts and minds of people and transform practices in our corporations, governments and societies.

In Chapter 1 ("Struggles and Successes of Transformative Learning for the SDGs: a Case Study"), authors Cottafava, Corazza, and Cavagliá discuss a successful pilot project in the University of Torino, Italy, that pioneered new pedagogical approaches. These use transdisciplinary and transformative learning to teach "education for sustainable development" skills such as envisioning, critical thinking and partnership building.

Goralski in the second chapter ("Using Our Time on the Planet to Make a Difference – the Sustainability Mindset") highlights the struggles and successes in the work life of Isabel Rimanoczy, the founder of LEAP! (Leverage resources, Expand awareness, Accelerate change and Partner) and the chair of the UN PRME Working Group on the Sustainability Mindset. Rimanoczy advocates a Sustainability Mindset Model, for personal reflection, decision-making and teaching.

In Chapter 3 on "Deep Sustainability," Martin discusses how a system of sovereign nation-states and a global economic system based on perpetual growth are fundamentally incompatible with the maintenance of a sustainable human civilization. Martin proposes ideas for our human society to regain "deep sustainability" in the midst of the current global crises.

The fourth chapter is on inclusive leadership. Sander, van Dellen, Hartmann, Burger-Klosen, and Keller discuss how unconscious biases shape personnel decisions in companies and organizations, and they propose ideas for human resource decision makers to recognize their own implicitly held biases and take steps to counteract them. Addressing unconscious biases can help organizations make progress toward more inclusive leadership and toward greater diversity and transparency.

Part II: Addressing SDGs at industry levels

The four chapters in this section present compelling case studies on how individuals, often working in partnership with others and in the context of local communities, bring entrepreneurial spirit and missionary zeal to bear in advancing the cause of global sustainability. Each case offers lessons on how the struggles of protagonists have brought about progress and successes in their industries.

Chapter 5 by Herbst and Grant-Smith presents a case study on Australia's Hepburn Wind project as a success story in the emerging community renewable energy industry. It is a grassroots initiative that effectively redresses the reticence and obstacles in adopting renewable energy and serves as an example to others seeking to advance the transition to low-carbon energy.

Gunarathne and Peiris's sixth chapter chronicles the trials and tribulations in the development of a community-driven sustainable waste management program in plantations in Sri Lanka. The case shows that, with the full participation and ownership of stakeholders at the grassroots level, communities can produce innovative waste management systems that can replace the wasteful and expensive traditional centralized forms of waste disposal.

In Chapter 7 on information and communication technology for development (ICT4D) research, Wynn and Jones analyze ICT as an enabler of widespread change across geography and national boundaries. The authors assess the different ways in which the ICT industry can help to advance the SDGs and discuss the emerging issues in the current research on ICT4D.

The eighth chapter, written by Mikić, is on creative industries in Pirot, Serbia. Mikić discusses the role of creative industries entrepreneurship as an engine for sustainable socioeconomic development in rural Serbia. The chapter also ties creative industries' contributions to the advancement of the SDGs and provides insights for implementing sustainability-sensitive projects in rural and less-developed areas.

Part III: Gender equality and women's empowerment

This section provides powerful case studies related to gender perspectives, women's rights and the broader issues of social inclusion embodied in SDG #5 (Gender equality and empowerment of women and girls) and in SDG #10 (Reduced inequalities). Each case demonstrates how entrenched discrimination, gender insensitivity and various forms of social exclusion can be rolled back with well-conceived social action and carefully formulated policies and practices.

In Chapter 9 ("Women's Empowerment through Indigenous Social Enterprises in Latin America"), Vázquez-Maguirre writes about three social enterprises involving indigenous rural communities in Mexico, Peru and Guatemala. Vázquez-Maguirre analyzes how the male-dominated culture and economic systems in these communities have prevented women's economic participation and community decision-making. The chapter demonstrates how empowerment mechanisms, such as access to job opportunities, gender equality practices and governance practices based on local values, can help reduce discrimination against indigenous women and advance their education, access to employment and community power.

In Chapter 10, El Jadidi, Arsi, and Ghoneim examine trends in gender equality and women's empowerment following the people-power movements of the Arab Spring. While several North African countries witnessed major political and social reforms in favor of gender equality, women's participation and empowerment in many areas of society are still lacking. The authors study the women on corporate boards in Egypt, Morocco and Tunisia to chronicle progress and shortfalls and to draw lessons on advancing gender equality in the boardroom.

Chapter 11 on the renaissance of gender equality research (by Zayer et al.) argues that while there is reluctance of business school academics to embrace gender equality in their work, gender research in the field of marketing is experiencing a "renaissance," driven by global, political and social movements of this time. The chapter advocates for continuing efforts in promoting gender sensitivity and a sustainability focus in the marketing field.

Kilgour (Chapter 12) elaborates on Canada's "feminist foreign policy" and its implications on global sustainability. The author discusses the Canadian government's formulation of "feminist" foreign policy in 2017 and the early successes and challenges in the policy's implementation. The chapter further elaborates on how Canada's feminist policy affects business practices abroad and impacts the SDGs in the affected countries.

Part IV: Programs and partnerships in developing countries

This section focuses on specific examples of collaborative projects and partnerships that promote various Global Goals in the contexts of three developing countries in Africa: Morocco, Nigeria and Malawi. These three case studies highlight critical aspects of pioneering and managing sustainability work in some of the most challenging social, economic and political environments. Using the analyses of "what works and what does not," lessons are drawn for pursuing similar projects in other contexts.

In Chapter 13, Moroccan authors El Ghaib and Allali examine case studies of social entrepreneurship and social innovations that promote sustainable development in their country. Two innovative social enterprises, Go Energyless Solutions and HydroBarley, spin-offs from a social incubator, Enactus Morocco, are discussed. The former promotes the use of energy-saving products while the latter provides low-cost green fodder to rural farmers. Lessons learned from the development of these businesses are then examined.

Next, Nwagwu in Chapter 14 writes about multi-stakeholder partnerships that advance the cause of sustainable development in Nigeria. The author analyzes two illustrative cases, the Food and Beverage Recycling Alliance and the Committee Encouraging Corporate Philanthropy, and their contribution to the Global Goals. The analyses focus on the opportunities and the obstacles inherent in partnerships for driving sustainable development.

Last, but not least, Blanks and Winter in Chapter 15 present a compelling case study based on several years of fieldwork to provide culturally responsive, sustainable and disabilities-focused technical assistance to teachers in rural primary schools in Malawi. The chapter chronicles painful lessons on how to engage local stakeholders across cultural chasms and to develop locally appropriate development-assistance interventions.

All in all, the chapters in this book show how some the most ingenious and sustainable solutions to problems of sustainable development can come from unexpected places. Individuals and organizations experimenting with ideas and innovations on a small scale, and with bottom-up processes, are key players. The stories and cases demonstrate that top-down government interventions and corporate mega projects are not the only ways that nations can work toward the 17 SDGs. Much can be learned from the struggles and successes of individual entrepreneurs and small groups of activists, who work tirelessly and undaunted, to make, at times, incremental but significant advances toward global sustainability. We hope the book inspires readers to challenge assumptions and to play key roles in the ongoing pursuit of sustainable development.

PART I

The big picture

1

STRUGGLES AND SUCCESSES OF TRANSFORMATIVE LEARNING FOR THE SDGS

A case study

*Dario Cottafava, Laura Corazza
and Gabriela Cavagliá*

Abstract

The 17 Sustainable Development Goals (SDGs) have shed light on the concept of Education for Sustainable Development (ESD) expressed through the knowledge of targets and indicators. Consequently, UNESCO has invoked the adoption of new pedagogical approaches for SDGs – that is, transdisciplinary and transformative learning, to overcome mere knowledge teaching and to teach, new generations of young leaders, ESD skills such as envisioning, critical thinking and partnership building. This paper discusses the struggles and successes of a pilot project in transformative learning in an institution of higher learning for the advancement of the SDGs. This project has been carried out at the University of Torino (UniTo) and focuses on merging sustainable development with open innovation. Recognized as one of the best practices regarding sustainable development by the Italian Association of Universities for Sustainability (RUS) in 2017, the case involves students in a transdisciplinary, creative and open learning environment. With this approach, students learn about SDGs, the complexities of sustainability and the use of valuable tools to contribute to their local communities and organizations.

Introduction

This chapter refers to the Education for Sustainable Development Goals (ESDGs) as a specific subset of the traditional and vast Education for Sustainable Development (ESD). Due to their intrinsic nature, a theoretical training on SDGs might be ineffective (Spangenberg, 2017), as the scope of the ESDGs goes beyond the formal knowledge and should stimulate leadership skills in learners (Efthimiou, 2017). By 2030, SDG #4 seeks to ensure inclusive and equitable quality education and promote lifelong learning opportunities for all. Its Target 4.7 explicitly explains the importance of cognitive and noncognitive aspects of learning, to boost such a leadership approach (UNESCO, 2017).

The ESDGs are defined as a "holistic and transformational education that addresses learning content and outcomes, pedagogy and the learning environment" (UNESCO, 2015, 2017). At its core, it has an interdisciplinary nature (Annan-Diab and Molinari, 2017) and a transdisciplinary approach (Sipos et al., 2008). Consequently, innovative pedagogies connecting the learners to the external environment are needed. Of particular relevance, transformative learning (Mezirow, 2000) seems to demonstrate its effectiveness in considering the importance of the physical place (Bergvall-Kareborn and Stahlbrost, 2009; Romero Herrera, 2017) where the training happens as well as the relevance of the training provider. The coherence between what is practiced and what is preached becomes relevant in transformative learning (Lozano et al., 2017; Molderez and Fonseca, 2018; Scheyvens et al., 2016).

Besides, UNESCO calls universities to provide students with the knowledge, skills and motivation to understand and address the challenges of the SDGs. According to a recent report of Sustainable Development Solution Network Australia, universities can provide training especially aimed at improving cross-cutting skills and "key competencies." These would include systems thinking, critical thinking, self-awareness and integrated problem-solving as well as anticipatory, normative, strategic and collaboration competencies. They could also address creativity, entrepreneurship, curiosity and learning skills, design thinking, social responsibility, partnership competencies and the ability to be comfortable in interdisciplinary settings (Sustainable Development Solutions Network Australia/Pacific, 2017).

This chapter addresses the range of managerial soft skills for sustainable development. Managerial skills are needed to deal with uncertainty and ambiguity (Parente et al., 2012). They can be identified as soft skills useful to strategize, plan, organize and control (Robbins and Hunsaker, 2000). A pilot project carried out at the University of Turin (UniTo) tested the role of managerial soft skills on transformative learning for the SDGs, highlighting the struggles and successes experienced. Students from different courses and disciplines were involved. The project was recognized as one of the best practices regarding sustainable development by the Italian Association of Universities for Sustainability (RUS) and selected as best practice by the International Sustainable Campus Network (ISCN) for the World Economic Forum 2018.

The chapter is structured as follows: The ESD Training Program section introduces the case study and provides an overview of the design of the ESD Leadership Training. It brings valuable insights to those interested in approaching the concept of ESDGs, to facilitate replication of the described methodology. A detailed description of each module comprising the overall input-output transformative learning experience is provided. The Assessment Methodology section describes the adopted assessment approach based on two participants' surveys and experts' evaluation. The Struggles and Successes section presents a SWOT (Strengths, Weaknesses,

Opportunities and Threats) analysis. The SWOT analysis is a managerial framework that helps managers identify their organization's competitive position. It has also been applied to evaluate the learning project's outcome by Cho and Brown (2013). Moreover, a review of some general criticisms of the ESDGs is presented as well as some tips and suggestions on how to overcome these struggles. Finally, in the Conclusion section, further studies and investigation are recommended to enhance the strengths and opportunities for universities and to reduce the threats and weaknesses of the proposed case study.

The ESD training program

Within the Global Action Programme (GAP) on Education for Sustainable Development of UNESCO (UNESCO Education, 2005), the University of Torino organized a program titled Education for Sustainable Development: Leadership Training. The workshop was designed to teach the basic knowledge of the 17 SDGs and to highlight their interlinkages, two essential features of ESDGs (Weitz et al., 2014). The empowerment of the learners through the development of leadership skills is one of the main planned outcomes of such a workshop (Cottafava et al., 2019).

The training was based on an input-output transformative learning approach – that is, a two-day workshop designed by modular blocks of topics in which each block represents a module. A module output provides the input of the next module. Each block consisted of one to two hours of active learning to acquire a specific managerial skill, facilitated by an expert with a background relevant to the topic for promoting inter- and transdisciplinary learning (Sunley and Leigh, 2017). The workshop was aimed at undergraduate and graduate students of all courses and disciplines with an interest in sustainable development. This workshop was held by experts in active learning and engagement. They took an active part during the whole project, from the conceptualization of the modules to the evaluation phase. They acted as facilitators during the training, offering support to guarantee an effective co-designed process.

Experts were selected from among the available researchers of the Green Office (UniToGo) and the UNESCO Chair in Sustainable Development and Territory Management of the University of Torino. External organizations like the World Water Assessment Programme of UNESCO and the Italian Accenture Foundation were also engaged through one of their representatives. The workshop had the support of Cinedumedia (a multidisciplinary center on Cinema, Education and New Media) and the university's business incubator, namely, 2i3t.

Training overview

This section provides a discussion of the modules of the case study, while the theoretical underpinning of this new transformative learning approach has been described in detail in Cottafava et al. (2019). The ESD Leadership Training methodology

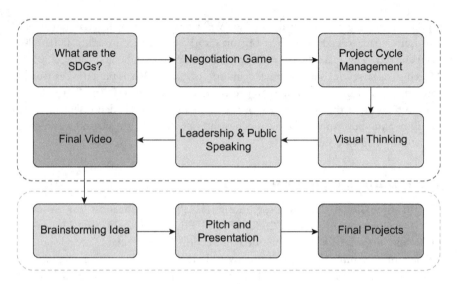

FIGURE 1.1 The ESD leadership training of the University of Torino

included two main components, each based on a different teaching approach. Thus, the basic structure, critical to this methodology, depends on two main parts, shown in Figure 1.1. The first one focuses on teaching the basic knowledge of the SDGs, their targets' and indicators' interconnectivity. The second part is centered on the plan and the design process for business ideas starting from the SDG challenges. In this way, a design for viable solutions and their implementation is established. Besides, students may imagine and conceive innovative solutions with a preliminary analysis of certain SDGs and a general sight on the complexity of all SDG interactions.

First, a non-formal teaching approach, the Learning of the SDGs, based on the ESD principles, was adopted to support the creation of a uniform learning path for students. Facilitators guided them from the basic understanding of the SDGs ("What Are the SDGs?" module) to the complexity of the stakeholder engagement behind a practical application of the SDGs in the university's context (Negotiation Game module). Other modules were the analysis of SDGs through their targets, indicators and their respective interlinkages (Project Cycle Management and Visual Thinking modules) and the design of workable solutions (Leadership and Public Speaking module) and their evaluation.

The second part of the transformative learning process, the Open Innovation Learning, aimed to encourage participants to conceive, design and plan innovative projects linking as many SDGs as possible. Two modules were provided: a Brainstorming Ideas module, in which participants, working in transdisciplinary teams, define their projects through a "business model canvas" (Osterwalder and Pigneur, 2010), and a Pitch and Presentation module, where the teams deliver five-minute presentations.

The learning of the SDGs

During the first part of the training, students discovered the complexity of sustainability and acquired basic knowledge about sustainable development by exploring goals, targets and indicators of the SDGs, thanks to an experiential learning approach and the adoption of managerial tools.

- *What are the SDGs?*
  This first module is organized as a "serious game" where a simulation emphasizes the added pedagogical value to fun and competition. Each participant represents one of the 17 goals and must discover information related to all the other SDGs by interacting with the other participants. The participants' interaction is facilitated by stimulating a debate around three thought-provoking questions: i) Goal name?, ii) Why? (list some data) and iii) What can I do?

- *Negotiation and conflict management*
  This second module is designed to show how to manage a multi-stakeholders' problem related to the SDGs. The case study focuses on access to education. Each group of participants interprets a stakeholder – for example, the Ministry of Education, students and their families, academic staff and the University Board of Directors. The four groups interact in a public debate according to the needs, aims and constraints of the game.

- *Project cycle management (PCM)*
  The third module introduces SDG targets and indicators. Students have to analyze the SDGs by using a root-cause tree graph (Wilson, 1993) and by identifying common causes among the SDGs. Root-cause analysis refers to any problem-solving method, and it is used to trace an issue from its origin to its present state. The complexity of the interactions among different targets and indicators are at the core of such modules.

- *Visual thinking*
  This module aims to develop a graphical synthesis using the Ishikawa diagram (Ishikawa and Loftus, 1990) – that is, a cause-effect visualization tool used by students to explore more in-depth the specific causes of each SDG.

- *Leadership and public speaking*
  Simulated interviews are at the core of this module. Participants split into three-person groups (one interviewer, with two interviewed experts), simulated to enact the situation of an interview in front of a camera. Students' interviews are played back and discussed in real time with all other participants with the help of the facilitators. The interviews, subsequently, are publicly shared on social media networks (Facebook, Twitter and Instagram), on the YouTube channel of the Green Office of the University of Torino and the related website.

The open innovation learning

During the second part of the training, students are encouraged to conceive, design and plan innovative projects linking as many SDGs as possible.

- **Brainstorming ideas**

  Within this activity, participant solutions related to real-world challenges, focused on the local territory and community, are presented and explained. Then, the five most promising ideas are selected, and transdisciplinary groups are created. Finally, all groups work on a business model canvas starting from the selected ideas. The entire process is facilitated and guided by business practitioners of the business incubator and SDG experts.

- **Pitch and presentation**

  This block aims to wrap up the group ideas into five-minute presentations according to five questions i) What? – idea description, ii) How? – innovation and necessary technology, iii) Scalability and modularity, iv) Environmental and social sustainability and interdependence with the SDGs and v) Economic feasibility.

The assessment methodology

The assessment methodology was conducted through two surveys, one ex ante and one ex post, the transformative training case study, the expert evaluation of the students' outputs, and a final SWOT analysis. The ex ante survey was a questionnaire focused on the students' motivations and interest in the topic, on their attitudes to develop projects and business ideas, and finally on their previous experiences in sustainable development. The ex post survey was conducted to understand the outcome of the workshop and to identify any improvement in the participants' knowledge and skills after the training.

Struggles and successes

In this section, struggles and successes, as well as lessons learned and suggestions, are presented for each module of the training. Instead of structuring the narrative by distinguishing between struggles and successes, we consider it appropriate to use a narrative approach based on the SWOT analysis of the entire process. The use of the SWOT analysis allows researchers to highlight strengths and weaknesses within each step, but at the same time, it brings out any opportunity in the sense of factors that can be further emphasized. The so-called threats are also useful to take into account certain areas of risk that may impair the effectiveness of the project itself. All feedback, both from experts and students, has been reviewed and analyzed using a SWOT analysis, shown in Figure 1.2. In particular, the internal strengths (top-left) and weaknesses (top-right) are related to the first part of the training and refer to the positive and negative impacts on the students' and participants' knowledge. The external opportunities (bottom-left) and threats (bottom-right), instead, refer to the second part of the transformative learning process and to the envisaged and produced impacts on the local territory.

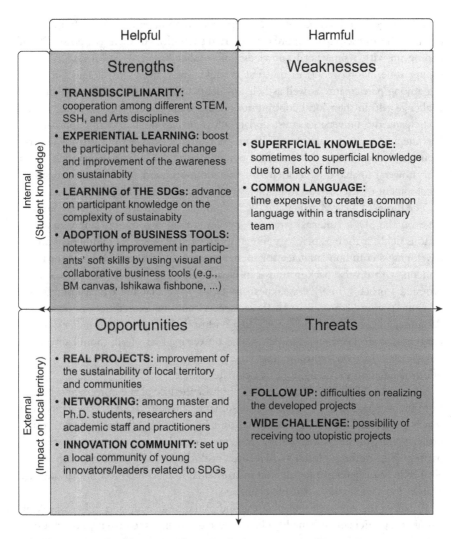

	Helpful	Harmful

FIGURE 1.2 SWOT analysis of the ESD leadership training program

The training modules

The What Are the SDGs? Module focuses on the acquisition of basic knowledge related to the SDGs through an experiential learning approach (internal strength) and the networking among participants to set the basis for a future community leader within the local territory (external opportunity). The main weakness of the module was the allotted time given to the participants, which was criticized as too short. Indeed, the experiential learning process – that is, obtained by stimulating the interaction and the debate among participants – could require more time than one to two hours.

The Negotiation and Conflict Management module emphasizes a full experiential and transdisciplinary approach (internal strength), but there is a possibility of ending up with a superficial knowledge of content (internal weakness), given the timing issue. Moreover, as in the first module, this activity encourages networking among participants as well as helps students to understand a real problem and challenge within their local community (external opportunity). According to one participant, the universities must update and renovate their teaching approach to become an "open-air laboratory allowing a dialogue between the various departments and degree courses too often perched behind old baronial models (such Ivory towers) unable to collaborate for the common good, for the knowledge and development of science and humanity."

The Project Cycle Management (PCM) module strengthens the students' knowledge on the SDGs (internal strength) by developing a common language across various fields, spanning sociology to economics and ecology. As highlighted above, developing a common language for such a broad field of knowledge and engaging students with diverse backgrounds can be a challenging task. It may need a more protracted process (internal weakness) to avoid superficial and trivial insights and to assure training continuity. All these aspects could be exceedingly improved by designing a learning path fully integrated within the bachelor's and master's degree programs, as declared by a student: "The university, first of all, should set up an obligatory course on environmental emergencies, workable solutions, and the role of our generation in the fight against climate change."

The Visual Thinking module points out how the role of the university is crucial from the perspective of cocreation. One student affirmed, "It affects the generation that is capable of the change. It should start by increasing the awareness through projects and workshops and later by implementing solutions and by letting students participate in finding solutions." Moreover, both the Visual Thinking and the Project Cycle Management modules are instrumental in teaching professional business analysis tools applied to a real-life challenge.

In one of the videos produced at the end of the Leadership and Public Speaking segment, a participant affirmed: "The purpose of my life is to give my contribution to make the world a better place for future generations than the current scenarios, and my university should be practically committed to letting me become a leader."

During, the Brainstorming Ideas module, the experts point out that this module is particularly effective in facilitating networking among the participants and in setting up a local innovation community (external opportunity), but that it must be improved in the follow-up process (external threats).

At the end of the Pitch and Presentation module, the experts' final evaluation of the presented projects was satisfactory even if none of the ideas continued with the business incubator follow-up. This aspect needs to be further discussed. The unsatisfactory results in the follow-up process could be due to several reasons. For instance, the far-reaching challenge based on the SDGs in some groups of students caused them to imagine unachievable solutions, at least in the short to medium term. This process can be further improved by clearly declaring, during the application process of the participants, specific interests from engaged stakeholders to fund some innovative solutions in order to achieve more SMART ideas (specific, measurable, achievable, realistic and time bound) during the workshop. A reasonable approach could be to identify a real budget for the sponsoring institutions devoted to realizing one or more projects. In this case, ideas presented may have a substantial budget constraint, and participants would be forced to undertake a more achievable project.

Finally, the ESD Leadership Training methodology, according to the engaged experts and stakeholders, proved to be a valid approach to spread the needed ESD skills, such as envisioning, critical thinking, systemic thinking and partnership building. They agree on how students might learn about the SDGs and sustainability complexity and may contribute to the sustainability of the local territory, becoming active citizens of their local communities.

Student knowledge

Regarding student knowledge, the main strengths declared by the students of the ESD Leadership Training program are the transdisciplinary, experiential learning and the focus on understanding the SDGs complexity. Moreover, some of the engaged stakeholders – for example, the Sustainability Report team and the Business Incubator 2i3t of the University of Torino – were recognized to be valuable assets in the teaching of professional business analysis tools. The Ishikawa diagram, project cycle management and the business model canvas were the managerial tools students appreciated the most.

In the ex post survey, at least half of the participants declared that they increased their acquisition of soft skills. The majority declared to have improved their skills in public speaking, teamwork, systemic thinking and stakeholder governance as well as in the understanding of the open innovation concept.

On the contrary, a few students and practitioners pointed out the main weakness was the lack of time. To be successful, the transdisciplinary approach needs much time to create a common language among students from entirely different disciplines and participants with varied backgrounds. The lack of a common ontology has negatively influenced the amount of new knowledge explicitly acquired on sustainable development as a concept. On the soft skills side, the most challenging skills were identified as public speaking and project idea definition, because they represent the stage where the students' engagement becomes proactive, and consequently, their personal commitment should be different, and it should be finally transformed.

Local territory and communities

Regarding the impact on the local territory and communities, three main opportunities were identified: the development of real and concrete projects, transdisciplinary networking and the creation of an innovators' community related to SDGs. For a generalist university such as the University of Torino, the creation of a transdisciplinary innovator community among students, researchers and academic staff is a very crucial challenge. The project methodology revealed that focusing on the fields related to the SDGs and sustainable development in general, was a powerful catalyst for learning by future leaders and innovators. The SDGs act as an excellent challenge to stimulating cooperation and collaboration among students from STEM (science, technology, engineering and mathematics), SSH (social sciences and humanities) and arts disciplines.

Finally, some threats emerged, especially related to the achievability of the developed projects. For example, a few facilitators recognized that the broadness of the content of the SDGs could affect the students' ability to provide attainable projects. The SDGs may be too general, and they may be difficult to operationalize into innovative solutions. A second noteworthy threat was related to the feasibility and implementation of the presented projects. Even if the declared goal of the workshop was to enable participants to "develop a real and achievable project," a few of the discussed solutions were far from being realistic for implementation.

In particular, the facilitators recognized some critical issues under a managerial perspective. Examples of such issues are technical feasibility, economic viability, intellectual property management and the risk of developing a sort of "SDG-washing" projects. For "SDG-washing" projects, they intend to develop a business idea that instead of matching the SDG, decouples it from the business perspective. For example, some students developed a communication strategy based on an SDG with the risk of creating a project that negatively impacts the same SDG, instead of producing a positive outcome. This is a case of using gamification to incentivize responsible consumer behavior for waste recycling, with the double-edged sword of incentivizing overconsumption of plastic bottles to gain credits, thanks to reverse machines. An intense debate emerged between facilitators on the critical and ethical issues of creating a conscious branding strategy for the SDGs.

Conclusions

The applied input-output process was conceived to provide a uniform learning path for students to guide them from a basic understanding of the SDGs to the analysis of targets and the interlinkages among the SDGs. It was designed to give all participants a common language with shared meanings and some basic knowledge of the SDGs as well as necessary management tools.

Practitioners, researchers and teachers who want to replicate this case study's approach are free to substitute each module with an alternative one; also, other modules may be added or removed. The input-output learning flow could replace the entire process to improve some specific features and knowledge or to focus more on a precise local challenge.

The SWOT analysis highlighted how the applied teaching methodology is suitable for ESD principles and was able to create a transdisciplinary and experiential learning process. On the contrary, the necessity to develop newer and stronger approaches emerged in order to improve the ESD Leadership Training methodology.

Further in-depth investigations are needed to reveal how to implement SDG #17 "building partnerships" between academia and local stakeholders. A critical issue remains in the follow-up stage of the workshop, that without a regular budget the learners might lose interest.

Finally, the allocation of adequate time is essential for conquering a complete learning process in order to avoid trivial contents and to adequately set up a common transdisciplinary language. Designing a fully integrated, transdisciplinary learning path for sustainable development into a bachelor's or master's degree program could overcome this weakness.

Bibliography

Annan-Diab, F. and Molinari, C. "Interdisciplinarity: Practical Approach to Advancing Education for Sustainability and for the Sustainable Development Goals." *International Journal of Management Education*, 15(2), 2017: 73–83. Doi: 10.1016/j.ijme.2017.03.006.

Bergvall-Kareborn, B. and Stahlbrost, A. "Living Lab: An Open and Citizen-Centric Approach for Innovation." *International Journal of Innovation and Regional Development*, 1(4), 2009: 356–370.

Cho, Y. and Brown, C. "Project-Based Learning in Education: Integrating Business Needs and Student Learning." *European Journal of Training and Development*, 37(8), 2013: 744–765.

Cottafava, D., Cavaglià, G. M. and Corazza, L. "Education of Sustainable Development Goals through Students' Active Engagement: A Transformative Learning Experience." *Sustainability Accounting, Management and Policy Journal*, 10(3), 2019: 521–544. doi: 10.1108/SAMPJ-05-2018-0152.

Efthimiou, O. "Heroic Ecologies: Embodied Heroic Leadership and Sustainable Futures." *Sustainability Accounting, Management and Policy Journal*, 8(4), 2017: 489–511. Doi: 10.1108/SAMPJ-08-2015-0074.

Ishikawa, K. and Loftus, J. H. *Introduction to Quality Control.* Tokyo: 3A Corporation, 1990.

Lozano, R., Merrill, M., Sammalisto, K., Ceulemans, K. and Lozano, F. "Connecting Competences and Pedagogical Approaches for Sustainable Development in Higher Education: A Literature Review and Framework Proposal." *Sustainability*, 9(11), 2017: 1889. Doi: 10.3390/su9101889.

Mezirow, J. "Learning to Think Like an Adult: Core Concepts of Transformation Theory." In J. Meziro, et al. (eds.), *Learning as Transformation: Critical Perspectives on a Theory in Progress.* San Francisco, CA: Jossey-Bass, 2000: 3–33.

Molderez, I. and Fonseca, E. "The Efficacy of Real-World Experiences and Service Learning for Fostering Competences for Sustainable Development in Higher Education." *Journal of Cleaner Production*, 172, 2018: 4397–4410. Doi: 10.1016/j.jclepro.2017.04.062.

Osterwalder, A. and Pigneur, Y. *Business Model Generation: A Handbook for Visionaries, Game Changers, and Challengers.* New Jersey: John Wiley & Sons, 2010.

Parente, D. H., Stephan, J. D. and Brown, R. C. "Facilitating the Acquisition of Strategic Skills: The Role of Traditional and Soft Managerial Skills." *Management Research Review*, 35(11), 2012: 1004–1028. Doi: 10.1108/01409171211276918.

Robbins, S. P. and Hunsaker, P. L. *Training in Management Skills.* Upper Saddle River, NJ: Prentice-Hall, 2000.

Romero Herrera, N. "The Emergence of Living Lab Methods." In D. V Keyson, O. Guerra-Santin and D. Lockton (eds.), *Living Labs: Design and Assessment of Sustainable Living.* Cham: Springer International Publishing, 2017: 9–22. Doi: 10.1007/978-3-319-33527-8_2.

Scheyvens, R., Banks, G. and Hughes, E. "The Private Sector and the SDGs: The Need to Move beyond 'Business as Usual'." *Sustainable Development*, 24(6), 2016: 371–382. Doi: 10.1002/sd.1623.

Sipos, Y., Battisti, B. and Grimm, K. "Achieving Transformative Sustainability Learning: Engaging Head, Hands and Heart." *International Journal of Sustainability in Higher Education*, 9(1), 2008: 68–86. Doi: 10.1108/14676370810842193.

Spangenberg, J. H. "Hot Air or Comprehensive Progress? A Critical Assessment of the SDGs." *Sustainable Development*, 25(4), 2017: 311–321. Doi: 10.1002/sd.1657.

Sunley, R. and Leigh, J. S. A. "Introduction." In R. Sunley and J. S. A. Leigh (eds.), *Educating for Responsible Management: Putting Theory into Practice*, New York: Routledge, 2017: 1–12.

Sustainable Development Solutions Network Australia/Pacific. *Getting Started with the SDGs in Universities: A Guide for Universities, Higher Education Institutions, and the Academic Sector.* Melbourne. 2017. http://ap-unsdsn.org/wp-content/uploads/2017/08/University-SDG-Guide_web.pdf.

UNESCO. *Rethinking Education: Towards a Global Common Good?* Paris: UNESCO, 2015.

UNESCO. *Unpacking Sustainable Development Goal 4 Education 2030.* 2017. http://unesdoc.unesco.org/images/0024/002463/246300E.pdf.

UNESCO Education. *United Nations Decade of Education for Sustainable Development (2005–2014): International Implementation Scheme.* Paris: UN Education, 2005.

Weitz, N., Nilsson, M. and Davids, M. "A Nexus Approach to the Post-2015 Agenda: Formulating Integrated Water, Energy and Food in the SDGs." *Review of International Affairs*, 34(2), 2014.

Wilson, P. F., Dell, L. D. and Anderson, G. F. *Root Cause Analysis: A Tool for Total Quality Management.* Milwaukee, WI: ASQ Quality Press, 1993.

2

USING OUR TIME ON THE PLANET TO MAKE A DIFFERENCE – THE SUSTAINABILITY MINDSET

Margaret A. Goralski

Abstract

This is a chapter about Isabel Rimanoczy – an advocate, educator and author – who wants people worldwide to think about global sustainability before they make decisions. She wants them to learn about the Sustainability Mindset and the value of, and values in, their lives. Rimanoczy wants people to make decisions that are good for themselves but that are also good for the earth and for future generations. She sets forth a Sustainability Mindset Model, for personal reflection, decision-making and teaching so that people will have a framework to follow. This chapter recognizes the struggles and successes that Rimanoczy has encountered on her journey. It concludes with the impact that her work has had on the United Nations (UN) Sustainability Development Goals (SDGs) and the people whom she has touched through her words and actions.

Introduction

Pulitzer Prize winner Mary Oliver's "The Summer Day" (Oliver, 1990) is a poem that Isabel Rimanoczy takes to heart as she suggests that we all ask ourselves how we could use our one wild and precious life on this planet to make a difference.

Rimanoczy began her journey into the Sustainability Mindset as she pursued her doctoral degree in education at Columbia University by asking what it means to be a leader who makes a difference in the world. She researched what motivated business leaders and what inspired them to venture into a world of sustainable thinking, that in many ways was anathema to the ways of Western business – for example, capitalist economies and societies of consumerism (Rimanoczy, 2010, 2013b). As Rimanoczy listened to the words and stories of leaders, she recognized a pattern of common elements – a way of connecting the dots of a problem to create a solution that she termed the "Sustainability Mindset." She recommended slowing down, living at a less hectic pace and taking time to reflect and ask oneself, "Why am I doing what I am doing?"

A key milestone in Rimanoczy's journey was her first TED Talk video on You-Tube, where she quotes Oliver and talks about the things in her own life that compelled her to create LEAP!, "Leverage resources, Expand awareness, Accelerate change, and Partner with forward thinking individuals to develop a generation of sustainability-minded leaders" (What Do You Do . . ., 2016).

Rimanoczy advocates for a Sustainability Mindset every day of her life. She has brought together a group of like-minded thinkers in education, business and government to talk together in webinars, to think together and to gather for a yearly retreat. In addition, Rimanoczy is bringing the Sustainability Mindset to the next and future generations of youth, to open their eyes through courses and mindful management education.

> A mindset for sustainability is defined as a particular lens through which an individual analyzes information and makes decisions, therefore, having a positive impact on the environment and the community. The impact is not always direct or immediately visible, i.e., when a leader decides to consider both the short- and long-term environmental impact of a project and seeks to accomplish both over a specific time period. By developing awareness and progressively embedding a sustainable way of viewing what we do, we take a path towards a more all-encompassing outlook for sustainability. The elements of the Sustainability Mindset relate to how we think, i.e., do we consider all stakeholders including nature and the next generations? Do we seek innovative solutions that transcend either/or options and aim at inclusive decisions? Also, the "being" dimension plays a central role in the mindset for sustainability, as individuals observe and reflect on their values, assumptions, and mental models, as well as their life purpose, as these are all expressed tacitly in our daily actions.
>
> *(Rimanoczy, personal communication, November 7, 2018)*

The "being" dimension means that one should look inside oneself to determine: 1) what is important to self and 2) how to make decisions that affect not just the self but also the broader, and in some ways, more abstract and less understood, larger world. Creation of a Sustainability Mindset in students could be a key factor in mobilizing citizens and organizations to reverse damage like loss of natural habitat and extinction of species by observing, reflecting and recognizing one's life purpose prior to making a decision.

This chapter investigates the depth of Rimanoczy's belief in human beings and their combined capability to use their time on this planet to make a difference and to embrace a Sustainability Mindset and share it with others. Margaret Meade, American scientist and anthropologist stated, "Never doubt that a small group of thoughtful, committed citizens can change the world; indeed, it's the only thing that ever has."

In *Exploring my Soul*, one of her books of poetry, Rimanoczy reflects on her own being and the core values that inform her passion to engage in this endeavor to spread the word about a Sustainability Mindset. She writes about birds, water, people, life and death. Rimanoczy's poetry is about humanity's dependence on nature, air and water and breath, which shape our perception and commitment to the care of the natural environment (Rimanoczy, 2013a).

In 2014, Rimanoczy created LEAP!, a network for academics interested in developing new mindsets. It began with a group of professors from 16 countries with a common vision to promote change and develop a mindset for sustainability in their students. Its members are curious to learn, share and connect and document their journey. LEAP! was instrumental in bringing together the initial cohort of pioneer professors into AIM2Flourish, to teach the Sustainability Development Goals (SDGs) while identifying and nominating business leaders who make a profit while addressing one or more of the SDGs. Since its inception, Rimanoczy has served as a Global Ambassador for AIM2Flourish. Its mission is to change the story about business from best *in* the world, to best *for* the world by connecting students with business innovators who are aligned with the UN Global Goals (AIM2Flourish, 2018).

In May 2015, LEAP! became the UN PRME (Principles for Responsible Management Education) Working Group on the Sustainability Mindset. UN PRME originated in 2007. It sets forth principles for business schools and a global engagement platform for academic institutions to inspire responsible management education, research and thoughtful leadership (Forray et al., 2015). As of December 2019, there are more than 805 university signatories from over 91 countries worldwide. The transition from LEAP! to the UN PRME Sustainability Mindset Working Group was a major strategic decision.

> Having seen how the UN PRME working groups were organized, I realized that LEAP! met all of the criteria. Principle One about Purpose was core to the work of LEAP! as members explored what is not only the purpose of business, but the purpose of education, of the courses we teach, and of the courses that students choose. Principle Two on Values directly related to LEAP!'s focus on developing critical revision of the values behind our actions in the world. We were also discussing what new pedagogical Methods (Principle Three) had to be used to develop a more holistic and sustainable mindset. We promoted collaborative Research (Principle Four) among members, a result visible in the many scholarly papers and books produced by members of this group. In our mission from the start, Partnering (Principle Five) was a key component, something called forth by PRME. And, lastly, Principle Six calls for creating inclusive Dialogue which is at the foundation of LEAP!'s essence.
>
> *(Rimanoczy, personal communication, November 7, 2018)*

Beyond this alignment, becoming connected to a respected initiative of the UN gave all members of LEAP! increased visibility within their own institutions. This was an important benefit considering that members were already pioneers in researching and teaching sustainability. Teaching a Sustainability Mindset through discourse and experiential learning allowed students to engage in dialogue about personal values, which are most often avoided beyond conceptual theories within a course.

Stop Teaching – Principles and Practices for Responsible Management Education explores the ways in which teaching methods need to evolve in order to develop a new generation of business leaders who connect profits with purpose and who see in social entrepreneurship and innovation key opportunities for addressing our planetary challenges (Rimanoczy, 2016).

Amelia Naim Indrajaya, IPMI Business School, Jakarta, Indonesia, utilizes Rimanoczy's teaching principles in her various courses. Her students state:

> We learn about SDG and SDG values. . . . Through this we can find ideas to solve problems in many ways. . . . This session teaches me to care for each other and also the world that we live in, and SDG is so important for us and to the better future of the world.
>
> *(Ghozidion Taufiqakbar Hanartyo)*

> By being more aware of our surroundings, we might be surprised at how much we have been missing out. We might also even start building up our commitment to contribute in making the world a better place.
>
> *(Tania Lasmaya Putritami)*

> The session has given me insights about particular knowledge of sustainable development goals. . . . Each session guides me little by little to understand what's happening in the world and how we can tackle challenges in the future.
>
> *(Shifa Mahdiya Ainiyah)*

The Sustainability Mindset

The Sustainability Mindset Model was codeveloped by Kerul Kassel, Shelley Mitchell and Isabel Rimanoczy. It was "officially" introduced in the *Handbook of Sustainability Management Education: In Search of a Multidisciplinary, Innovative and Integrated Approach* (Rimanoczy, 2017). The model outlines the four elements of innovative and collaborative action: an ecological worldview, a systems perspective, emotional intelligence and spiritual intelligence.

Each element of the model is then broken down into its individual dimensions so that academics can incorporate various ideals of knowledge/thinking like systems theory, self-awareness and purposeful mission into their teaching. By including the values/being dimension, educators can expand student learning by incorporating a sense of interconnectedness and compassion, which then enhances a student's ability to make decisions on a more cognizant level. Finally, incorporation of the competency/doing dimension, which includes stakeholder engagement, global sensitivity and contemplative practices, allows a student time to think about an issue and then put that thought into action by utilizing an innovative and collaborative mindset. Examples of how the elements and dimensions of the Sustainability Mindset Model are incorporated into faculty curriculum and teaching as well as in the understanding of students are explained in more detail through testimonials in this chapter.

Recently, Rimanoczy partnered with Kassel to coedit *Developing A Sustainability Mindset in Management Education* designed to help educators frame curricula to facilitate broad and deep systemic learning (Kassel and Rimanoczy, 2018). The book seeks to create future leaders who will utilize a Sustainability Mindset to analyze complex management challenges and generate innovative solutions. Chapters are included from 23 individuals across the world who share the ways in which they are developing a mindset for sustainability through unique conceptualizations and pedagogical approaches.

Support and mentoring for the Sustainability Mindset Working Group

Rimanoczy provides individual support and mentoring to UN PRME Sustainability Mindset Working Group members in a virtual introductory fast-track course and faculty development session via Zoom. The course includes seven modules. Members receive YouTube video links, readings and assignments via email prior to a module opening, so the attendee will be ready for a vibrant discussion. The course is structured like a "teachers' room discussion": there are no lectures, but a conversation among the participants, facilitated by Rimanoczy. Educators exchange insights about the teaching materials, considerations for using them with their students, alternatives they may have used for similar learning goals, and so on. Members in attendance during the session bring knowledge from around the world into the forum, so participants are learning from each other as well as from Rimanoczy. These global interactions are an important part of the modules. Members feel enriched by their experience and the learning that has taken place. In addition, members come to know each other through these discussions and form a more cohesive network in the PRME Working Group.

Some comments at the end of the fast-track course include:

> I especially liked the exercises we did during the course and the readings and I did not let anything interfere with my doing the readings; it was my special time. . . . I got new ideas for my courses and plan to implement them next year. I enjoyed this wonderful experience and nurturing environment provided by Isabel. I felt like coming home, to the caring people who are sustainability advocates.
>
> *(Judita Peterlin, University of Ljubljana, Slovenia)*

> Because of this course, I again, could remember the importance of slowing down and have been meditating daily for over a month now, something that I never "had time" for. Lesson number one in our world: we need to make

the time, because there is always something else luring our attention. . . . This course has enriched my life very much, creating the space to discuss these topics that we usually leave on the back burner and I am happy and grateful for the opportunity.

(Marina Williams, Sustainability professional, Argentina)

Much has happened during this course. The readings and process of learning have been the greatest transformation. Yet drifting my mind through those words has felt more like a familiar reconnection rather than a discovering of newness. . . . I have come to better understand the importance of being connected.

(Melissa Edwards, University of Technology Sydney, Australia)

LEAP Café offers members an opportunity to get together virtually the first Monday of every month to talk informally about the things that are important around the world. Every third Monday of the month, Storytelling Circle allows one member to begin the conversation by sharing his/her experience of the Sustainability Mindset with others, who learn and share during the ensuing conversation. The sessions are conducted virtually on Zoom and last for about one hour. Peer coaching is the newest addition. Members share their most current challenges and receive valuable input, which they can use to find a solution or to hear how someone else might handle the same challenge. Quarterly, members receive a newsletter via email from Rimanoczy to keep abreast of what's new, conferences that members have attended, AIM2Flourish updates, upcoming meetings, and so on.

Struggles

For Rimanoczy, struggles in developing a Sustainability Mindset have branched in three directions: establishing the Sustainability Mindset and the values/being dimension into business school curricula, creating a learning community for a Sustainability Mindset and procuring financial support in sustaining her initiative.

Not being associated with a host university creates a challenge for Rimanoczy, since she is not intimately aware of the politics of a university and its schools and departments. In addition, she does not fully recognize the practical issues and constraints related to business school core curricula. Many students in today's Western techno-society pursue a degree in business to get a great job, earn a good income and live a good life. Hence, developing a Sustainability Mindset must identify its value proposition for students and educators. What will one gain by acquiring a Sustainability Mindset? What will one lose if he/she does not shift into a new mindset for sustainability?

Developing a mindset for sustainability involves a dimension that educators and students might not be familiar with in business/management education – the values/being dimension. This dimension questions whether one observes and reflects on his or her own values and assumptions, as well as his or her own life purpose, prior to making a decision. Establishing the importance and strategic urgency of introducing a Sustainability Mindset to students, educators and administrators is critical in order to have it considered for the business core curriculum. Students understand the importance of the knowledge/thinking and the competency/doing dimensions. What is the argument for the necessity of the values/being dimension? Rimanoczy's research on individuals engaged in sustainability initiatives indicates that their key capabilities rely on what they already know about social or environmental challenges (knowledge) and innovation to solve them (competency). These initiatives, however, were anchored on how these individuals viewed themselves, their life purpose and their personal mission, which are, in fact, based on deep-felt values (being) (Rimanoczy, 2010, 2013b).

Many authors have stated that the values/being dimension is foundational for a needed paradigm shift in education to prepare students to play a meaningful role in society (Cseh et al., 2013; Scharmer and Kaufer, 2013; Taylor, 2017). When one is contemplating the long term, the most important decisions of one's life for this generation and generations to come, the Sustainability Mindset is of paramount importance (Barnett et al., 2018; Godfrey and Lewis, 2018).

Creating a learning community, providing a space and structure for people to align around a shared goal on the topic of Sustainability Mindset, is a less difficult struggle. Rimanoczy has spoken to thousands of people through her academic presentations and webinars between 2014 and 2019. The percentage of PRME Working Group members who are actively engaged and implementing the Sustainability Mindset into their courses is close to 70 percent. These professors teach thousands of students per year. Moreover, Rimanoczy's learning community has extended far beyond the people she has met personally on a one-to-one basis. Adding into the equation her multiple papers and books, YouTube videos and blogs in the *Huffington Post*, one can easily understand that Rimanoczy's learning community is extensive and continuing to expand.

Rimanoczy has been financing her efforts on behalf of LEAP! and UN PRME Sustainability Mindset Working Group on her own; however, she has recently sought outside funding by writing and submitting grant proposals. So far, she has submitted two grant proposals; however, those two proposals did not meet with success. The granting organization does not give feedback on submissions, so no lessons could be learned from these submissions. She has not had the finances available to hire a grant writer. Since the fast-track course has met with success, Rimanoczy is contemplating charging tuition for the course. And finally, Rimanoczy has asked for sponsorship from members of the UN PRME Sustainability Mindset Working Group. Many have been willing to offer that sponsorship.

Successes

There have been many successes for Rimanoczy. She has taken Oliver's question seriously. She discovered during her doctoral research that this powerful Sustainability Mindset could be intentionally developed. She made it her purpose to inspire and spread the word, so people worldwide could learn from her and others' experiences.

Rimanoczy delved into global teaching methods and identified those that she believes best match the goal of creating a Sustainability Mindset in students. She has highlighted these teaching methods to others through webinars so that each person can take this methodology back to her/his college or university. And, as noted above, she has documented her findings in a book, *Stop Teaching: Principles and Practices for Responsible Management Education* that others can use to update their teaching methods or to apply best practices to their own teaching (Rimanoczy, 2016).

Through Rimanoczy's commitment to LEAP! and the UN PRME Sustainability Mindset Working Group, she has found a community whose work she supports and who support her mission for change. This synergy among world educators and Rimanoczy establishes a sense of belonging to something larger than one's self. Rimanoczy inspires and encourages members to present and publish their work. Members of LEAP! are breaking new ground, such as Shelley Mitchell, Hult International Business School – Boston, who presented *Research Agenda 2020: Exploring the Impacts of Sustainability in Management Education*, which received the Management Education Award for Best Professional Development Workshop, Academy of Management, 2018. Radha Sharma's symposium paper 'Leadership Self Awareness through Western & Eastern Lenses: An Empirical Study' received Best Symposium Award of the Management Education Division, Academy of Management, 2018.

The value of creating a Sustainability Mindset is now understood and being taught by many whom Rimanoczy has touched worldwide, including, for example: Judita Peterlin, Slovenia; Amelia Naim Indrajaya, Indonesia; Eunice Mareth Areola and Pia Manalastas, the Philippines; Ekaterina Ivanova and Yulia Aray, Russia; Jan Hermes, Finland; Aixa Ritz, Kent Fairfield, Jim Stoner, and Shelley Mitchell, the United States; Soraia Schuttel and Alba Torres, Brazil; Mary Grace Neville, Morocco; Ali Awni, Egypt; Aline Popowski, France; Mauricio Cardenas, Colombia; Javier Ruano, Ecuador; Aleandra Scafati, Argentina; Karthyeni Sridaran and Melissa Edwards, Australia; Henrietta Onwuegbuzie, Nigeria; Rohana Ulluwishewa, Sri Lanka; Shirley Mo Ching Yeung, China; and many others too numerous to name in this chapter.

The comments of a few Working Group members:

> I offer Developing a Sustainability Mindset. This course's content has developed and increased a great interest and commitment to sustainable practices not only in my students, but in myself as well. I am thankful . . . for how much our students benefit from learning about Sustainability Mindset.
>
> *(Aixa Ritz, Fairleigh Dickinson University, USA,*
> *Personal Communication, November 20, 2018)*

> In the last three years I have been actively using innovative pedagogical approaches that I learned from Isabel. AIM2Flourish is a truly transformational experience for the students who write mini-cases about sustainable

businesses as a force for good. Students are developing a better connection to their inner self and the world around them. Their empathy grows. They strive to be more conscious customers. Many consider becoming sustainable entrepreneurs.

(Ekaterina Ivanova, Higher School of Economics, Moscow Russia,
Personal Communication, November 20, 2018)

[Rimanoczy] with her course . . . gave direction to wondering and made me realize that even though this wondering makes my job much more demanding and much less standardized . . . it is also much more rewarding to think you have the ability to change lives not only of your students but also their surroundings – for the better. . . . I have incorporated Sustainability Mindset at the core of the courses in Ljubljana.

(Judita Peterlin, University of Ljubljana, Slovenia,
Personal Communication, November 20, 2018)

In keeping with the quote of Margaret Meade, "Never doubt that a small group of thoughtful, committed citizens can change the world; indeed, it's the only thing that ever has," Rimanoczy recognizes that she has brought together a small core group of thoughtful citizens who can change the world through their commitment to developing the Sustainability Mindset. Rimanoczy's mentoring role is key to the growth and professional impact of her increasing network of members.

Initiatives fostered by Rimanoczy's leadership continue to emerge: A Center for Sustainability Mindset and Corporate Social Responsibility was established by Amelia Naim Indrajaya, International Business School, Indonesia, who is collaborating with Shirley Mo Ching Yeung, School of Business, Gratia Christian College, Singapore, in offering a Quality Education in Sustainable Development Executive Training Program. The idea is to encourage the development of an innovative business model that supports one or more of the SDGs of the United Nations (UN). Yeung is also managing a UN Office for South-South Cooperation (UNOSSC) partnership that includes Eunice Areola from the BIG Institute, Manila, Philippines (UN Office for South-South Cooperation [UNOSSC], 2019). Indrajaya has also begun a new journal titled *IPMI International Journal of Business Studies*. A new book titled *Sustainability Leadership*, to be edited by Working Group member Aixa Ritz, Fairleigh Dickinson University, USA, is seeking contributors. It too will address several of the SDGs.

Member Jan Hermes, University of Oulu, Finland, has recently collaborated with Rimanoczy to publish a paper titled "Deep Learning for a Sustainability Mindset" (Hermes and Rimanoczy, 2018). Members Jody Fry and Eleftheria Egel, (the United States and Germany) in collaboration with psychologist Vanessa Prins-Goodman created The Being-Centered Leadership Team to support personal and organizational transformation. Other initiatives suggested at a recent Sustainability Mindset Retreat include certification programs to be offered at universities to fill a worldwide gap of knowledge around the topic of Sustainability Mindset and creation of a collective power of Sustainability Mindset academics to touch not just the minds of students but also their hearts to embrace a Sustainability Mindset.

Rimanoczy has begun to develop a Sustainability Mindset Indicator (SMI), which will assess and map the profile of a Sustainability Mindset in individuals. The SMI will take the Sustainability Mindset from theory to practice to measurement. Rimanoczy's SMI Project has recently won two awards: The Gold Award in the Social Sciences Track and the Silver Award in the category of Sustainability at the Reimagine Education event sponsored by Wharton and QS Reimagine Education.

Conclusion

Rimanoczy has begun to make a real difference in some people's lives worldwide. Her work has had a concrete impact on specific SDGs including #3 good health, #4 quality education, #5 gender equality, #10 reduced inequalities, #11 sustainable cities and communities, #12 responsible consumption, #13 climate action and #17 partnerships for the goals. In addition, the UN Working Group on Sustainability Mindset, chaired by Rimanoczy, has advocated for the PRME principles of purpose, values, methods, research, partnering and dialogue. Rimanoczy in her webinars and through her YouTube videos and presentations at various organizations has met many people of like minds.

Rimanoczy's successes have far outweighed the struggles, especially when one considers how far Rimanoczy and her idea for Sustainability Mindset have grown from when she first read Mary Oliver's poem and questioned what she should do with her one wild and precious life.

References

AIM2Flourish. "Celebrating Business Innovations for the Global Good." 2018. https://aim-2flourish.com.

Barnett, M. L., Henriques, I. and Husted Corregan, B. "Governing the Void between Stakeholder Management and Sustainability." In *Sustainability, Stakeholder Governance, and Corporate Social Responsibility (Advances in Strategic Management, Volume 38)*. Bingley, West Yorkshire, England: Emerald Publishing Limited, 2018: 121–143.

Cseh, M., Davis, E. B. and Khilji, S. E. "Developing a Global Mindset: Learning of Global Leaders." *European Journal of Training and Development*, 37(5), 2013: 489–499.

Forray, J., Leigh, J. and Kenworthy, A. L. "Special Section Cluster on Responsible Management Education: Nurturing an Emerging PRME Ethos." *Academy of Management Learning & Education*, 14(2), 2015: 293–296.

Godfrey, P. C. and Lewis, B. W. "Pragmatism and Pluralism: A Moral Foundation for Stakeholder Theory in the 21st Century." Brigham Young University. 2018. https://scholarsarchive.byu.edu/cgi/viewcontent.cgi?referer=www.google.com/&httpsredir=1&article=3115&context=facpub.

Hermes, J. and Rimanoczy, I. "Deep Learning for a Sustainability Mindset." *The International Journal of Management Education*, 16(3), 2018: 460–467.

Isabel Rimanoczy. "What Do You Do With Your Time?" *TEDxNSU*. 2016. www.youtube.com/watch?v=0e-ylVkGzWY.

Kassel, K. and Rimanoczy, I. (eds.). *Developing a Sustainability Mindset in Management Education*. London: Routledge, 2018.

Oliver, M. *House of Light*. Boston, MA: Beacon Press, 1990.

Rastogi, P. and Sharma, R. "Ecopreneurship for Sustainable Development." In S. Dhiman and J. Marques (eds.), *Handbook of Engaged Sustainability*. Cham, Switzerland: Springer International Publishing AG, 2018: 991–1016.

Rimanoczy, I. B. "Business Leaders Committing to and Fostering Sustainability Initiatives." (Doctoral dissertation, Teachers College, Columbia University, New York, 2010).

Rimanoczy, I. B. *Exploring My Soul*. Fort Lauderdale, FL: Legacy Coaching Press, 2013a.

Rimanoczy, I. B. *Big Bang Being: Developing the Sustainability Mindset*. Sheffield, UK: Greenleaf Publishing Ltd, 2013b.

Rimanoczy, I. B. *Stop Teaching: Principles and Practices for Responsible Management Education*. New York, NY: Business Expert Press, 2016.

Rimanoczy, I. B. "Developing the Sustainability Mindset." In J. A. Arevalo and S. F. Mitchell (eds.), *Handbook of Sustainability Management Education: In Search of a Multidisciplinary, Innovative & Integrated Approach*. Cheltenham, UK: Edward Elgar Publishing Limited, 2017: 221–241.

Scharmer, O. and Kaufer, K. *Leading from the Emerging Future from Eco-System to Echo System Economies*. Oakland, CA: Berrett-Koehler Publishers, 2013.

Taylor, E. W. "Transformative Learning Theory." In *Transformative Learning Meets Bildung*. Rotterdam: SensePublishers, 2017: 17–29.

UN Office for South-South Cooperation (UNOSSC). *South-South Entrepreneurship Academy*. 2019. www.asia-pacific.unsouthsouth.org/2019/02/building-global-citizenship-and-harnessing-entrepreneurial-skills-and-mindset-through-south-south-cooperation-technology-financial-innovation-and-entrepreneurship-3-4-april-2019/.

3

DEEP SUSTAINABILITY

Really addressing our endangered human future

Glen T. Martin

Abstract

The chapter "Deep Sustainability: Really Addressing Our Endangered Future" argues that the UN Sustainable Development Goals (SDGs) are wholly inadequate to the task of creating a sustainable future for humankind. It reviews some of the fundamental principles that science has revealed about our planetary biosphere, the multidimensional interrelatedness of all living things. Ecology here is consistent with the holistic paradigm discovered throughout the sciences during the 20th century, replacing the early-modern Newtonian paradigm. The essay examines some of the features of the SDGs and shows that these goals presuppose the fragmented and anachronistic political and economic assumptions that we inherited from four centuries ago when the world operated according to a different paradigm. It gives examples of how both the fragmented system of so-called sovereign nation-states and the global economic system necessarily defeat the creation of a sustainable civilization. Finally, the essay examines some features of the *Constitution for the Federation of Earth*, founded on holistic principles. This constitution treats human political and economic affairs with the same holism that operates within our planetary biosphere. The chapter argues that holism under the *Earth Constitution* will give us the "deep sustainability" that can make a real future possible for humankind.

Introduction

The Brundtland Report *Our Common Future* (2015) defines sustainable development as "development that meets the needs of the present without compromising the ability of future generations to meet their own needs."[1] The key phrases in this definition are loaded with profound meanings. What are the "needs of the present," and how are these related to the ecology of Earth and its living systems? Are the "needs of the present" being addressed in the world we live in today? How will our future generations be able to meet their own needs in relation to a climate that is severely disrupted and a world order that remains deeply fragmented?

In order to address these questions we must proceed in a systematic fashion. First, we need to examine what science has revealed to us about the ecological character of Earth and its biosphere that supports all life. Second, we need to look at the complex set of factors that are disrupting our planetary biosphere and address these both serially and as a set of interrelated factors. Third, we must ask what kind of economic and political structures can provide the holism necessary to establish a sustainable world civilization. The UN Sustainable Development Agenda that came into effect in 2016 ostensibly attempts to do these things.

However, we will see that there are major flaws and omissions in this approach that do not address the deeper causes of climate disruption and, therefore, will not result in truly sustainable development. The UN system and the nation-states systems are hopelessly outdated and fundamentally unsustainable. I will show below that a truly sustainable world system requires ratification of the *Constitution for the Federation of Earth* and the creation of a democratic World Parliament.[2] Both politics and economics must *mirror* the holism of the biosphere that is the overwhelming message of contemporary science.

Ecological holism and our planetary biosphere

Climate crisis is upon us. It is worldwide and very serious. Former NASA climate scientist, James Hansen, who testified before the US Congress on global warming wrote, in 2012, "my colleagues and I have revealed a stunning increase in the frequency of extremely hot summers, with deeply troubling implications for not only our future but also for our present." As early as 1989, economist Jeremy Rifkin wrote, "we have been extracting, processing, and discarding energy and matter faster than the earth's ecosystems can recycle the waste and replenish the resources. The buildup of polluted waste in the form of dissipated energy and organic and inorganic garbage now threaten the survivability of the earth. The statistics are grim" (1989: 192).

Environmental scientist, James Gustive Speth, examined "ten global scale concerns" in his book *Red Sky at Morning*. These ten areas of crisis, he affirms, are mutually interacting and reinforcing: ozone layer depletion, climate change, desertification (agricultural and grazing lands worldwide turning into deserts), deforestation, biodiversity loss, population growth, diminishing freshwater resources, marine environment deterioration (dying or dead fisheries in every part of the world), toxification (tens of thousands of harmful artificial chemical compounds in every environment on Earth), and acid rain. With each passing year, he writes, "the problems have become deeper and truly urgent. The steps that governments took over the past two decades represent the first attempt at global environmental governance. It is an experiment that has largely failed" (2004: 1–2).

The scientific revolutions of the 20th century initiated a *paradigm shift to holism* that carries immense consequences for our understanding of our planetary biosphere. Along with all the other sciences, ecology has discovered the same holism throughout the natural world, with many thousands of ecosystems holistically related to one another and to our planetary ecosystem. This means that everything is "internally" related to everything else; a change in one feature of the world impacts upon all its interrelated dimensions (Birch and Cobb, 1990: 83).

The fish living in one of the coral reefs of the world are not independent of a vast multiplicity of *internal relationships* that they share with water temperature, other fish, the coral reef, the health of undersea plant life, the seasons, the rhythm of the tides, the ozone layer, the acidity and oxygenation of the water it inhabits, and so on endlessly. To understand the fish and its life, one must understand all these aspects of its environment, as the fish interacts with an ecosystem that encompasses and sustains it. Internal relationships mean that parts of the ecosystem are always interdependent with the wholes of which they are a part. Changes in any part alter not only other parts but the whole system.

The pre-holistic, early-modern paradigm assumed a world that was atomistic, mechanistic, and fragmented among incommensurable parts, such as space, time, energy, and matter (Harris, 2000). The new holism demands that we think differently and begin acting as integral parts of the whole that encompasses and sustains us, not as isolated entities who stand apart from the rest of the civilizational and ecological worlds.

Yet many of today's efforts toward sustainability retain these early-modern assumptions and therefore fail to effectively address not only the concept but the very real problems of a collapsing global environment. Philosopher Errol E. Harris, writes: "If the implications of this scientific revolution and the new paradigm it produces are taken seriously, holism should be the dominating concept in all our thinking. In considering the diverse problems and crises that have arisen out of practices inspired by the Newtonian paradigm, it is now essential to think globally" (2000: 90).

The UN Sustainable Development Goals versus our fragmented world system

The UN has created an elaborate website with many supporting documents to articulate the details of each of the SDGs. The central document is called "Transforming Our World: The 2030 Agenda for Sustainable Development." At its annual meeting in New York, the UN General Assembly adopted the Resolution on September 25, 2015. The SDG agreement commits the nations of the world to the pursuit of the 169 economic, social, and environmental "targets" that concretize the 17 SDGs. It is a global agenda that necessarily includes businesses, civil organizations, individuals, and governments worldwide. This must be a global, cooperative effort, if it is to succeed.

The SDG Resolution appears to recognize the danger facing today's world caused by unsustainable development. Item 14 declares, "We are meeting at a time of immense challenges to sustainable development. . . . Natural resource depletion and adverse impacts of environmental degradation, including desertification, drought, land degradation, freshwater scarcity and loss of biodiversity, add to and exacerbate the list of challenges which humanity faces." It appears that the document grasps the severity of the threat before the world and the need for a coordinated and comprehensive response.

Yet an immense *cognitive dissonance* appears when one reflects on these idealistic sounding goals in relation to the world we experience daily, a world we experience not only from the global news media but also from the work of scholars and observers of the world system itself. Every item on the list stems from an elaborate global context that is denied in practice by the world's institutions. To illustrate, item 16.3 in the list of the 169 objectives of the SDGs focuses on promoting the rule of law at national and international levels. Omitted here is the large body of literature within the scholarly community that argues that so-called international law is not binding and has minimal enforcement effects on the behavior of the nation-states (see Martin, 2016). The concept of law as a set of rules regulating the actions of states is incompatible with the concept of sovereign nation-states, since a sovereign state by definition recognizes no effective authority above itself.

The document does not mention the fact that some powerful countries routinely ignore international law, including treaties they signed. The SDGs completely ignore this reality of our global order consisting of sovereign nation-states. There is no mention of the crying need to abolish the US$1.8 trillion per year now wasted on militarism worldwide and convert these immense resources to the sustainability effort. The SDG document also *inauthentically* tiptoes around the systems of domination, imperialism, power corruption, and exploitation that most fundamentally define our world today (Petras and Veltmeyer, 2005). This may appear necessary since the UN is an intergovernmental organization created to serve the interests of nation-states, and not the common good of the peoples of Earth. Item 16.6 calls for the development of "transparent institutions" at all levels, yet there is no mention of the vast and rapidly growing security, private policing, and prison industries that, along with rampant worldwide militarism and "national security" interests, promote regimes of oppression and secrecy in various countries worldwide.

Finally, just as the concept of war is downplayed and avoided in the document (despite its demand for a comprehensive and cooperative approach), the word "population" appears only five times in the document. *None* of these uses of the word "population" intimates that the continuing global population growth might be a runaway crisis of our planet, pushing the use and exploitation of natural resources beyond the carrying capacity of the planet. The figures are widely known and recognized (Erlich and Erlich, 1990). In 1950 Earth had some 2.5 billion human inhabitants. Some population scientists predict about 9 billion people by the year 2050. The impact on the environment of this vastly expanding number of people is immense and devastating. In *Earth Federation Now*, Errol E. Harris calls population the number-one issue that human beings are faced with in dealing with climate disruption (2014: 23). It is controversial, and there are very powerful forces that want to obscure or deny this global population crisis. And the SDGs substantially ignore this crucial problem. There is simply no way the SDG goals can be achieved unless we confront the population explosion problem as well as the problems of militarism and war head on and integrate solutions to these issues as central features of our conception of sustainability.

The present world system defeats the UN Sustainable Development Goals

The dominant global institutions that govern most of human life on Earth arose during the early-modern era and are based on atomistic and fragmented assumptions. Global capitalism has its roots in the Italian Renaissance and gradually replaced the economic systems of feudalism during the 16th and 17th centuries. The rise of the contemporary system of nation-states replaced feudal modes of governance and authority during this same period. The key date given by scholars is the signing of the 1648 "Peace of Westphalia" treaty document that, in effect, defined the system of sovereign nation-states. Each nation now had absolute territorial boundaries, and each had, in principle, an effective government with authority to make and enforce law within its boundaries. Between nations or above nations, there are substantially no enforceable laws.

Capitalism, as philosopher Michael Luntley (1990) points out, is based on an atomistic view of human beings and their relationships. It treats human beings as independent economic units in external relationships with other such units. Corporations and business enterprises under capitalism are likewise treated as units (atoms) expected to pursue the self-interest (maximized profit margins) of investors. Under these basic assumptions, there is a major incentive for persons and businesses to *externalize* the costs of production and consumption onto society, the natural world, or other persons (Caldicot, 1992).

Economist Herman E. Daly develops the parameters of a sustainable economics that are necessarily "beyond growth" as well as beyond consumerism and all other unsustainable features of the current global economic system. A correct definition of sustainability is "development without growth beyond environmental carrying capacity, where development means qualitative improvement and growth means quantitative increase" (1996: 9). The resulting picture of a truly sustainable world involves a transformed ecological economics where "input" from the natural resource base of our planet is extremely restricted, and energy sources are now redirected to include the vast quantities of free, clean energy coming each day from the sun.

To curtail the unsustainable resource extraction that is wrecking the ecological fabric of Earth and to vastly curtail the immense release of greenhouse gases and other harmful wastes into the environment, requires a unity of authority and integrity of purpose that is currently lacking in the fragmented system of mostly militarized nation-states. As Speth asserts, all attempts at "global environmental governance" thus far have been failures. The system of sovereign nation-states shares a similar fragmented atomism and operational dynamic with capitalism. Today, militarism in all its forms has been exposed as environmentally toxic and unsustainable, a fact not addressed or mentioned in the SDG document. The weapons that are developed and could be used to destroy people and property in countries around the world have a profoundly adverse environmental impact (Sanders, 2009).

World-systems theorists show that the global capitalist system developing over the past five centuries is one that is simultaneously organized around sovereign nation-states, each competing and cooperating with one another in the promotion of interests, which are highly shaped by their respective capitalist ruling classes (Shannon, 1989). The basic model of capitalism is perpetual growth in profits, production, consumption, and size of enterprises. This model is used to measure the economic success of nations (always treated as *fragments* as if the world were not one integrated economic system): the Gross Domestic Product (GDP), which annually measures the economic performance of individual nations for production growth and exchange within their borders. However, as Daly and many others have pointed out, you cannot have limitless growth on a finite planet (see Heinberg, 2011).

We have discovered, therefore, major contradictions at the heart of the SDG document. The world must unite to combat climate disruption and global warming, but it must unite through the capitalist dogma in which growth in GDP is the primary measure of a country's economic well-being and success. It must also somehow unite for sustainable development while retaining the devastating fragmentation of absolute sovereign, mostly militarized nation-states.

In the SDG document, both the endless growth of capitalism and autonomous nation-states are taken for granted or uncritically assumed. Item 18 states that, "We reaffirm that every State has, and shall freely exercise, full permanent sovereignty over all its wealth, natural resources and economic activity. We will implement the Agenda for the full benefit of all, for today's generation and for future generations."[3] Are the resources of Earth really the property of sovereign nation-states and to be used as they see fit? Is the absolute sovereignty of militarized nation-states compatible with the holism necessary for sustainable development and the continuing survival of the planet?

The forests of the Amazon basin are often referred to as "the lungs of Earth" because of the fundamental, multiple roles they play in the maintenance of a life-giving planetary biosphere. Does the government of Brazil, or the other countries occupying the Amazon basin, have the right to destroy the lungs of Earth? Many articles on the internet describe the project promoted by some wealthy Brazilian politicians to build 40 major dams and a number of smaller secondary dams in the Tapajós River Basin.[4] This would flood some 1,000 square miles of rain forest to create navigable waters for commercial ships exploiting the resources of the basin.

Does Brazil as a sovereign nation and the commercial interests of companies it hosts have to right to exploit Earth's critical resources in this way? According to the SDG document, it does have the *legal right* to do this. Does the United States have the right to exit from an agreement, such as the Paris Climate Accord, that may affect the fate of the entire earth and future generations? (Shear, 2017). According to the SDGs (and today's "international law"), it does have the *legal right* to do this.

Item 55 of the SDG document makes clear that the SDGs are *merely a treaty among sovereign nations*, just as the UN Charter itself is a treaty among sovereign nations committed to "the principle of the sovereign equality of all its Members" (Article 2.1). Some treaties, for example, concerning human rights, have attempted to build (largely) self-monitoring and other incentives into their agreements (Donnelly, 2003). In the same way, the SDGs and the Paris Climate Agreement are *voluntary* commitments by certain governments and are subject to noncompliance, withdrawal, or self-decided exceptions of the governments of signatory states.

A model for a sustainable world system: *the Constitution for the Federation of Earth*

Holism is the fundamental reality of our planetary biosphere as well as the human situation. We are one species characterized by the unity in diversity of holism (see Ricoeur, 1992). In any organized system, the principle of order governing the whole applies to all the parts, and the responses of the parts are *internally* related to the health of the whole and the harmony with the other parts within the whole. Parts are not autonomous fragments in external relationships with one another. Yet this is precisely what the global economic system, as well as the world system of sovereign nation-states, assumes. Under these conditions sustainability is difficult, if not impossible, and the SDG goals for 2030 are next to impossible to accomplish.

The Universal Declaration of Human Rights, perhaps the highest vision of human unity and dignity attainable under the early-modern paradigm, affirms so-called first generation political rights of assembly, speech, habeas corpus, and political participation. It also affirms so-called second generation economic and social rights to decent wages, adequate leisure time, and social security for disability and old age. However, it does *not* embody the "third generation rights" that have become evident with the advent of holism and planetary consciousness since the mid-twentieth century: the rights to peace and a protected planetary environment (Wacks, 2008: 149–150).

Clearly, the first two generations of rights cannot be fully actualized without both world peace and planetary sustainability. These third-generation rights are focused on the *common good* of the people of Earth and demand a global democratic public authority to sustain and protect them. A framework for such a global public authority was developed between 1968 and 1991 by hundreds of world citizens from many countries concerned for the future of humankind. This is known today as the *Constitution for the Federation of Earth*, translated into some 23 languages, and available online and in print.[5]

These third-generation rights permeate the *Earth Constitution* from beginning to end. Unless sustainability is more than a mere moral obligation but rather a legal requirement elaborated for every sphere of life arising from our common humanity and the demands of our life-giving biosphere (from extraction to production to consumption to disposal), we will never have a sustainable civilization.

Under the *Earth Constitution*, no nation, corporation, or individual any longer has the *legal right* to destroy the environment or threaten the welfare of future generations. For the first time in human history, the rule of force in nation-states and fragmented self-interest of countries is subsumed by the *rule of law* serving the common good of our planet and future generations. The global rule of law over all individual persons, of course, is the key not only to sustainability, but to ending war and promoting planetary justice as well.

The *Earth Constitution* does not eschew "development" or "free trade" but insists that sustainable development be available to all through global public banking (development financing not just for the wealthy who have property and the collateral to secure loans). The history of private, for-profit banking under the capitalist system has proven a failure. It has only made the wealthy more and more wealthy and the majority of people on Earth poor and penniless (see Brown, 2007). The issue is not the abolition of all private property (the *Constitution* affirms this right in Articles 12.1 and 12.16), but the responsible and sustainable use of Earth's resources that derives from an authentic economic and political holism of the people of Earth.

It is well known that today all governments are caught in the web of debt financing to the private banking system. Even wealthy nations have sunk into trillions of dollars in debt to the private banking system like the Federal Reserve Bank in the United States, and poor countries around the world are forced to seek convertible currency through external trade for the purposes of debt servicing, depriving them of revenues for education, healthcare, social security, or sustainable development needed by their citizens. Items 17.4 and 69 of the SDG Resolution declare that "Debtors and creditors must work together to prevent and resolve unsustainable debt situations."

In a document dedicated to "development that meets the needs of the present without compromising the ability of future generations to meet their own needs," it seems strange to advocate for "sustainable debt situations" so that the poor can sustainably *continue to pay* on the interest and principal of loans contracted to governments that will eventually hamper the ability of future generations to escape from poverty and underdevelopment. In a document that claims that the world must unite to address the climate crisis, this reveals that "uniting" does not even go so far as to forgive third-world debt in order to save the planet for future generations.

Conclusion

These facts underline my thesis that the SDG Resolution is premised on a *fundamental contradiction* between the goals of environmental sustainability and the fragmented *global institutional means* that are assumed for the attainment of these goals. *First,* the chapter has shown that the system of the absolute sovereignty of nations defeats the holistic political integration necessary for a sustainable world system.

Second, we have seen that fragmented, for-profit global economics also defeats sustainability. The *Earth Constitution* establishes global banking available worldwide, debt-free money creation for the planet, and public financing for sustainable development. Planetary money and banking become a *democratic public utility* designed to serve human needs (including both peace and sustainability) rather than private profit.

Third, it makes no sense for nations, corporations, or individuals to have the *legal* right to the unsustainable exploitation of Earth's resources at the expense of the rest of humanity and future generations. There must be public ownership of the critical resources necessary to protect the planetary biosphere. The *Earth Constitution* places "under world controls essential natural resources which may be limited or unevenly distributed about the Earth" (Article 4.30). It places the water supplies, oceans, and atmosphere of Earth in the hands of the global public authority. These are the real foundations of sustainability – a legally mandated and morally grounded *common good* for Earth, represented by the World Parliament and the Earth Federation Government.

Fourth, the SDGs include the goal of "full productive employment and decent work for all" by the year 2030 (Goal #8). In an economic system based on an employment "market" that seeks to maximize profit through offering the lowest wages to people desperate for work, the prospect of "full productive employment" is very unlikely. Capitalism thrives (the rich get richer) because of unemployment. However, with the *power to create money* in the hands of the World Parliament (representing the common good of the people of Earth), rather than in the hands of private bankers as today (see Brown, 2007), and with the goal of a happy and healthy world population living sustainably on Earth as embodied in the *Earth Constitution*, the Earth Federation will easily establish the World Service Corps (Article 4.36), possibly employing hundreds of millions of people, dedicated to *restoring* the planetary environment, replanting the forests, improving the air quality, creating fresh water supplies everywhere on Earth, reinvigorating the soil, and revitalizing the oceans.

In sum, it should be clear that only a global public authority can accomplish these goals. The World Parliament created with ratification of the *Constitution* is *legally mandated* to end war, demilitarize the world, protect human rights, end severe poverty, address the population crisis, and "to protect the environment and the ecological fabric of life from all sources of damage" (Article 1). Without the holistic infrastructure and proper means to sustainability, it will not happen. The SDG goal of sustainability is *contradicted* by today's fragmented global set of institutions that defeats this goal at every turn.

Since sustainability requires a united human civilization that complements and interfaces with a holistic planetary biosphere, the only way to really achieve sustainability is to **unite humanity legally, economically, morally, and culturally under the principle of unity in diversity** that respects and protects differences while legally embracing us as one species living on a single, fragile planet (see the Preamble to the *Earth Constitution*). This is both the function of the *Earth Constitution* and the very definition of "deep sustainability." The UN Sustainable Development goals cannot be achieved apart from ratification of the *Constitution for the Federation of Earth*.

Notes

1 https://www.sustainabledevelopment2015.org/AdvocacyToolkit/index.php/earth-summit-history/historical-documents/92-our-common-future.
2 The Constitution was collectively written by many world citizens working together between 1968 and 1991 as organized by the World Constitution and Parliament Association (WCPA). It was certified as completed at the final meeting in Troia, Portugal, May 1991: www.earth-constitution.org; www.earthfederationinstitute.org
3 *Transforming Our World: The 2030 Agenda for Sustainable Development: A/RES/70/1.* Declaration Introduction, Item 18: https://sustainabledevelopment.un.org/post2015/transformingourworld
4 "Battle for the Amazon: Tapajós Basin Threatened by Massive Development" by Sue Branford and Maurício Torres, 3 January 2017, Mongabay Website: https://news.mongabay.com/2017/01/battle-for-the-amazon-tapajos-basin-threatened-by-massive-development/.
5 The history of the composition of the *Constitution for the Federation of Earth* can be found at Martin, Glen T. *Constitution for the Federation of Earth: With Historical Introduction, Commentary, and Conclusion.* Appomattox, VA: Institute for Economic Democracy Press, 2010. See also: www.earth-constitution.org. See Martin (2010).

References

Birch, Charles and Cobb, John B., Jr. *The Liberation of Life.* Denton, TX: Environmental Ethics Books, 1990.
Branford, Sue and Torres, Maurício. "Battle for the Amazon: Tapajós Basin Threatened by Massive Development," January 3, 2017, Mongabay Website:https://news.mongabay.com/2017/01/battle-for-the-amazon-tapajos-basin-threatened-by-massive-development/.
Brown, Ellen Hodgson. *Web of Debt: The Shocking Truth about Our Money System.* Baton Rouge, LA: Third Millennium Press, 2007.
Caldicott, Helen. *If You Love This Planet.* New York: W.W. Norton & Co, 1992.
Daly, Herman E. *Beyond Growth: The Economics of Sustainable Development.* Boston: Beacon Press, 1996.
Donnelly, Jack. *Universal Human Rights in Theory and Practice.* Ithaca: Cornell University Press, 2003.
Erlich, Paul R. and Erlish, Anne H. *The Population Explosion.* New York: Simon & Schuster, 1990.
Hanson, James. "Climate Change Is Here: And Worse Than We Thought." *The Washington Post*, Washington, DC, August 3, 2012. www.washingtonpost.com/opinions/climatechange-is-here-and-worse-than-wethought/2012/08/03.
Harris, Errol E. *Apocalypse and Paradigm: Science and Everyday Thinking.* London: Praeger, 2000.
Harris, Errol E. *Earth Federation Now: Tomorrow Is Too Late*, 2nd ed. Appomattox, VA: Institute for Economic Democracy Press, 2014.
Heinberg, Richard. *The End of Growth: Adapting to Our New Economic Reality.* Gabriola Island, BC: New Society Publishers, 2011.
Luntley, Michael. *The Meaning of Socialism.* La Salle, Illinois: Open Court Publishing, 1990.
Martin, Glen T. (ed.). *Constitution for the Federation of Earth: With Historical Introduction, Commentary and Conclusion.* Appomattox, VA: Institute for Economic Democracy Press, 2010.

Martin, Glen T. (ed.). *One World Renaissance: Holistic Planetary Transformation through a Global Social Contract*. Appomattox, VA: Institute for Economic Democracy Press, 2016.

Petras, James and Veltmeyer, Henry. *Empire with Imperialism: The Globalizing Dynamics of Neo-Liberal Capitalism*. London: Zed Books, 2005.

Ricoeur, Paul. *Oneself as Another*. Kathleen Blamey, trans. Chicago: The University of Chicago Press, 1992.

Rifkin, Jeremy. *Entropy: Into the Greenhouse World*, rev. ed. New York: Bantam Books, 1989.

Sanders, Barry. *The Green Zone: The Environmental Costs of Militarism*. Oakland, CA: AK Press, 2009.

Shannon, Thomas Richard. *An Introduction to World-System Perspective*. Boulder, CO: Westview Press, 1989.

Shear, Michael. "Trump Will Withdraw U.S. From Paris Climate Agreement." *The New York Times*, June 1, 2017. www.nytimes.com/2017/06/01/climate/trump-paris-climate-agreement.html.

Speth, James Gustive. *Red Sky at Morning: America and the Crisis of the Global Environment*. New Haven: Yale University Press, 2004.

Wacks, Raymond. *Philosophy of Law: A Very Short Introduction*. Oxford: Oxford University Press, 2008.

4

INCLUSIVE LEADERSHIP

How to deal with unconscious biases in human resources decisions

*Gudrun Sander, Bianca van Dellen,
Ines Hartmann, Dominik Burger-Kloser
and Nora Keller*

Abstract

How do unconscious biases shape crucial personnel decisions recruitment and promotions in companies and organizations? This chapter shows how implicit biases about gender, race, looks, nationality or age can crucially influence managers' and human resources (HR) personnel's decision-making without their ever being aware of it. This can create companies that are not inclusive of heterogeneous backgrounds, where decision-making is not transparent and where employees feel unfairly treated. While inclusive, transparent workplaces for all genders and minorities are intrinsically desirable, this chapter also discusses how unconscious biases can negatively affect companies' bottom lines. Conversely, if managers learn to critically reflect on their own implicitly held biases and implement HR processes designed to counteract unconscious biases, this is a big step in the direction of inclusive leadership and diverse, inclusive and transparent companies. In this chapter, we primarily address SDGs #5 (gender equality) and #10 (reduced inequality) but also SDG #8 on decent work, as inclusive, unbiased leadership can create a place of work where everyone, irrespective of background, feels included, safe and empowered.

Introduction

How do unconscious biases shape crucial personnel decisions in companies and organizations? Managers – often together with human resources (HR) professionals – decide on new hires, promotions, salaries, salary increases, training initiatives, further education and team composition. In addition, managers are decisive in setting the tone for company culture. Hence, they should critically reflect on their unconscious biases when making such important decisions. Successfully doing so will contribute significantly to a more inclusive company.

Unconscious (or implicit) biases are automatic associations or stereotypes about groups of people happening outside our conscious awareness. According to Herbert (2013), "unconscious bias . . . is a bias that happens automatically and is triggered by our brain making quick judgments and assessments of people." Such judgments can be based on a difference in gender, sexual orientation or ethnicity and numerous other factors.

Managers who reflect on and counteract their unconscious biases are more likely to be inclusive leaders. Inclusive leaders embody a leadership approach that appreciates diversity, invites everyone's individual contribution and encourages full engagement during joint tasks (Bortini et al., 2016). Particularly for minority or underrepresented employee groups, such as women or people of color, inclusive leadership is an important prerequisite to feel fully included in teams (Shore et al., 2011). However, the benefits of inclusive leadership are not limited to minority groups; inclusive work environments offer equal opportunities to all employees to develop their full potential.

Apart from considerations of fairness and transparency, companies can reap tangible benefits from actively promoting diversity. If managed effectively, diverse teams are more likely to reexamine facts and remain objective, process information more carefully and come up with more creative solutions than homogeneous teams (Rock and Grant, 2016). Employees will be more content and motivated if promotion processes are as unbiased and transparent as possible. In turn, highly motivated and engaged employees will work harder, identify more strongly with their company and stay there longer. Thus, a climate of inclusion can decrease the turnover rate within a company, saving it from spending money on retraining new employees (Nishii, 2013). The 2015 "Diversity Matters" McKinsey report of 366 public companies even indicated that those in the top quartile for ethnic and racial diversity in management were 35 percent more likely to experience financial returns above their respective industry mean (McKinsey, 2015).

Unconscious biases at the workplace are connected closely to several sustainable development goals (SDGs), and limiting the influence of unconscious biases at work can get us a step closer to achieving several of these important milestones. First, gender stereotypes are a widespread cause of unconscious biases, which can prevent women from getting important opportunities or well-deserved recognition and remuneration for their work. Thus, SDG #5 (gender equality) is particularly relevant here. Second, unconscious biases can exacerbate workplace inequality (SDG #10): Biases can cause us to judge women, minorities, obese people and elderly people by different standards than members of the dominant group in an organization, eventually considering them less skilled and qualified. This reinforces existing patterns of inequality at the workplace. Finally, inclusive, unbiased leadership can contribute to a place of work where everyone, irrespective of their background, feels included, safe and empowered (SDG #8 on decent work).

This chapter explores how inclusive leadership helps companies reduce unconscious biases in HR processes and decisions. It argues that both managers reflecting on their own unconscious biases and de-biasing management processes are crucial prerequisites for inclusive leadership. First, the term "unconscious bias" is defined and then it is shown why it is important for managers to critically examine their own biases and alter their behavior accordingly. The chapter then focuses on recruitment and promotion processes, taking into account that both line managers and HR professionals are involved in these. Reference is made to the authors' own long-term research projects on diversity and inclusion practices with clients from different industries (banking, insurance, public sector, etc.) at the Competence Centre for Diversity & Inclusion (CCDI) at the University of St. Gallen (www.ccdi-unisg. ch) and to other seminal studies to show the impact of biased decision-making on companies and their employees.

Unconscious biases

Also known as implicit biases, unconscious biases are automatic stereotypes about groups of people outside our conscious awareness (Herbert, 2013). We all have unconscious biases regardless of how open minded we consider ourselves, and our implicit biases may run counter to our consciously held values. Unconscious biases stem from our tendency to stereotype people as members of particular groups (based on gender, sexuality, race, etc.) and to ascribe positive or negative attributes to them (Taylor,1981). People typically feel comfortable with those who are like them (the so-called in-group), and less comfortable with those they do not recognize as members of this group (members of the "out-group"). By identifying someone as a member of the in-group or out-group, we implicitly limit our assessment of another person to a single attribute, ignoring many others (Crisp and Nicel, 2004).

At their core, unconscious biases are mental shortcuts to make sense of enormous complexity: Neuroscientists estimate that we absorb ten million bytes of information every second. However, the human brain only consciously processes 0.00004 percent of this (von Kopp, 2015). In other words, we constantly filter and sort information upon which to base value judgments, decisions and actions outside our conscious awareness (Kahneman, 2011). Unconscious biases come from our particular experiences, education, media, cultural influences and other external influences.

Biases are not inherently negative (Herbert, 2013). Human ancestors would not have survived without the ability to tell friend from foe in a split second. Unconscious biases help us reduce unfathomable complexity, simplify our daily lives, speed up decision-making, compensate for knowledge gaps and help us preserve mental stability and a sense of security. Conversely, by their reductive nature, unconscious biases affect our ability to make fair and objective decisions and misinterpret situations and information as our brain presents us with a foregone conclusion. Because we are not consciously aware of many of our biases, their effect is difficult to control. Unconscious biases multiply as we grow older, and they are particularly prominent within homogeneous groups of people, in stressful situations and during moments of uncertainty.

Unconscious biases can lead to discriminatory decisions and actions if we allow stereotypes to guide us. A stereotype is a generalization, idea or judgment about a group of people that is applied to a single person we identify as part of that group (Crisp and Nicel, 2004). For example, a common stereotype is to associate obesity with laziness. If hiring managers subscribe to this stereotype, they will conclude an obese job applicant is lazy and therefore unsuited for the position – and not hire him or her (Baitsch and Steiner, 2004). In this way, unconscious biases have led to discrimination – for example, the unfair or prejudicial treatment of people and groups based on characteristics such as race, gender, age or sexual orientation (American Psychological Association, 2018).

There are three types of unconscious biases relevant in this chapter. Through *confirmation bias*, we search for and focus on information that confirms beliefs we already hold, discounting information that runs counter to our ideas. The *similarity or affinity bias* makes us gravitate toward people similar to us, evaluating their ideas more positively than others'. This "mini-me effect" confirms the holder as a person and my special attributes in a positive way. This leads to homogeneous groups at risk of not considering all possible alternatives and making wrong decisions. Finally, *attribution bias* makes us falsely attribute other people's actions to some flawed personal characteristic rather than situational factors. In a business context, supervisors attribute successful projects largely to the work of male collaborators while discounting the female labor that went into them (Kelley, 1973; Pohl, 2004; Gruman et al., 2017; Singh and Yan Ho, 2000).

It is crucial for business leaders to undergo the process of recognizing and examining their own unconscious biases. Most managers want to be good leaders who do not purposefully discriminate. When they make biased decisions, this has a huge impact on companies, especially on recruitment and promotions (hiring and promoting the "wrong" people). In turn, this influences employees' ability to achieve their full potential. Therefore, managers should acknowledge and reflect upon their unconscious biases and change their behaviors and patterns in terms of more inclusive leadership. This is not only a discussion about fairness and equal opportunity; it also has an impact on the bottom line, development of talents, performance and the image of the organization. Crucially, organizations should offer unconscious bias training to both managers and employees to highlight the pervasiveness and effects of unconscious biases and help people to confront their own biases, which often is uncomfortable and difficult. Unconscious bias training should be on a voluntary basis to guarantee high levels of engagement and motivation of training participants (Dobbin and Kalev, 2016).

Unconscious biases and recruitment

When it comes to vacancies, employment ads and recruitment, managers' biased decisions strongly influence whether certain groups have a chance to enter the company. Unconscious biases can permeate the entire recruiting process, starting with job postings and ranging from the invitation to interview and the interviews themselves to making an offer to the favored candidate.

Biases play a poignant role during initial candidate selection, where recruiters field a large number of applicants with little time to get a full picture of each. The similarity or affinity bias can play a significant role: Companies risk excluding high potentials from continuing in the hiring process only because they are different from the interviewer or the incumbent holding the position. As companies are not recruiting the best person for the job in this way, they are left less productive and profitable than they could be otherwise (Singh and Yan Ho, 2000).

Studies show the pervasiveness of biased decision-making during recruitment. For example, Weichselbaumer (2016) reports that foreign-sounding names and wearing a headscarf significantly depress positive responses and candidate preselection for otherwise identical job applications. In an experiment, 1,474 applications were submitted in response to job advertisements of companies located in Germany (where adding photos to CVs is the norm). The applicant with the German name was the most successful, receiving positive feedback from 18.8 percent of her applications. The applicant with the Turkish name wearing no headscarf had a response rate of 13.5 percent and the applicant with a Turkish name and headscarf fared worst, receiving positive feedback from only 4.2 percent of all companies contacted.

Not only should companies deliberately counteract biases during the initial screening of applications, they should also be vigilant about having a well-balanced candidate pool throughout the entire recruitment process. In a series of widely cited studies, Johnson et al. (2016) found that if there is only one woman in a finalist pool during a candidate search, there is virtually no chance that she will be hired. According to their experiment, a woman's hiring chances increased by almost 80 times if there were two or more women in the finalist pool. One explanation is that a single woman in a group of men will be viewed as the "token" woman – and therefore not as deserving and qualified as men (Johnson et al., 2016; Kanter, 1977).

How can companies avoid the pitfalls of unconscious biases during recruitment? Luckily, several strategies can minimize bias and discrimination. When reviewing incoming applications, it may make sense to remove identifying information from résumés to avoid being influenced by applicants' gender. A pilot study conducted by the German Anti-Discrimination Commission from 2010 to 2011 asked eight major companies and organizations to anonymize their application procedures (Krause et al., 2012). In this study, various anonymization methods were used to conceal any information that could point to gender, including names, photos, or even membership in gender-specific organizations. Recruiters were able to find equally well-qualified candidates as with traditional recruiting strategies, and many appreciated not being "distracted" from job-relevant information. Forty-one percent of applicants indicated that they believed anonymization increased their chances of being invited to interview. Overall, all organizations found that the rate of discrimination decreased due to the intervention, though the anonymization procedure should be chosen with care to avoid the loss of crucial information.

Apart from anonymization, recruiters may consider women's and men's résumés separately and pick top candidates from each, then compare them against each other at the end. Candidates should be screened by multiple people, asked the same questions in the same order during interviews and evaluated based on identical criteria (Herbert, 2013). This minimizes the amount of leeway for recruiters to judge candidates based on unconscious biases. During each round of candidate eliminations, recruiters or line managers should reconsider the number of minorities still in the running and ask themselves honestly whether the small percentage of minorities in the final round is due to unconscious biases. The order of interviews can be used strategically: Recruiters should consider inviting a favorite candidate to interview last, to allow interviewers to keep an open mind while interviewing less favored candidates (and the recruiters may be surprised by the results). After the interviews, recruiters should ask themselves honestly: Would I have asked a man/woman this question? Would I have asked this question to an older/younger person? Would I have asked this question to someone from my own/another nationality?

Unconscious biases and promotions

Even if an institution is able to onboard a diverse staff, this unfortunately does not mean that they are also able to develop them. How do unconscious biases influence human resource development regarding promotions and retention?

Many companies have a quite diverse workforce overall. For example, the recent McKinsey and Lean In (2018) study found that women made up 48 percent of the entry-level workforce in the United States. ADVANCE and CCDI (2018) found similar patterns for Swiss companies. Nevertheless, at higher management levels, especially on the board or top-management level, the degree of diversity decreases significantly (Hambrick, 2007; Kilduff et al., 2000). In the United States in 2018, at the top level of management, 22 percent of employees were women (McKinsey and Lean In, 2018). In Switzerland, 51 percent of nonmanagement employees were women, but only 15 percent at the top-management level (ADVANCE and Competence Centre for Diversity and Inclusion, 2018). This means that retention and promotion of a diverse workforce remains a significant challenge for companies and business today that must (and can) be addressed.

Biased decision-making plays a crucial role during professional development and promotion processes. Similarity and attribution biases can cause male supervisors to unconsciously view other men more favorably and attribute successful projects largely to male collaborators. Supervisors may also evaluate men based on their potential and women based on their specific experience (Ibarra et al., 2010).

Age and age differences can also trigger unconscious biases. A CCDI study (2017) shows that the age difference between employee and supervisor can have a significant impact on performance evaluation. If the supervisor is younger than the employee, the performance evaluation significantly worsens as age difference increases. If the supervisor is older than the employee, the opposite is the case – the larger the age difference, the better the performance evaluation. The study further reveals that men receive significantly more positive evaluations of their development potential than women do. Another study by the chapter authors' organization shows a marginalized group effect (CCDI, 2017), whereby members of the dominant group tend to evaluate members of its group more favorably than members of the marginalized group. Members of the marginalized group are stricter in their evaluations in general, but especially when it comes to evaluating employees of their own (marginalized) group (CCDI, 2017). One possible reason for this is that minority managers, due to their small number, feel like they are under closer scrutiny than their non-minority peers. According to this logic, they are more scrupulous in their evaluations, especially of other members of their minority group, to avoid charges of favoritism. If employees feel their evaluation was unfair, they are more likely to leave the company for opportunities elsewhere.

The 2018 Gender Intelligence Report for Switzerland by ADVANCE and CCDI shows evidence that both promotions in general and promotions to management clearly favor employees working full time. In Switzerland, women often work part time. As such, women face higher obstacles to promotion than men, even when working very close to full time (80 percent and above) and even during the initial promotion from nonmanagement to the first management level. What are some strategies to mitigate unconscious biases during promotion processes, thereby reducing the turnover rate and retaining a more diverse workforce at all hierarchy levels?

It is vital that managers be trained and sensitized to foster, promote and model sustainable approaches to diversity and unconscious biases during the personnel development and promotion processes. Managers should ask themselves if they are really promoting the best team members (based on objective, verifiable criteria) or if they are favoring the "loudest" team member exhibiting the most confidence. Are members of the team periodically overlooked because they are more introverted or because they work part time or from home. Which team members do managers pay the most attention to? In which team members do they see the most development potential? Why? Not only should managers ask these questions and urge those below them in the hierarchy to do the same, but they should make it very clear that they strive for bias-free, transparent promotion and HR processes.

All HR processes should be "de-biased." Effects should be measured regularly and processes adapted in response. For instance, a proposal to promote a specific employee should not only depend on the evaluation of the direct supervisor. Rather, feedback from different perspectives such as clients, peers and team members should also matter. All promotions should be discussed with several carefully composed circles that take potential biases and fair promotion goals into account in their decision-making. Another possibility is to shift promotion processes to follow an "opt out" logic. At Deloitte Switzerland, all women and all employees who work on 80 percent contracts are automatically part of the promotion pool. This puts line managers into the purposely uncomfortable position to argue against a woman's (or minority group member's) promotion instead of arguing why a woman should be promoted. This leads to a higher promotion rate for women, minorities and part-time employees.

Crucially, HR processes should not be "de-biased" in isolation; they should be part of a holistic diversity strategy driven by upper management. To foster an inclusive culture and leadership, a company must have a corporate culture that views diversity as important for the whole organization (Sander and Hartmann, 2019). This is best achieved through a so-called systemic approach (Dass and Parker, 1999) to managing diversity and inclusion, where diversity is viewed as a strategic issue, clearly communicated to both employees and stakeholders as such and linked to existing systems and core activities. It is important that supervisors be assigned diversity-related goals and monitored accordingly and that there are rewards and sanctions associated with (non)compliance (Dobbin and Kalev, 2016). Sometimes, one hears the criticism that such an approach might lead to a less qualified minority candidate being hired over a more qualified candidate without a diverse background. If quotas are worded and implemented smartly ("at equal qualification levels") and coupled with transparent evaluation criteria to measure respectively how qualified candidates are, it is highly unlikely that this would happen. Day-to-day management processes should be reconsidered from an inclusion angle, ranging from core business processes like products and services offered to customers to support processes like quality management, human resources and accounting. This can help de-biasing management processes and also reduce unconscious biases in HR processes.

Conclusion

In order to lessen the impact of unconscious biases in company leadership and HR processes, it is crucial to examine personal unconscious biases and foster an inclusive working environment. It takes personal courage and a willingness to consider potentially unwelcome and uncomfortable aspects of our mental frameworks; after all, most people do not like to acknowledge their own potentially racist or sexist beliefs. By understanding the value in reducing personal biases, leaders and managers can move past the discomfort inherent in confronting implicit biases at odds with consciously held values and begin to acknowledge and eliminate blind spots. There are concrete mental steps to take in specific situations to avoid judgments and actions based on unconscious biases. For instance, to overcome confirmation bias, it helps to set clear and tangible criteria to form the basis of the decision-making process (Pohl, 2004). To sidestep attribution bias, it helps to question why we judge others as competent or incompetent, respectively (Heilman and Haynes, 2005). To avoid affinity bias, it can help to evaluate each team member's individual contributions to a project as transparently as possible (Kanter, 1977).

Leaders who critically examine their own unconscious biases and consciously implement strategies to prevent unconscious biases from affecting decision-making are well on their way towards inclusive leadership. According to Shore et al. (2011), inclusive leadership is a prerequisite to boost inclusion in teams as managers shape the culture of the organizations, as their decisions influence the level of inclusiveness in teams and in the organization. Therefore, it is particularly important to raise awareness for unconscious biases on the managerial level and to de-bias management processes in order to guarantee high levels of inclusion and equal opportunities for all employees. In this regard, tracking key performance indicators for diversity and inclusion and measuring to what extent the employees perceive the work environment as inclusive can also help unconscious bias training for managers (and employees) support organizations and managers to overcome the danger of excluding diverse employees with high potential from key opportunities. Inclusive leadership skills will allow leaders to utilize to the fullest the advantages of diversity in those they manage, while leaders without inclusive leadership skills may get left behind.

Both de-biasing management processes and managers who reflect on their unconscious biases are important prerequisites for inclusive leadership, which in turn can lead to more inclusive work environments with an adequate representation of women and other minorities in the organization.

References

ADVANCE and Competence Centre for Diversity & Inclusion. "Gender Intelligence Report." (Online report, ADVANCE and HSG, University of St. Gallen, 2018). Accessed November 9, 2018. https://advance-hsg-report.ch.

American Psychological Association. "Discrimination: What It Is, and How to Cope." (Online report, 2018). Accessed November 9, 2018. www.apa.org/helpcenter/discrimination.aspx.

Baitsch, C. and Steiner, E. *Zwei tun das Gleiche. Kommunikation zwischen Frauen und Männern im Berufsalltag.* Zürich: Verlag der Fachvereine, 2004.

Bortini, P., et al. "Inclusive Leadership: Theoretical Framework." (Online report, 2016). Accessed November 15, 2018. https://inclusiveleadership.eu/il_theoreticalframework_en.pdf.

Competence Centre for Diversity & Inclusion (CCDI). "Biases in Performance and Potential Evaluations." (Research project report, University of St. Gallen. St. Gallen, 2017).

Competence Centre for Diversity & Inclusion (CCDI). "The Marginalized Group Effect in Employee Evaluations." (Research project report, University of St. Gallen. St. Gallen, 2017).

Crisp, R. and Nicel, J. "Disconforming Intergroup Evaluations: Asymmetric Effects for In-Groups and Out-Groups." *Journal of Social Psychology*, 144(3), 2004: 247–271.

Dass, P. and Parker, B. "Strategies for Managing Human Resource Diversity: From Resistance to Learning." *Academy of Management Perspectives*, 13(2), 1999: 68–80.

Dobbin, F. and Kalev, A. "Why Diversity Programs Fail." *Harvard Business Review*, online, 2016. Accessed November 28, 2018. https://hbr.org/2016/07/why-diversity-programs-fail.

Gruman, J., Schneider, F. and Coutts, L. *Applied Social Psychology: Understanding and Addressing Social and Practical Problems*, 3rd ed. Los Angeles: Sage Publications, 2017.

Hambrick, D. "Upper Echelons Theory: An Update." *Academy of Management Review*, 32(2), 2007: 334–343.

Heilman, M. and Haynes, M. "No Credit Where Credit Is Due: Attributional Rationalization of Women's Success in Male-Female Teams." *Journal of Applied Psychology*, 90(5), 2005: 905–916.

Herbert, C. "Unconscious Bias and Higher Education." London: Equality Challenge Unit. 2013. Accessed November 28, 2018. www.ecu.ac.uk/wp-content/uploads/2014/07/unconscious-bias-and-higher-education.pdf.

Ibarra, H., Carter, N. and Silva, C. "Why Men Still Get More Promotions Than Women." *Harvard Business Review*, online, 2010. Accessed November 28, 2018. https://hbr.org/2010/09/why-men-still-get-more-promotions-than-women.

Johnson, S., Hekman, D. and Chan, E. "If There's Only One Woman in Your Candidate Pool, There's Statistically No Chance She'll Be Hired." *Harvard Business Review*, online, 2016. Accessed November 28, 2018. https://hbr.org/2016/04/if-theres-only-one-woman-in-your-candidate-pool-theres-statistically-no-chance-shell-be-hired.

Kahneman, D. *Thinking, Fast and Slow*. London: Penguin Books, 2011.

Kanter, R. M. *Men and Women of the Corporation*. New York: Basic Books, 1977.

Kelley, H. "The Process of Causal Attribution." *American Psychologist*, 28(2), 1973: 107–128.

Kilduff, M., Angelmar, R. and Mehra, A. "Top Management-Team Diversity and Firm Performance: Examining the Role of Cognitions." *Organization Science*, 11(1), 2000: 21–34.

Krause, et al. *Pilotprojekt "Anonymisierte Bewerbungsverfahren"*. *Abschlussbericht*. Berlin: KOWA and IZA. 2012. Accessed November 28, 2018. http://ftp.iza.org/report_pdfs/iza_report_44.pdf.

McKinsey. *Diversity Matters*. New York: McKinsey. Online, 2015. Accessed November 9, 2018. www.mckinsey.com/~/media/mckinsey/business%20functions/organization/our%20insights/why%20diversity%20matters/diversity%20matters.ashx.

McKinsey and Lean In. *Women in the Workplace*. Online, 2018. Accessed November 9, 2018. https://womenintheworkplace.com.

Nishii, L. "The Benefits of Climate for Inclusion for Gender-Diverse Groups." *Academy of Management Journal*, 56(6), 2013: 1754–1774.

Pohl, R. *Cognitive Illusions: A Handbook on Fallacies and Biases in Thinking, Judgement and Memory*. New York: Psychology Press, 2004.

Rock, D. and Grant, H. "Why Diverse Teams Are Smarter." *Harvard Business Review*, online, 2016. Accessed November 28, 2018. https://hbr.org/2016/11/why-diverse-teams-are-smarter.

Sander, G. and Hartmann, I. "Diversity as Strategy." In M. Danowitz, E. Hanappi-Egger and H. Mensi-Klarbach (eds.), *Diversity in Organizations: Concepts & Practices*, 2nd ed. Basingstoke: Palgrave Macmillan, 2019.

Shore, L., et al. "Inclusion and Diversity in Work Groups: A Review and Model for Future Research." *Journal of Management*, 37(4), 2011: 1262–1289.

Singh, R. and Yan Ho, S. "Attitudes and Attraction: A New Test of the Attraction, Repulsion and Similarity-Dissimilarity Asymmetry Hypotheses." *British Journal of Social Psychology*, 39(2), 2000: 197–211.

Taylor, S. "A Categorization Approach to Stereotyping." In D. Hamilton (ed.), *Cognitive Processes in Stereotyping and Intergroup Behavior*, 1st ed. London: Psychology Press, 1981: 83–114.

Von Kopp, D. "11 Millionen vs. 40 Bit." In D. von Kopp (ed.), *Focusing: Die Sprache der Intuition*, 1st ed. Heidelberg: Springer, 2015: 27–28.

Weichselbaumer, D. *Discrimination against Female Migrants Wearing Headscarves*. Bonn: Forschungsinstitut zur Zukunft der Arbeit, 2016.

PART II

Addressing SDGs at industry levels

5

TAPPING INTO NEW POWER

Opportunities and challenges for growing community renewable energy

Judith M. Herbst and Deanna Grant-Smith

Abstract

Traditional energy sources, such as oil, coal and gas are subject to supply shortages and have significant environmental impacts. A range of renewable energy sources, including solar photovoltaic, geothermal, hydroelectric and wind power, have been posited as more sustainable alternatives to meet current and future energy demands. Despite its potential to deliver affordable and clean energy, the adoption of renewable energy has experienced a varied rate of support in governmental policy and uptake in electricity markets. Community renewable energy has emerged as a grassroots approach to redress this general policy failure to adopt renewable energy as a major contributor to energy supplies and to advance the transition to low-carbon energy. It represents an important shift toward an affordable, reliable, sustainable, decentralized and clean energy supply. Using an illustrative example of global good practice and innovation, this chapter critically explores the potential for community renewable energy projects to positively respond to Sustainable Development Goals #7 (affordable and clean energy), #13 (climate action) and #17 (partnerships for the goals). Australia's Hepburn Wind project is highlighted as a paradigmatic case to draw attention to the complexities and promise of introducing and scaling up community renewable energy projects.

Introduction

It is estimated that energy accounts for a substantial 42 percent of greenhouse gas emissions (International Energy Agency [IEA], 2016). Despite their contribution to emissions and reported health and environmental impacts, oil, coal and gas remain leading power sources. With energy demand expected to increase and predicted energy supply shortages looming (Yergin, 2011), the adoption of renewable energy sources has the potential to reshape the global energy sector. Renewable energy is poised to provide solutions to meet current and future energy requirements (Hoffmann, 2014) and remedy the energy poverty experienced by vulnerable and disadvantaged citizens. The deployment of renewable energy also promises the advancing of inclusive and sustainable development using low-carbon technologies to deliver affordable and clean energy. There has, however, been inconsistent adoption of renewable energy into governmental policies and electricity markets.

Community renewable energy (CRE) has emerged as a grassroots approach to rectify this general policy failure and to advance the transition to low-carbon energy. CRE projects empower citizens to generate their own small-scale distributed power using renewable energy sources (Heffron and McCauley, 2014). Cooperatives, sharing ownership of CRE initiatives with private entities, offer leverage to tackle social injustice, offset energy shortages and abate climate change. CRE projects may thus positively respond to the United Nations' (UN) Sustainable Development Goals (SDGs) #7: Affordable and clean energy, #13: Climate action and #17: Partnerships for the goals. Despite these opportunities, the energy market and regulators have not easily adapted to the governance of decentralized energy production through such collective citizen undertakings (Saintier, 2017) to generate their own power and savings (Seyfang et al., 2013).

This chapter provides an overview of the global CRE landscape. Although CRE projects are multifaceted and diverse (Hicks and Ison, 2018), CRE is explored here in the context of common institutional and other intersecting forces that shape CRE project viability. The chapter begins by discussing these forces alongside the motivations and benefits that drive a project forward. Contextual factors that may help or hinder CRE project development are then considered. While it is not possible to replicate CRE experiences across communities (Walker et al., 2010), Australia's Hepburn Wind project is discussed to provide an account of a successful CRE project. Ideas for expanding CRE globally and locally conclude the chapter.

Key considerations for CRE projects

Conventional public or private utilities using fossil fuel reserves dominate the global marketplace, but a growing number of countries are phasing out 'dirty' energy sources and investing in an array of renewables (Kennedy, 2012). These include solar, wind, biogas and geothermal energy. Many of the leaders in renewable energy production and consumption are smaller countries (UN Department of Economic and Social Affairs [UNDESA], n.d.). Sweden aims to become the world's first 100 percent renewable energy nation. Costa Rica, Scotland and Uruguay are committed to achieving 99, 97 and 95 percent renewable energy, respectively (The Climate Reality Project, 2016).

There are considerable differences in the degree of civic participation and cost savings achieved between countries to pursue renewable energy (Ruggiero et al.,

2018). There is strong evidence of an increased interest by energy 'prosumers'[1] in establishing CRE enterprises across Europe, spanning Spain (Kunze and Becker, 2015), the Netherlands (Oteman et al., 2017), Italy (Wirth, 2014), Germany (Walker, 2008) and Finland (Varho et al., 2016). In 2017, England, Wales and Northern Ireland alone documented 228 community organizations – comprising 48,000 members and more than 1,800 volunteers that generated up to 170 MWh of energy (Community Energy Association England [CEAE], 2018). These numbers demonstrate how a groundswell of support can play a crucial role in delivering local energy solutions. Indeed, a key strength of CRE lies in its ability to mobilize residents and businesses to facilitate increased transitions to energy efficiency (Kostevsek et al., 2013; Rutherford and Coutard, 2014). However, a number of technological, sociocultural, political, economic, locational and environmental forces can affect the viability of CRE projects.

Technological considerations

CRE projects entail significant planning and operational considerations (Mallon, 2006), especially to ensure technological feasibility (Jacobsson and Bergek, 2004). Technological issues vary depending on the energy type, local conditions, available natural and community assets and community needs (Wiseman and Bronin, 2013). It is important that uncertainties associated with variable feed-in to the grid are also recognized and innovative solutions developed (Jones, 2017). These uncertainties include accounting for weather conditions to permit 'smoothing out' of energy generation (Teleke et al., 2010).

CRE projects require the installation of digitally monitored systems such as smart grids or smart meters. These interface with a standard electricity network to increase energy efficiency and build in security through distributed sources of power that guard against power interruptions (Sioshansi, 2011). Technological developments in energy storage systems offer advantages in increased performance, cost savings and reduced emissions (Ruggiero et al., 2018).

Sociocultural considerations

Equally essential to CRE development is gaining a social license to operate in a community. Participatory decision-making should be encouraged from the outset, as successful CRE projects rely on local cooperation (Wirth, 2014) and the commitment of a range of actors. Evidence from biogas cooperatives in Tyrol, northern Italy, demonstrates how intermixing appropriate institutional forces with norms of locality and resident responsibility can bolster support for a CRE proposal. To gain traction at the community level, trusting relationships must be developed within local communities (Walker et al., 2010). However, social bonds can be difficult to establish. This is particularly so when there are dissenting views about likely costs and benefits of CRE projects or where projects threaten emotional attachments to a place (van Veelen and Haggett,

2017). For example, CRE developments in Scotland were impacted when locals believed projects were at odds with conserving natural heritage (Fiona and Mackenzie, 2006).

Research indicates the presence of a positive relationship between awareness of the environment and the likelihood of participating in a CRE project (Boon and Dieperink, 2014.) Moreover, where a local area has at least two favorable influences such as conditions for generating wind or solar power, and locals have established social bonds, then a higher level of social acceptance for a CRE project can result (Gormally et al., 2014). The trust required to successfully introduce and manage CRE projects also depends on developing relationships with banks and finance companies, renewable energy experts and state and national governmental agencies. Agreements with each of these parties should be negotiated separately. These relationships contribute to achieving partnerships for sustainable development (SDG #17).

In the absence of strong community leadership, the local government can become a renewable energy prosumer. One such local government–driven CRE project is occurring in the Sunshine Coast region, Australia. The Sunshine Coast Regional Council has installed solar photovoltaic panels to completely offset the area's energy requirements (see Photo 5.1). This project also allows the council to act on behalf of ratepayers to improve residents' health, lower emissions by stimulating a 'clean tech' hub and provide long-term cost savings (Sunshine Coast Regional Council, 2019).

PHOTO 5.1 Solar farm of the sunshine coast regional council in Australia

Political considerations

Galvanizing support by a local government authority, such as a mayor who can act as a policy entrepreneur (Young and Brans, 2017), can also positively impact the outcome for a CRE proposal. Connections with energy providers and local residents (Magnani et al., 2017) can create the momentum required to carry a project forward. Local government can also be instrumental in leading public consultation and enhancing positive relationships between the public and developers (Devine-Wright, 2014).

Advocacy by policy makers at higher tiers of government is another critical element for CRE. Generally, market and land-use planning mechanisms tend to favor large commercial projects funded by large corporations, diminishing prospects for CRE (Strachan et al., 2015). When state and federal policy makers enact favorable energy policies, change can take place. For example, when the United Kingdom introduced a Shared Ownership Policy as a voluntary strategy to support local initiatives and it established a norm for "new commercially-developed onshore renewable projects" (UK Government, 2015: 35), developments increased. Later policy changes associated with feed-in tariffs, and tax relief seemed to negatively impact growth in CRE projects (CEAE, 2018). Therefore, different policies may cancel each other out.

Economic considerations

Inconsistencies in the provision of government incentives with financing can place additional burdens on residents to secure their own resources to pursue CRE initiatives. Raising capital to defray the investment and operational costs can be particularly difficult. The Energy Saving Trust, a social enterprise that oversees disbursement of grants and loans and provides advice to interested communities helped to fill this void after the abolition of the Community Renewables Initiative in the United Kingdom, Wales and Scotland (Walker et al., 2007).

Alternative funding arrangements may come from floating member shares, offering bonds, collecting donations or engaging in crowdfunding. There are many cases of successful CRE projects where communities created hybrid approaches by setting up a cooperative or joint ownership/governance arrangement to pool citizen funding with external sources to realize a project (Strachan et al., 2015). These types of investment models are often implemented in rural areas where agreements are formed to share ownership and management of initiatives among communities, private enterprises and local governments (Magnani et al., 2017). PPP (public-private-partnership) business models can stimulate communities to underwrite CRE projects and may precipitate fringe benefits in community funding programs. These programs can enhance a community's capacity to access additional equipment or services for other community projects. Additionally, obtaining financial viability for CRE can protect disadvantaged consumers through energy equality (Saintier, 2017).

Locational considerations

Some countries have mobilized a high participation of locals alongside capital reserves or properties to house collective energy systems. Clustering energy production sites can lead to higher rates of CRE development and diffusion. Further, having a wider coverage of wind farms across climate zones can increase grid reliability (Blakers et al., 2017). Such colocation of CREs is seen in collectively owned wind energy sites (Garud and Karnoe, 2003) and agricultural biogas plants in Denmark (Geels and Raven, 2007) and in solar energy-generated power stations in Germany (Dewald and Truffer, 2011).

Larger schemes for CRE in the United States are being achieved through leveraging programs and planning processes by state and municipal decision makers working around potential national constraints (Cook et al., 2016). Thus, a trend is growing toward building networks of solar, wind, hydroelectric and bio sources to increase the capacity of renewable energy, strengthen innovation for resilience and improve marketplace competitiveness. Nevertheless, complex planning processes combined with high grid-connection costs and an inability to access suitable sites have prevented or stalled projects. Introducing specific development controls can offer the potential to promote and protect CRE project development in suitable locations (Caripis and Kallies, 2012).

Environmental considerations

In the Anthropocene Age, which recognizes the influence of mankind on nature, there is a rising concern for climate change. Climate action (SDG #13) is becoming an impetus for embracing clean energy technologies, as there is growing scientific evidence and international consensus on the existence and impacts of global warming. Moreover, recent reports of the Intergovernmental Panel on Climate Change (IPCC, 2018) point to benefits of green energy in local communities. Although CRE projects can be perceived as sustainable energy sources, tensions can arise regarding potential negative environmental impacts. Wind power projects, for example, have been directly implicated in wildlife mortality through collision with turbines and indirectly through impacts on foraging habitat availability and migration and foraging patterns (Hull and Cawthen, 2013; Millon et al., 2018). Community resistance has also been raised in relation to noise, impacts on adjacent property values, health concerns, aesthetics of wind farms (Newton, 2015) and general opposition to what may be perceived as promoting a "green political agenda" (Barrett, 2015: 132). These issues must be addressed in CRE planning in order to gain community support (Kuch and Morgan, 2015).

The Hepburn Wind project

Like many countries, Australia has experienced pervasive challenges in its CRE projects. This case explores how the above considerations affected the development of Hepburn Wind. In a cooperative situated 100 kilometers northwest of

PHOTO 5.2 Twin Turbines at Hepburn Wind that generate enough energy for the towns of Hepburn and Daylesford in Victoria

Melbourne, Hepburn Wind's champions worked to overcome obstacles to bring its 4.2 MW wind farm to fruition (See Photo 5.2).

It took years of campaigning by locals to assemble a consensus and fund the wind farm that was designed to service the needs of its immediate community. The project initially struggled against technological costs for grid connection and low returns due to a decrease in commodity prices for oil that would have helped to offset its deficit (Herbst, 2017). The company faced political intentions to abolish the renewable energy target (Department of the Environment and Energy [DEE], 2018). The implication of this was a lessening of government support for CREs more generally. Then wind and solar energy subsidies provided via feed-in tariffs through large-scale generation certificates (LGC) that traded around AU$80 MWh significantly decreased (Parkinson, 2018). Spot prices at the end of September 2018 were recorded at $71.90 (Clean Energy Regulator, 2018). These combined factors delayed the payment of dividends to investors.

Notwithstanding these pressures, the company maintained open communication with its shareholders and applied participatory decision-making in its governance to counter issues. In doing so, it survived, and its shareholders influenced the overturning of state-based planning amendments that imposed a ban on wind farms in Victoria. The ban effectively gave the owner of any dwelling within two kilometers of a proposed wind farm the power to decide whether or not development should proceed (Caripis and Kallies, 2012). Today, Hepburn Wind honors its pledge to distribute AU$1 million (one million Australian dollars) in community benefit funds that help to cultivate other community renewable energy projects in nearby communities, and it has substantially reduced its debt (Hepburn, 2016).

Legislation by the federal government still poses continuous uncertainty, most recently through its failure to adopt a National Energy Guarantee (Australia Government, Clean Energy Regulator, 2018). Had a guarantee been adopted, renewable energy would have made up 28–36 percent of total energy generation by 2030 (Clean Energy Council, 2014). The goal of current reforms is to achieve 23.5 percent of national electricity via renewable energy sources by 2020. Lower prices to install renewable energy are expediting the development of infrastructure, but oil and coal power generators remain the primary sources of energy at 53 percent compared to 6 percent for renewable energy (Australian Energy Update, 2017). The pursuit of renewable energy targets is contested with some industry and fossil-fuel generation/retailer groups opposed to renewable energy targets. By contrast, NGOs and the renewable sector have been more likely to support them (Simpson and Clifton, 2014). Hepburn Wind is a testament to the power of having renewable energy experts and locals persevere to make a project operational. Moreover, it is believed by many to exemplify best practice in CRE (World Wind Energy Association [WWEA], 2015).

Beyond fulfilling company objectives, several Hepburn Wind executives and partners started a peak advocacy body, Embark, to disseminate knowledge, so other communities can set up their own CRE projects. Embark concentrates on wind, solar and micro-hydro power and functions as an online learning platform (Herbst, 2017). It includes links to intermediaries that can achieve small-scale initiatives (Guerreiro and Botetzagias, 2017; Embark, 2013). This case therefore highlights how CRE actors can become powerful agents to transition to affordable and clean energy (SDG #7) (Young and Brans, 2017) by taking climate action (SDG #13). It also shows how power is increased when working together to advance partnerships for sustainable development (SDG #17). In addition, it demonstrates how one can catalyze change to advance other SDGs (UNDESA, n.d.) including industry, innovation and infrastructure (SDG #9); sustainable cities and communities (SDG #11) and responsible consumption and production (SDG #12).

Conclusion: realizing the untapped potential of CRE

Although interest in renewable energy projects has been impacted by fluctuations in the cost of fossil fuels (Newton, 2015) these have now, in many respects, been subsumed by social and environmental concerns. This situation is particularly relevant to CRE (Lowy Institute, 2018). Increasing global energy demands, climate change and calls to action under the SDGs compel all levels of government to take seriously the potential contribution of renewable energy for global energy portfolios (Ehrlich, 2013) to heighten energy security (Yergin, 2011). Civil society, in partnership with government and business, has the capacity to play a significant role in promoting a clean energy future through CRE projects (Magnani et al., 2017).

Research from Finland looked at ways to create opportunities for scaling up the energy sector. Although evidence of learning between CRE projects may be limited, 'system change projects' (i.e., when members want to diffuse specific innovative technologies or knowledge about producing renewable energy) demonstrate increased engagement in learning, networking and developing interest (Ruggiero et al., 2018). These aspects can create a strategic niche to facilitate wider adoption (Seyfang and Smith, 2007). To broaden reach at a global level, there should be clarity of vision by communities, coordination of logistics by competent intermediaries and support by favorable policy and regulatory frameworks (Ruggiero et al., 2018).

The Coalition for Action of the International Renewable Energy Agency [IRENA] (2018) recognizes renewable energy investment as urgent to accelerate transformation that is in line with achieving the SDGs. It provides an international forum where pioneers and startups can exchange ideas, gain knowledge and learn from the experiences of CRE operators. IRENA recommends communities seek additional assistance from nearby advisory services and finance providers. It urges governments to avoid energy auction systems and support adjustable feed-in tariffs that allow for higher capacity CRE projects. In developing nations, governments could spearhead a business model whereby finance institutions could offer public loan guarantees that could curtail energy injustices suffered by disadvantaged citizens (IRENA, 2018).

Policies to reduce costs and barriers to CRE, combined with opinion leaders applying "salient social pressure" (Kalkbrenner and Roosen, 2016: 67) could transform CRE initiatives from niche projects into mainstream enterprises. However, as Cass (2017: 24) argues, "[i]n order to win hearts and minds the renewable energy industry needs to shift from describing technologies to illustrating the benefits they bring." This includes ensuring that deep consultation and ongoing communication with affected stakeholders are undertaken so that ineffective efforts do not negatively impact the reputation of the wider CRE industry (Hall and Jeanneret, 2015). Increasing the uptake of CRE schemes and supporting their expansion present numerous economic, social and environmental benefits. These accrue at an individual, community and regional scale for improving cost-competitiveness in the marketplace. They also provide employment and training opportunities in local communities and offer a truly sustainable energy alternative for energy consumers and the planet.

Note

1 "Prosumers undertake a proactive behaviour by managing their consumption, production and energy storage, while traditional consumers assume a passive behaviour when it comes to their energy consumption" (Sousa et al., 2018: 2).

References

Australian Government. "Australian Energy Update." 2017. Accessed September 26, 2018. www.energy.gov.au/sites/g/files/net3411/f/energy-update-report-2017.pdf.
Australian Government. "Large-Scale Generation Certificate Market Update – October 2018." *Clean Energy Regulator.* 2018. Accessed September 24, 2018. www.cleanenergyregulator. gov.au/.

Barrett, N. "Against the Wind: Wind Power Opposition in Australia." In D. E. Newton (ed.), *Wind Energy: A Reference Handbook*. Santa Barbara, CA: ABC-CLIO, LLC, 2015: 131–137.

Blakers, A., Lu, B. and Stocks, M. "100 Percent Renewable Electricity in Australia." *Energy*, 133, 2017: 471–482.

Boon, F. P. and Dieperink, C. "Local Civil Society Based Renewable Energy Organisations in the Netherlands: Exploring the Factors That Stimulate Their Emergence and Development." *Energy Policy*, 69, 2014: 97–307.

Caripis, L. and Kallies, A. "Victorian Wind Farm Laws: A Blow to Australia's Clean Energy Future?" *National Environmental Law Review*, (3), 2012: 45–46.

Cass, D. "Policy: Murky Communication Won't Help Clean Energy." *Ecogeneration*, 98, 2017: 24–25.

Clean Energy Council. "National Energy Guarantee." 2014. Accessed November 29, 2018. www.cleanenergycouncil.org.au/policy-advocacy/national-energy-guarantee.html.

The Climate Reality Project. *Follow the Leader: How 11 Countries Are Shifting to Renewable Energy*. Washington, DC. 2016. Accessed September 24, 2018. www.climaterealityproject. org/blog/follow-leader-how-11-countries-are-shifting-renewable-energy.

Community Energy Association England. "State of the Sector Report 2018." 2018. Accessed September 26, 2018. https://communityenergyengland.org/pages/state-of-the-sector-report-2018.

Cook, J. J., Aznar, A., Dane, A., Day, M., Mathur, S. and Doris, E. "Clean Energy in City Codes: A Baseline Analysis of Municipal Codification across the United States." (No. NREL/TP-6A70-66120, National Renewable Energy Lab, Golden, CO, 2016).

Department of the Environment and Energy. "The Renewable Energy Target (RET) Scheme." Australian Government. 2018. Accessed September 27, 2018. www.environment.gov.au/climate-change/government/renewable-energy-target-scheme.

Devine-Wright, P. (ed.). *Renewable Energy and the Public: From NIMBY to Participation*. Oxford, UK: Routledge, 2014.

Dewald, U. and Truffer, B. "Market Formation in Technological Innovation Systems: Diffusion of Photovoltaic Applications in Germany." *Industry and Innovation*, 18(3), 2011: 285–300.

Ehrlich, R. *Renewable Energy: A First Course*. Boca Raton, FL: CRC Press, February 27, 2013.

Embark (n.d.). "Home." 2013. Accessed December 21, 2017. www.embark.com.au/display/WebsiteContent/Home.

Fiona, A. and Mackenzie, D. "A Working Land: Crofting Communities, Place and the Politics of the Possible in Post-Land Reform Scotland." *Transactions of the Institute of British Geographers*, 31, 2006: 383–398.

Garud, R. and Karnoe, P. "Bricolage versus Breakthrough: Distributed and Embedded Agency in Technology Entrepreneurship." *Research Policy*, 32, 2003: 277–300.

Geels, F. and Raven, R. "Socio-Cognitive Evolution and Co-Evolution in Competing Technical Trajectories: Biogas Development in Denmark (1970–2002)." *International Journal of Sustainable Development and World Ecology*, 14, 2007: 63–77.

Gormally, A. M., Pooley, C. G., Whyatt, J. D. and Timmis, R. J. "'They Made Gunpowder . . . Yes Down by the River There, That's Your Energy Source': Attitudes Towards Community Renewable Energy in Cumbria." *Local Environment*, 19(8), 2014: 915–932.

Guerreiro, S. and Botetzagias, I. "Empowering Communities: The Role of Intermediary Organisations in Community Renewable Energy Projects in Indonesia." *Local Environment*, 23(2), 2017: 158–177.

Hall, N. L. and Jeanneret, T. "Social Licence to Operate: An Opportunity to Enhance CSR for Deeper Communication and Engagement." *Corporate Communications: An International Journal*, 20(2), 2015: 213–227.

Heffrom, R. and McCauley, D. "Achieving Sustainable Supply Chains through Energy Justice." *Applied Energy*, 123, 2014: 435–437.

Hepburn Wind. "Hepburn Wind Community Energy." 2016. Accessed September 24, 2018. http://hepburnwind.com.au/.

Herbst, J. "How Australian Social Enterprises Use Strategic Marketing and Social Marketing to Drive Accountability and Change for Sustainable Development." (PhD thesis, Queensland University of Technology, 2017). Accessed December 21, 2017. https://eprints.qut.edu.au/103631/.

Hicks, J. and Ison, N. "An Exploration of the Boundaries of 'Community' in Community Renewable Energy Projects: Navigating between Motivations and Context." *Energy Policy*, 113, 2018: 523–534.

Hoffmann, W. *The Economic Competitiveness of Renewable Energy: Pathways to 100% Global Coverage*. West Sussex, UK: John Wiley & Sons, 2014.

Hull, C. L. and Cawthen, L. "Bat Fatalities at Two Wind Farms in Tasmania, Australia: Bat Characteristics, and Spatial and Temporal Patterns." *New Zealand Journal of Zoology*, 40(1), 2013: 5–15.

Intergovernmental Panel on Climate Change. *Renewable Energy Sources and Climate Change Mitigation*. Geneva, Switzerland. 2018. Accessed January 15, 2019. www.ipcc.ch/site/assets/uploads/2018/03/SRREN_FD_SPM_final-1.pdf.

International Energy Agency. *World Energy Outlook 2016*. Paris, France. 2016. Accessed September 26, 2018. www.iea.org/newsroom/news/2016/november/world-energy-outlook-2016.html.

International Renewable Energy Agency. "Community Energy: Broadening the Ownership of Renewables." Abu Dhabi, United Arab Emirates. 2018. Accessed September 25, 2018. http://coalition.irena.org/-/media/Files/IRENA/Coalition-for-Action/Publication/Coalition-for-Action_Community-Energy_2018.pdf.

Jacobsson, S. and Bergek, A. "Transforming the Energy Sector: The Evolution of Technological Systems in Renewable Energy Technology." *Industrial and Corporate Change*, 13, 2004: 815–849.

Jones, L. E. (ed.). *Renewable Energy Integration: Practical Management of Variability, Uncertainty, and Flexibility in Power Grids*, 2nd ed. Waltham, MA: Academic Press, 2017.

Kalkbrenner, B. J. and Roosen, J. "Citizens' Willingness to Participate in Local Renewable Energy Projects: The Role of Community and Trust in Germany." *Energy Research & Social Science*, 13, 2016: 60–70.

Kennedy, D. *Rooftop Revolution: How Solar Power Can Save Our Economy and Our Planet From Dirty Energy*. Oakland, CA: Berrett-Koehler Publishers, 2012.

Kostevsek, A., Cizeli, L., Petek, J. and Pivec, A. "A Novel Concept for a Renewable Network within Municipal Energy Systems." *Renewable Energy*, 60, 2013: 79–87.

Kuch, D. and Morgan, B. "Dissonant Justifications: An Organisational Perspective of Support for Australian Community Energy." *People, Place and Policy*, 9(3), 2015: 177–189.

Kunze, C. and Becker, S. "Collective Ownership in Renewable Energy and Opportunities for Sustainable Degrowth." *Sustainability Science*, 10(3), 2015: 425–437.

Lowy Institute. *2018 Lowy Institute Poll*. Sydney, Australia. 2018. Accessed June 22, 2018. www.lowyinstitute.org/publications/2018-lowy-institute-poll.

Magnani, N., Maretti, M., Salvatore, R. and Scotti, I. "Ecopreneurs, Rural Development and Alternative Socio-Technical Arrangements for Community Renewable Energy." *Journal of Rural Studies*, 52(2017), 2017: 33–41.

Mallon, K. (ed.). *Renewable Energy Policy and Politics: A Handbook for Decision-Making*. London: Earthscan, 2006.

Millon, L., Colin, C., Brescia, F. and Kerbiriou, C. "Wind Turbines Impact Bat Activity, Leading to High Losses of Habitat Use in a Biodiversity Hotspot." *Ecological Engineering*, 112, 2018: 51–54.

Newton, D. E. *Wind Energy: A Reference Handbook*. Santa Barbara, CA: ABC-CLIO, LLC, 2015.

Oteman, M., Kooji, H. J. and Wiering, M. A. "Pioneering Renewable Energy in an Economic Energy Policy System: The History and Development of Dutch Grassroots Initiatives." *Sustainability*, 9(550), 2017: 1–21.

Parkinson, G. *The Rapidly Disappearing Subsidies for Solar and Wind in Australia*. May 14, 2018. Accessed September 24, 2018. https://reneweconomy.com.au/the-rapidly-disappearing-subsidies-for-wind-and-solar-in-australia-42300/.

Ruggiero, S., Martiskainen, M. and Onkila, T. "Understanding the Scaling-Up of Community Energy Niches through Strategic Niche Management Theory: Insights from Finland." *Journal of Cleaner Production*, 170, 2018: 581–590.

Rutherford, J. and Coutard, O. "Urban Energy Transitions: Places, Processes and Politics of Socio-Technical Change." *Urban Studies*, 51(7), 2014: 1353–1377.

Saintier, S. "Community Energy Companies in the UK: A Potential Model for Sustainable Development in 'Local' Energy?" *Sustainability*, 9(1325), 2017: 1–18.

Seyfang, G., Park, J. J. and Smith, A. "A Thousand Flowers Blooming? An Examination of Community Energy in the UK." *Energy Policy*, 61, 2013: 977–989.

Seyfang, G. and Smith, A. "Grassroots Innovations for Sustainable Development: Towards a New Research and Policy Agenda." *Environmental Politics*, 16(4), 2007: 584–603.

Simpson, G. and Clifton, J. "Picking Winners and Policy Uncertainty: Stakeholder Perceptions of Australia's Renewable Energy Target." *Renewable Energy*, 67, 2014: 128–135.

Sioshansi, F. P. (ed.). *Smart Grid: Integrating Renewable, Distributed and Efficient Energy*. Waltham, MA: Academic Press, 2011.

Sousa, T., Soares, T., Pinson, P., Moret, F., Baroche, T. and Sorin, E. *Peer-to-Peer and Community-Based Markets: A Comprehensive Review. arXiv preprint arXiv: 1810.09859*, 2018.

Strachan, P. A., Cowell, R., Ellis, G., Sherry-Brennan, F. and Toke, D. "Promoting Community Renewable Energy in a Corporate Energy World." *Sustainable Development*, 23(2), 2015: 96–109.

Sunshine Coast Regional Council. *Sunshine Coast Solar Farm*. Nambour, Australia. 2019. Accessed December 19, 2018. www.sunshinecoast.qld.gov.au/Environment/Sunshine-Coast-Solar-Farm.

Teleke, S., Baran, M. E., Bhattacharya, S. and Huang, A. Q. "Rule-Based Control of Battery Energy Storage for Dispatching Intermittent Renewable Sources." *IEEE Transactions on Sustainable Energy*, 1(3), 2010: 117–124.

UK Government. *Community Strategy Energy Update*. 2015. Accessed September 27, 2018. https://assets.publishing.service.gov.uk/government/uploads/system/uploads/attachment_data/file/414446/CESU_FINAL.pdf.

United Nations Department of Economic and Social Affairs. *Sustainable Development Knowledge Platform*. New York. n.d. Accessed February 19, 2018. https://sustainabledevelopment.un.org/sdgs.

Van Veelen, B. and Haggett, C. "Uncommon Ground: The Role of Different Place Attachments in Explaining Community Renewable Energy Projects." *Sociologia Ruralis*, 57(S1), 2017: 533–554.

Varho, V., Rikkonen, P. and Rasi, S. "Futures of Distributed Small-Scale Renewable Energy in Finland: A Delphi Study of the Opportunities and Obstacles Up to 2025." *Technology Forecasting Social Change*, 104, 2016: 30–37.

Walker, G. "What Are the Barriers and Incentives for Community-Owned Means of Energy Production and Use?" *Energy Policy*, 36, 2008: 4401–4405.

Walker, G., Devine-Wright, P., Hunter, S., High, H. and Evans, B. "Trust and Community: Exploring the Meanings, Contexts and Dynamics of Community Renewable Energy." *Energy Policy*, 38(6), 2010: 2655–2663.

Walker, G., Hunter, S., Devine-Wright, P., Evans, B. and Fay, H. "Harnessing Community Energies: Explaining and Evaluating Community-Based Localism in Renewable Energy Policy in the UK." *Global Environmental Politics*, 7(2), 2007: 64–82.

Wirth, S. "Communities Matter: Institutional Preconditions for Community Renewable Energy." *Energy Policy*, 70, 2014: 236–246.

Wiseman, H. and Bronin, S. "Community-Scale Renewable Energy." *San Diego Journal of Climate & Energy Law*, 14, 2013: 165–194.

World Wind Energy Association. "15 Years of the World Wind Energy Association." 2015. Accessed September 24, 2018. www.wwindea.org/download/general_files/15years.pdf.

Yergin, D. *The Quest: Energy, Security, and the Remaking of the Modern World.* London: Penguin Random House, 2011.

Young, J. and Brans, M. "Analysis of Factors Affecting a Shift in a Local Energy System Towards 100% Renewable Energy Community." *Journal of Cleaner Production*, 169, 2017: 117–124.

6

SUSTAINABLE WASTE MANAGEMENT FOR THE PLANTATION SECTOR IN SRI LANKA

A. D. Nuwan Gunarathne and Mahendra Peiris

Abstract

There is an urgent need to find alternative waste management mechanisms in communities where local councils are not developed and that lack a proper waste collection system and infrastructure. This chapter presents a sustainable waste management program ("food yielding waste management system," FYWMS) implemented in the plantation sector in Sri Lanka. It highlights the possibility of creatively exploring locally acceptable and community-driven pragmatic solutions to overcome the waste management challenges that hinder the achievement of many of the Sustainable Development Goals (SDGs) in developing countries. With the participation of many stakeholders, the innovative waste management model described in the chapter offers an alternative to the traditional centralized system. The chapter also points to the impacts, challenges and lessons learned for those who aspire to initiate innovative solutions to the challenges faced in achieving the SDGs.

Introduction

Despite the progress made on advancing many of the United Nations' (UN) Sustainable Development Goals (SDGs), the challenges associated with achieving them are diverse and complex. Translating SDGs into pragmatic and locally acceptable action remains a challenge in many parts of the world, particularly in combating growing environmental and social issues such as waste management. This is particularly evident in some communities and regions whose social and economic development is comparatively low (Wilson and Velis, 2015; Gunarathne et al., 2019, 2020; Guerrero et al., 2013).

With rising living standards and consumerism the world over, the dominant linear economic model is characterized by the so-called take, make and dispose system, in which producers make products that consumers use and dispose. In this economic model, extracted virgin materials are used for production, and these products are used until they are disposed of as waste, as value creation is assumed by maximizing the amount of products produced and sold (Ellen MacArthur Foundation, 2013). However, its resultant huge quantities of waste pose major threats to the achievement of many of the SDGs that countries aspire to by 2030 (Gunarathne et al., 2020). For instance, "improper disposal of plastic waste [on land] . . . can contribute to the spread of diseases such as chikungunya, dengue, malaria and Zika" (UN, 2018: 14), which have become a serious threat to human health and well-being as outlined in SDG #3.

In many developing countries, the failures in municipal waste management systems could worsen this situation. The likely results could be environmental, social and economic losses including additional healthcare costs, loss of productivity, flood damage, deterioration of the standard of living, damage to businesses and tourism and even social unrest (Wilson and Velis, 2015). Therefore, there is an urgent need to find creative, pragmatic and acceptable solutions to the global sustainability challenges. This chapter presents a sustainable waste management program in the plantation sector in Sri Lanka.

In contrast to the linear economic model noted above, the circular economy principles for waste management underpin the promotion of closing the resource loops to provide an alternative to the conventional unidirectional concept of resource consumption (George et al., 2015). The circular economic model promotes "restoration and circularity in order to replace the traditional concept of end-of-life [waste disposal] . . . and aims for the elimination of waste through the superior design of material, products, systems and business models" (Michelini et al., 2017). Transition to a circular economy thus entails product and service redesign, creation of new business models and reverse supply chains and provision of supportive and enabling conditions (Ellen MacArthur Foundation, 2013; Gunarathne et al., 2020). This presents a global challenge, especially for developing countries for several reasons, including restricted funding for local authorities, insufficient integration of various stakeholders, problems of waste management–related infrastructure, inadequate regulatory systems and lack of awareness (Guerrero et al., 2013; Gunarathne et al., 2019).

Although much attention has been paid to the management of municipal solid waste, waste management in the suburban and rural areas has received little attention globally. It has become a severe problem in suburban and rural plantation communities, particularly in developing countries such as Sri Lanka, where the plantation sector plays a key role in creating employment and in earning foreign exchange. In Sri Lanka, these plantations are located mainly in the central highlands of the country where many rivers that source water to the entire island originate. The International Union for Conservation of Nature (IUCN) has declared the natural ecosystems in the central highlands of Sri Lanka a "biodiversity hot spot" on the planet (IUCN, 2017). Although there are traditional waste management systems, they have been found to be ineffective and inefficient despite the economic and environmental importance of the region (Gunarathne, 2020). Hence, an innovative program for managing domestic waste in plantations has been developed within Sri Lanka with the help of the plantation companies. This program, called "food yielding waste management system" (FYWMS), including its strengths and challenges, is the focus of this chapter.

This program is important for several reasons. First, as a developing country, Sri Lanka faces many sustainable development challenges in its pursuit of rapid economic growth in a post-conflict period. Waste management, one of the country's greatest challenges, has become a serious environmental issue at present (Fernando, 2019; Basnayake et al., 2014; Gunarathne et al., 2019, 2020). Second, although municipal solid waste management (MSWM) has received attention following recent catastrophes such as the Meethotamulla landfill collapse,[1] little attention has been paid to this in suburban and rural areas in the country. Third, several pilot projects to address the plantation sector's waste management problems have failed for want of multi-stakeholder and community support. Hence, the plantation communities that are socially, educationally and economically less empowered are now facing severe health and environmental problems. This project highlights how stakeholders can work effectively together in managing waste. Moreover, the principles involved can be applied to all types of change interventions aimed at resolving the problems of achieving SDGs.

To support this, the chapter presents how the traditional waste management system in the plantation sector operates and its associated problems. It also provides an overview of the recently introduced FYWMS program. It details the early positive impacts of this program and how the challenges encountered were overcome or are being addressed. Finally, the chapter presents the lessons learned and the way forward for other projects of this nature.

Traditional waste management in the plantation sector in Sri Lanka

This section demonstrates how the traditional MSWM system was not accepted by the local communities and how they had resorted to alternative ways of waste management – ways that were neither environmentally friendly nor healthy.

Waste management in developing countries is a complex, multidimensional affair that requires the support and involvement of many stakeholders (Guerrero et al., 2013; Anschutz et al., 2004). However, waste management often fails in developing countries when the systems are designed without due attention to such complexities. As highlighted in this chapter, the waste management system in the plantation sector of the central highlands in Sri Lanka has not been effective over the years, despite the many initiatives taken (Gunarathne, 2020). In the central highlands of Sri Lanka, waste is mainly managed by the local councils that provide regular door-to-door waste collection. The waste collected in a locality is either landfilled or sent to a recycling facility or both. (See Figure 6.1.) This MSWM system where waste is

Households and other entities

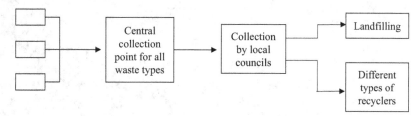

FIGURE 6.1 Centralized traditional waste management system

collected and sent to a central location for management has been largely unsustainable in this region for several reasons.

First, the local councils do not have sufficient resources for collecting and treating the collected waste. For instance, they do not have adequate manpower and other resources such as collection trucks nor recycling facilities with advanced technology and enough capacity for waste treatment. Further, due to the lack of awareness and regulations, the waste is collected in mixed form often in plastic bags, which creates a real challenge to processing them. Second, the residences of the plantation community are largely in scattered clusters widely spread over mountainous terrain. This makes most of these houses inaccessible to the collection vehicles of the local councils. Third, connected to the previous issue, are difficulties in collecting and transporting the waste due to the poor condition of the road networks stretching over steep, sloping territory. Fourth, is the lack of interest in, and the poor support for, waste management by the plantation community due to a lack of awareness and poor education levels. Rather than disposing waste through the MSWM system, they prefer to dump it in the nearby surroundings, polluting the environment.

This existing improper waste management situation in the plantation sector has created many problems for the environment and for human health. Perishables, including kitchen waste, have encouraged the propagation of pests, pathogens and vector species such as rats, houseflies, cockroaches, mosquitoes and fruit flies. As stated previously, almost all plantations are in and around the central highlands of Sri Lanka. As such, the larger portion of the waste generated in the region is washed away during the rainy season and gets into waterways due to the hilly terrain. This causes soil and water source contamination and pollutes the drinking water supply, causing serious threats to human health in the community.

Meanwhile, for the plantation companies, safe and proper disposal of domestic and industrial waste is a requirement for the certification standards of the Rainforest Alliance, Fairtrade Labeling Organization and ISO 22,000/2005. Therefore, these companies have taken several initiatives to deal with these improper waste disposal methods adopted by the plantation community. However, most of these efforts have been unsuccessful owing to the poor response of the worker community and local government bodies. (See Photo 6.1.) Some local government bodies have been reluctant to accept even the waste in segregated form, since they do not have proper

PHOTO 6.1 Improper waste disposal of the plantation communities

Note: Even though some plantation companies have made costly efforts such as constructing permanent structures to collect segregated waste, the waste is still disposed of in very unhealthy ways such as open burning as depicted in this picture.

recycling mechanisms to handle it. The senior manager of a plantation company explained the difficulties they encounter in managing household solid waste in the plantation sector with conventional methods:

> Efforts made by us to segregate and collect [household] waste were not successful as there was no proper way to dispose of it even after separation. Simply, there's no one to accept domestic solid waste generated in plantation households. . . . Municipal councils [in this area] are not equipped to handle the quantities of waste coming from all the plantations.

Thus, there is a long-felt need for a suitable mechanism and awareness program for these communities to counter their present highly unsafe and unhealthy waste disposal practices.

New approach to managing waste

With a view to providing a sustainable solution to the problems associated with the plantation sector waste management challenges, a novel system was first developed in one estate in 2015. FYWMS was later commenced as a pilot project in four estates in the Maskeliya region of Sri Lanka in early 2018. The initial funding, a major constraint in initiating a project in the region, was overcome with partial financial support from the UK-based nongovernmental organization "Save the Children

International" under the theme of an integrated home gardening promotion and water quality improvement project in plantation households. It was initiated as a Child Development Center (CDC)-based community nutrition enhancement program in which pregnant mothers and children below the age of two years formed the target group. (See Table 6.1 for the beneficiaries of the initial program.)

Later the project was extended to cover waste management with the support of the funding of the plantation company's corporate social responsibility (CSR) initiatives. FYWMS was implemented in several stages. First, the types of waste generated in households in selected plantation business units (estates) were identified through a survey. Second, project teams were set up comprising plantation managers and teams in charge of health and medical affairs of the plantation business units. Third, awareness programs on waste management were conducted for the community including households and children. (See Table 6.2.)

Technical guidance on sustainable home gardening and seed material for gardening were provided through the officers of the CDCs. Further, through this project sustainable home gardening models were established in schools. (See Photo 6.2.) Moreover, farm inputs and poultry were supplied to the identified families. In this

TABLE 6.1 Profile of initial beneficiaries of FYWMS project

Estate name	No. of pregnant mothers	No. of children below 2 years	No. of ladies in reproductive age	Total population
Estate 1	30	238	1,492	5,142
Estate 2	16	105	1,320	4,540
Estate 3	16	56	1,154	2,699
Estate 4	17	30	988	2,177
Total	**79**	**429**	**4,954**	**14,558**

TABLE 6.2 Details of the community-based workshops

Target Audience	Points Emphasized
Students [children]	• Potential to earn pocket money by collection and sale of waste • Need for proper collection of different domestic waste types at household level without mixing • Promotion of feeding of fresh food waste to poultry
Adults	• Possibility of low-cost practical ways of waste management and beautification of the home environment • Benefits of perishable kitchen waste management through poultry birds • Possibility of improving the family nutrition status through home gardening

PHOTO 6.2 An awareness campaign conducted in a school

process, government institutions including the Central Environment Authority (CEA), public schools and local government bodies played supporting roles as the other project facilitators.

The focus of this alternative waste management program was to separate food materials (biomass) from other types of household waste such as paper, glass, metal, plastics and e-waste at the point of origin. Poultry and small domestic ruminants (i.e., goats and sheep) were used as recycling agents for the separately collected food materials in this system. Organic materials such as fruit peel and vegetable waste were fed to goats and sheep, while cereals and other small grain food waste were used as poultry feed. In both cases, the food waste was converted to organic manure within one day while recycling part of the nutrient as animal feed.

This process is rapid and efficient compared to the conventional and widely used method of composting perishable domestic waste. Further, this method prevents the breeding of many pests and pathogens usually fostered by the traditional waste management systems operating in this region. FYWMS program promoted the use of animal dung for home gardening that converted the nutrients in organic waste to fertilizer for fruits and vegetables for human consumption. In effect, it completed the nutrient/resource cycle within the household itself. For each type of other non-perishable waste scrap, collectors were engaged for the collection. Plastic recyclers were encouraged to make plants in pots of various shapes in collaboration with the CEA of Sri Lanka. These recycled plastic pots were returned to the plantation communities to grow, completing an internal plastic cycle while promoting and facilitating home gardening. (See Photo 6.3.)

PHOTO 6.3 A model home garden set up under the project

Some important characteristics of this novel waste management system are as follows:

- Avoidance of central collection of waste whereby the waste collectors directly deal with the households and other entities. This transforms the present push system to a pull system of waste management. (See Figure 6.2.)
- Transformation of nutrients present in kitchen waste into eggs and meat (by using them as food for hens) and poultry manure within a short period. This is a more efficient and rapid way of converting nutrients than the traditional method of composting perishable waste.
- Focus on children as key actors in domestic waste segregation at the household level through the use of their motivation to earn pocket money by selling waste items.

Impacts of the new program

Although the project is still underway, its early impacts are visible on many fronts. The enthusiasm and acceptance of the community and the respective direct beneficiaries of the project reflect how well the project has been positioned to cater to their needs. They have made a very strong positive response to this novel concept of waste management because of its many apparent direct and indirect benefits. First, the households benefited by raising poultry and improving the intake of eggs and chicken and using poultry manure produced for home gardening, which strengthened the family nutrition status and household income. Second, households

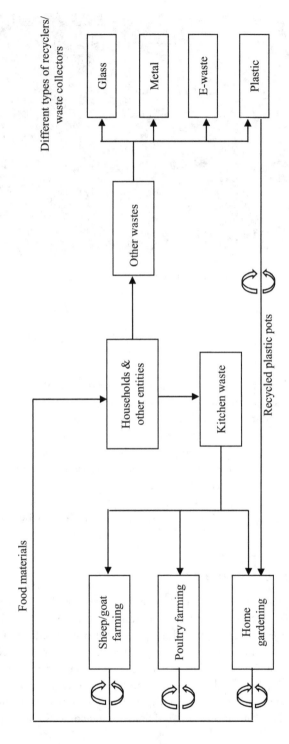

FIGURE 6.2 New community–centric waste management system (FYWMS)

benefited from the organized, hassle-free disposal of perishable kitchen waste, which greatly improved their health and living environment. A female estate worker confirmed the benefits of the new system thus:

> We never thought of disposing of [kitchen] food waste through animals and using their dung for home gardening systematically. The project introduced this concept and it really works well.

Third, the children of the community benefited by segregating and disposing of other waste forms at household level through scrap collectors to earn pocket money. In order to maintain the momentum with the students, regular follow-ups were conducted in the schools. A female high school student who participated in a follow-up workshop expressed her enthusiasm for the project:

> Now we know waste is money. In vain, we were burning and destroying a lot of money all this time. . . . There's a buyer who visits us in search of scrap materials at our homes.

The principal of a school participating in this program further explained the benefits and how students get involved in the project:

> Earlier open-waste heaps were everywhere in this estate. It was a real problem for this community, although they themselves caused it largely. Now you don't see them since the children are collecting and selling waste to the collectors. Actually, this is a good way to dispose of waste.

These responses demonstrate that the project has made a positive contribution to many of the SDGs including SDG #1 (to end poverty), SDG #2 (to end hunger and improve nutrition), SDG #3 (to ensure healthy lives and well-being), SDG #11 (to make the communities safe and sustainable) and SDG #12 (to ensure sustainable consumption and production). Further, the FYWMS program illustrates how broader stakeholder involvement and partnerships can facilitate the achievement of the objectives promoted in SDG #17 (to strengthen the partnerships for the goals).

Another stakeholder group, the plantation companies involved in the project, played a dual role as project beneficiaries and facilitators. They were among the primary facilitators who provided partial funding and necessary project teams, while at the same time being the beneficiaries, as they benefited from the hassle-free waste disposal mechanisms established within the plantation community. The project also placed the plantation companies in a win-win situation by being relieved of the burden of complying with certification standards.

Other actors in this plantation waste management system, such as scrap collectors and waste recyclers, benefited from these changes by not having to segregate waste at their end. In addition, waste materials supplied through this system were cleaner compared to the earlier situation. A self-employed domestic waste material collector expressed his satisfaction with the new system:

> This is a very good program. I am really benefited by this system because I do not have to do the stuff [i.e. waste separation, cleaning, etc.] now as I used to do before. My work time and operational expenditure have been considerably saved now.

Besides, local government bodies and the CEA were also spared costly waste management operations. A director from the CEA involved in the project said:

> It's commendable that plantations are coming forward to support the government's efforts to handle this national issue of managing solid waste. This is truly an innovative breakthrough in the field of domestic solid waste management [in this region].

Additionally, the other communities living within the plantations and the populations dwelling downstream of the water bodies add millions of additional beneficiaries since the project systematically removes pollutants and prevents the contamination of their drinking water. Owing to the proper waste management system, there is a positive impact on water quality flowing from the landscape, although a scientific study of the improvement has yet to be done. Thus, the project has resulted in positive contributions to other SDGs such as SDG #14 (to conserve water) and SDG #15 (to protect and conserve the use of land).

Challenges of the new program

Despite the positive impacts, the project faced some setbacks and challenges too. This novel waste management system involved changing the existing waste disposal behavior of the plantation community. As commonly experienced in introducing and implementing any other novel concept, the FYWMS program, too faced resistance. Ironically, the greatest resistance originated from some individuals in relatively high positions in the plantation sector. Some of the initially chosen trial sites had to be changed owing to the resistance of these high-ranking individuals, although lower-level team members were enthusiastically positive about the new program. Yet, the resistance from the communities was relatively easily overcome through constant realization of the benefits. However, constant dialogue with the project facilitators and the dedication and enthusiasm of rest of the team members and the community mitigated the negative effects of resistance.

Further, a few spells of extreme weather experienced in succession adversely affected the initial home gardening efforts and discouraged the beneficiary householders. However, home gardening was carried out by the community due to its strong wholehearted interest, despite the harm to their home gardens.

These hostile weather conditions affected the poultry birds distributed among beneficiary families. Different unexpected diseases, supposedly caused by severe weather conditions, resulted in a high percentage of animal deaths. Negotiations were soon made with the poultry-supplying farm for the replacement for the dead poultry birds. Further, it was agreed to do the replacement with grown-up animals, who would be more resistant to inclement weather as a remedy to the problem.

Although the project was originally designed to provide a win–win proposition for multi-stakeholders, community responses and experiences of the team members showed that the degree of success and the extent of the results differed from site to site. Hence, proper awareness programs and regular follow-up are needed to overcome the teething problems in novel community-based systems until such concepts are practically proven. Close monitoring of project performance was done regularly to identify common, as well as site-specific, problems to evaluate the success factors and the constraints.

Lessons learned and the way forward

An important lesson learned from FYWMS is the need to create win–win situations for all or at least for the majority of stakeholders involved in community-driven programs designed to address sustainability challenges. As already discussed, the benefits of this waste management program filtered down to many stakeholder groups including the community, plantation companies, waste collectors and recyclers and local governments. Sharing the positive synergies of a program among stakeholders is essential for establishing a self-running sustainable system. This highlights the need for innovative ways to provide sustainable solutions at the micro level where many stakeholders become winners and thereby solutions become locally acceptable and inclusive.

This project also highlights how a major environmental and social problem that hinders achievement of the SDGs in a community can be systemically diagnosed in order to identify its different components and processes and to practically deal with them using the right incentives and locally appropriate methods. This approach was adapted to deal with the domestic waste management problem in the plantation sector by identifying the different components of domestic waste and their unique features while understanding their interactions. The development of an effective way to prevent kitchen waste being mixed with other waste types was the objective of this process. First, this was achieved by using domestic farm animals where they were fed fresh food waste found in kitchen waste. This supported the trapping of nutrients and converting them quickly into animal biomass. Second, digested nutrients present in animal dung were transformed into safe human food material through home gardening to complete a nutrient cycle. This process was facilitated with the supply of recycled plastic pots for home gardening while establishing a closed internal path for disposed plastic and polythene as well.

FYWMS also more specifically highlights the following lessons learned for community-centric sustainable waste management:

- The endless possibilities of creatively exploring locally acceptable and community-driven alternative solutions to overcome the challenges that hinder the achievement of SDGs in contexts where even well-established solutions may fail (e.g., centralized MSWM systems) in some communities and regions.
- The possibility of overcoming resistance to change in waste disposal practices on the part of mature generations by modifying their behaviors to suit the SDGs by focusing on children as change agents. This not only creates internal pressure within households for behavior modification among family members but also paves the way for a future generation with sustainability awareness.
- The need to pass the center of ownership of sustainable waste management systems from external parties to the local communities once the initial teething problems are overcome, as a self-sustaining mechanism for long-term continuity.
- The urgent need for alternative waste management mechanisms in communities where local councils are not developed and a proper waste collection system and infrastructure are lacking – this is a common feature of some of the developing countries struggling to cope with the rising quantities of urban, suburban and rural waste.

Nonetheless, while FYWMS has been in operation for some period with overwhelming enthusiastic support from communities and stakeholders, these initial positive signs do not guarantee future success or sustainability. Hence, what is important is dynamic leadership and responsive and unwavering in its commitment to the project to find pragmatic solutions for the problems that emerge along the way. Yet, for this program to be more effective as a stakeholder-driven, community-centric, sustainable waste management system, there are several prerequisites. First, a waste management system of this nature will be more suited when space is available for gardening and rearing animals within a community for an adequate number of households. Second, the willingness of, and commitment to, farming activities by the community membership is a precondition for running this system effectively. Third, although this method can be practiced virtually anywhere under tropical and temperate climate conditions, except in apartment complexes, it is most recommended for suburban and rural landscapes such as in East Asia, Central Africa, the Caribbean Islands and South America, where the plantation sector plays a crucial role in the local agricultural economy.

Note

1 More than 30 meters high, the Meethotamulla landfill in the capital city of Sri Lanka, Colombo, collapsed in April 2017 killing more than 25 people and leaving hundreds of families displaced. This landfill was to have been shut down many years back but due to the unavailability of a suitable mechanism and facilities to manage waste generated daily in the capital city of Colombo, dumping continued until this tragic incident took place (National Building Research Organization (NBRO), 2017).

References

Anschutz, J., Ijgosse, J. and Scheinberg, A. *Putting Integrated Sustainable Waste Management into Practice: Using the ISWM Assessment Methodology as Applied in the UWEP Plus Programme (2001–2003)*. Gouda, the Netherlands: WASTE, 2004.

Basnayake, B. F. A. and Visvanathan, C. "Solid Waste Management in Sri Lanka." In A. Pariatamby and M. Tanaka (eds.), *Municipal Solid Waste Management in Asia and the Pacific Islands: Challenges and Strategic Solutions*. Berlin: Springer, 2014: 299–316.

Ellen MacArthur Foundation. *Towards the Circular Economy: Economic and Business Rationale for an Accelerated Transition*. Isle of Wight: Ellen MacArthur Foundation, 2013.

Fernando, R. L. S. "Solid Waste Management of Local Governments in the Western Province of Sri Lanka: An Implementation Analysis." *Waste Management*, 84, 2019: 194–203.

George, D. A., Lin, B. C. A. and Chen, Y. "A Circular Economy Model of Economic Growth." *Environmental Modelling & Software*, 73, 2015: 60–63.

Guerrero, L. A., Maas, G. and Hogland, W. "Solid Waste Management Challenges for Cities in Developing Countries." *Waste Management*, 33(1), 2013: 220–232.

Gunarathne, A. D. N. "Making Sustainability Work in Plantation Agriculture." In P. Flynn, M. Gudić and T. Tan (eds.), *Global Champions of Sustainable Development*. London: Routledge, 2020: 49–63.

Gunarathne, A. D. N., de Alwis, A. and Alahakoon, Y. "Challenges Facing Sustainable Urban Mining in the e-Waste Recycling Industry in Sri Lanka." *Journal of Cleaner Production*, 251, 2020. https://doi.org/10.1016/j.jclepro.2019.119641.

Gunarathne, A. D. N., Tennakoon, T. P. Y. C. and Weragoda, J. R. "Challenges and Opportunities for the Recycling Industry in Developing Countries: The Case of Sri Lanka." *Journal of Material Cycles and Waste Management*, 21(1), 2019: 181–190.

International Union for Conservation of Nature (ICUN). *Central Highlands of Sri Lanka 2017 Conservation Outlook Assessment*. Gland, Switzerland: ICUN, 2017.

Michelini, G., Moraes, R. N., Cunha, R. N., Costa, J. M. and Ometto, A. R. "From Linear to Circular Economy: PSS Conducting the Transition." *Procedia CIRP*, 64, 2017: 2–6.

National Building Research Organisation (NBRO). *Geotechnical Assessment on the Failure at Meethotamulla Waste Fill*. Colombo, Sri Lanka: Ministry of Disaster Management, 2017.

United Nations (UN). *World Economic and Social Survey 2018-Frontier Technologies for Sustainable Development*. New York: Department of Economic and Social Affairs, 2018.

Wilson, D. C. and Velis, C. A. "Waste Management: Still a Global Challenge in the 21st Century: An Evidence-Based Call for Action." *Waste Management & Research*, 33(12), 2015: 1049–1051.

7

THE SUSTAINABLE DEVELOPMENT GOALS, THE ICT INDUSTRY AND ICT4D RESEARCH

Martin Wynn and Peter Jones

Abstract

The Sustainable Development Goals (SDGs), agreed to at the United Nations (UN) in 2015, were an agenda for global change and sustainability for the next 15 years, but the programme made little mention of the potential role of the information and communications technology (ICT) industry. ICT is a key enabler of such widespread change, and this chapter assesses the potential involvement of the ICT industry in the advancement of the SDGs. A review of key reports from major industry entities reveals the significant business opportunities perceived by these ICT companies and highlights the critical role of governments in creating appropriate infrastructures for, and for funding of, ICT. The chapter also discusses key issues emerging from these reports in the context of current research in the ICT for Development (ICT4D) field. The rapid pace of technological development may revolutionise how the SDGs will be pursued and achieved around the world, but there are tensions between the imperatives of the SDGs and the pursuit of economic growth.

Key words: SDGs, Sustainable Development Goals, ICTs, ICT industry, technology change, ICT4D research

Introduction

It has been suggested that there are two issues of particular importance regarding the development of global economies and societies – "the challenge of environmental sustainability and the potential of information and communications technology" (Souter et al., 2010). This article examines the implications of the Sustainable Development Goals (SDGs) for the information and communications technology (ICT) industry and how this may align with current and future research initiatives in the developing world context (ICT for Development – ICT4D).

The 17 SDGs represent "the scale and ambition" of the UN 2030 Agenda for Sustainable Development, which is designed to "shift the world on to a sustainable and resilient path" (United Nations, 2015: webpage). To address these goals, the role of the business community, along with that of national governments, was highlighted by the UN. However Tim Unwin, Director of the ICT4D Collective, argued that "the almost complete omission of ICTs from the final agreed SDGs was a very serious failing" and that "those determining the SDG agenda for the next 15 years barely gave them any recognition at all" (Unwin, 2015: 2). This chapter puts forward a preliminary review of some key perspectives surrounding the relationships between ICT and the SDGs and comments on their resonance with current thinking in ICT4D research.

ICT and the SDGs

ICT is mentioned in just four of the 169 targets linked to the SDGs (Table 7.1). However, a number of frameworks have been developed for considering and measuring the relationships between ICT and both the environment and development. The Organisation for Economic Co-operation and Development (OECD), for example, outlined a model that identified both "ICT supply (producers, production and products) and ICT demand (users and uses)" as agents to improve environmental outcomes as well as a number of "indirect factors affecting ICT and the

TABLE 7.1 ICT targets related to the SDGs

SDG #4. "Ensure inclusive and equitable quality education and promote lifelong learning opportunities for all."

Target: By 2020, substantially expand globally the number of scholarships available to developing countries, in particular least developed countries, small island developing states and African countries, for enrolment in higher education, including vocational training and information and communications technology, technical, engineering and scientific programmes, in developed countries and other developing countries.

SDG #5. "Achieve gender equality and empower all women and girls."

Target: Enhance the use of enabling technology, in particular information and communications technology, to promote the empowerment of women.

SDG #9. "Build resilient infrastructure, promote inclusive and sustainable industrialization and foster innovation."

Target: Significantly increase access to information and communications technology and strive to provide universal and affordable access to the internet in least developed countries by 2020.

SDG #17. "Strengthen the means of implementation and revitalize the global partnership for sustainable development."

Target: Fully operationalise the technology bank and science, technology and innovation capacity-building mechanism for least developed countries by 2017 and enhance the use of enabling technology, in particular information and communications technology.

Source: United Nations (2015).

environment" (OECD, 2009: 8–12). Qureshi (2017: 7) offered a "theoretical lens" to help in "investigating ICTs in ways that offer development outcomes" and suggested that "this lens offers a view through which interventions, often seen as projects in which ICTs are used to support healthcare, education or agriculture, are investigated".

A number of ICT companies and organisations have suggested that their sector can play a central role in contributing to the achievement of the SDGs. Hans Vestberg, Ericsson's President and Chief Executive Officer, for example, argued that "Information Communication Technology offers an incredible platform for achieving the SDGs" (Ericsson, 2016: 6). Matt Granryd, Director General of the *Groupe Spécial Mobile* Association (GSMA), suggested "as an industry we have an important opportunity to leverage the mobile networks that we have built and the services we deliver to help achieve the Sustainable Development Goals" (GSMA, 2016: 5).

Some key perspectives on the relationships between ICT and the SDGs emerge from a reading of reports on the SDGs published by two leading ICT companies, namely, Ericsson and Microsoft, and two industry bodies, GSMA and the Global e-Sustainability Initiative (GeSI). GSMA represents the interests of more than 800 mobile telephone operators through industry programmes, working groups and industry advocacy initiatives. GeSI works in conjunction with some of the major global technology companies and provides information, resources and best practice guides aimed at achieving integrated social and environmental sustainability through ICT. A key theme in all four reports cited above is the leading role that the ICT industry believes it can play in the future achievement of the SDGs.

The shared value of ICT

Ericsson visualised ICT as a catalyst for achieving the SDGs and argued, "ICT, especially mobile broadband, will be the essential infrastructure platform for the SDGs" and that "rapid action is needed to harness the contribution that ICT can make toward the achievement of the Global Goals" (Ericsson, 2016: 8). It is clear that the ICT industry regards the SDGs as a major new business opportunity. For example, GeSI estimated that "the digital solutions that catalyse SDG achievement" could generate "$3.1 trillion of additional annual revenue to the sector" (GeSI, 2016: 32). It also noted that there could be a range of softer benefits, including brand enhancement and the increased demand for data-driven products and services generated by the improvements in lifestyles brought about by the advancement of the SDGs.

The industry's belief that it can make a major contribution to the achievement of the SDGs reflects the spirit of the concept of shared value, which has been defined as "policies and practices that enhance the competitiveness of a company while simultaneously addressing the economic and social conditions in the communities in which it operates" (Porter and Kramer, 2011: 78). However, Crane et al. (2014: 131) have highlighted some concerns regarding the shared value model and suggested it is "naïve about the challenges of business compliance". In a more positive vein, the Shared Value Initiative (Shared Value Initiative, 2015: webpage) suggests that the SDGs offer an "opportunity for people running businesses to cash in on the huge market potential in solving the most pressing issues of our time".

Microsoft prioritised eight SDGs because of their "particular alignment with Microsoft's business and philanthropic strategies" (Microsoft, 2016: webpage). These are:

> SDG #3 – good health and well-being; SDG #4 – quality education; SDG #5 – gender equality; SDG #8 – decent work and economic growth; SDG #9 – industry, innovation and infrastructure; SDG #11 – sustainable cities and communities; SDG #13 – climate action and SDG #16 – peace, justice, and strong institutions.

In addressing SDG #8, Microsoft claimed to work with a number of agencies around the world to promote economic development and to empower entrepreneurs and business leaders with the tools, skills and opportunities to stimulate and facilitate economic growth. In addressing SDG #3, Microsoft reported on its role in providing products, services and training to help governments and healthcare providers to "understand how to apply technologies like advanced data analytics and cloud solutions to transform healthcare" (Microsoft, 2016: webpage). In a slightly wider context, the ICT industry as a whole has a vital role to play with regard to SDG #17 – sustainable development through global partnerships – in encouraging and facilitating international cooperation and coordination, promoting technology transfer and capacity building and strengthening partnerships at local, national and global levels.

In the context of ICT4D research, this debate underlines the relevance of research approaches that recognise different ideologies of development (Figure 7.1). Van Biljon and Alexander (2014) have put forward a conceptual map of discipline, research paradigm, underlying theory, research methodology, data capturing strategy and data analysis. Heeks (2014) used the post-2015 development agenda to identify priorities for future ICT4D research within such a framework. Different development theories used in the ICT4D literature highlight the fact that a single development theory is unlikely to be sufficiently strong and widely accepted to provide overall coherence.

Walsham (2017: 29) has stressed the importance of creating "a cumulative research tradition" through "the development and application of theory" that enables "moving from a particular setting or application to more general statements or conceptual frameworks". Similarly, Sein and Harindranath suggest that to better understand the role ICT can play in national development, "ICT needs to be conceptualized in its many facets, perceptions, and in its manifold impact in societies". They go on to propose an integrative framework to study the role of ICT in development that "policymakers and donor agencies may find useful in evaluating the potential impact of development interventions using ICT" (Sein and Harindranath, 2004: 15).

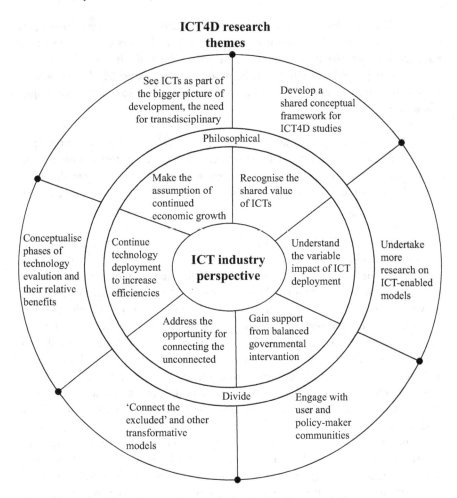

FIGURE 7.1 ICT industry perspectives and related ICT4D research themes

The variable impact of ICT deployment

The four reports point out that the role and impact of the ICT industry in contributing to the SDGs will vary in different contexts – for example, in urban and rural areas and in developed and less developed economies. More specifically, GSMA reported on variations in future opportunities for the mobile industry to affect economies at different stages of development and in different geographic regions. GSMA (2016: 73) reported that within developed economies, the mobile industry would have a high impact on SDG #13 (action for climate change), SDG #5 (gender equality), SDG #8 (decent work and economic growth) and SDG #11 (sustainable cities and communities).

Alternatively, GSMA predicted that the overall impact of the mobile industry within developing economies will be lower than the global average and that it would be most marked in relation to SDG #13 (action for climate change) and SDG #7 (affordable and clean energy). Variations in the future opportunities for the mobile industry to impact on the SDGs were also identified across geographical space. For example, in Sub-Saharan Africa, there are concerns that the impact of ICT on the SDGs is limited by low penetration of mobile services. GSMA also suggested that, in this region, "in addition to increasing the reach of its services, it is equally important for the industry to play a leading role to promote transparency and ethical business practices within its own operations" (GSMA, 2016: 83).

Within Europe, however, the impact of the mobile industry is seen to be high across most of the SDGs. GSMA suggested that there is scope to increase the impact of SDG #17 (sustainable development through global partnerships), particularly in enabling information sharing, diffusion of practices and other partnership-facilitating activities. This could be achieved through the ICT industry's leadership of "multi-stakeholder partnerships, driving co-ordination of the sustainable development agenda, as well as continuing to develop and implement open platforms that enable innovation ecosystems and provide a blueprint for other regions to follow" (GSMA, 2016: 79). New ICT-enabled models are relevant here because they can provide examples of where ICTs appear to make a significant difference. Unwin (2017: 49) has similarly called for the private sector to "draw on examples of existing good practices to develop new business models that focus on increased durability and sustainability of their technologies, whilst maintaining affordability". The research community has an important role to play in clarifying the agendas of various agencies involved, the impact on processes, the overall costs and benefits to all parties and the nature of sociopolitical transformation.

Balanced governmental intervention

The ICT industry has also argued that governments have a vital enabling role. Ericsson (2016: 17) suggested that "to harness ICT effectively for the 2030 Agenda . . . governments need to ensure that the entire public sector, including service delivery in health, education, energy and infrastructure, is fully supported by high-quality ICT infrastructure". Unwin (2017: 53) suggests that "governments should engage pro-actively in open, transparent and honest conversations with the private sector, civil society and citizens about how best to respond to the needs of the poorest and most marginalised, and the policies that should be in place to reduce inequalities through the use of ICTs". This raises questions about the role of the state within society and the respective policy and conceptual issues. As regards policy, many states have sought to promote sustainable development through "a restricted public sphere paradigm which places greater emphasis on the corporate imperative", namely, that the state must not jeopardise "the competitiveness of corporate interests in the wider global economy" (French, 2002: 41).

However, there are variations in the policy role that the ICT industry would like to see governments play. GeSI (2016: 36) has called on governments to play "their part in shaping policy and legal frameworks" by "liberalising some markets, improving the ease of doing business and bearing down on restrictive practices", thereby reducing the regulatory burden on businesses. For French (2002: 142), sustainable development raises fundamental questions about the coordination of "public/private-public/corporate" intervention, and he calls for "a more collaborative approach". This highlights the importance for future research in this area, but as Harris (2016) has pointed out, researchers are not generally inclined toward engaging with the users of their research and communicating their findings to a wider audience. Harris also notes that ICT4D researchers are not normally incentivised to adopt these engagement practices.

A liberal pluralist perspective sees the state as a neutral arbiter of social processes, which provides opportunities for all stakeholders to influence state policy and which works for the benefit of society as a whole. This is consistent with the ICT industry's position on the SDGs and also echoes the UN's call for governments and the private sector to collaborate to address the SDGs.

Connecting the unconnected

"Connecting the unconnected" (Ericsson, 2016: 24) is generally viewed as a realistic contribution that the ICT industry can make in the achievement of the SDGs. This resonates with Heeks' (2014) assertion that "connecting the excluded" was one particular area worthy of further study and analysis, with an example of job advertisements through SMS in a developing world context. Indeed, the GSMA (2016: 5) stressed the importance of "extending network coverage to rural areas" but arguably more importantly recognised that while connectivity "is a very important first step", the real prize is about "what this connectivity enables", namely, "connecting everyone and everything to a better future". In many ways this is globalisation positively cast, and Sachs (2016: webpage), for example, has described the SDGs as "a new kind of globalization", but as such, it might be seen to be in conflict with the underlying spirit of the SDGs in a number of ways.

In particular, the standardisation of products and services and the dominance of a relatively small number of global brands within the ICT industry constitute significant barriers to small local entrepreneurs and producers within less developed countries. There are also risks that increase in trade, often associated with globalisation, will accelerate the exploitation of nonrenewable natural resources and thereby increase pollution and greenhouse gas emissions and undermine the SDGs. Where local economies increasingly concentrate on the production of a limited range of products and services to meet the demands of global markets, a downturn in these markets can have damaging consequences for local economies. Ultimately, many critics would argue that globalisation does not offer a better future for everyone, rather it produces winners and losers, and that it can exacerbate, rather than reduce, inequalities between developed and less developed economies.

Technology increases efficiencies

The development and deployment of new technologies are often considered key contributing factors in the improvement of efficiencies across the sustainability spectrum and in helping to deliver sustainable growth. Clark and Dickson (2003: 8059) suggest that "the need for sustainable development initiatives to mobilize appropriate science and technology has long been recognized". More specifically, Ericsson (2016: 12) concluded that "ICTs have the potential to increase the rate of diffusion of a very wide range of technologies across the economy" and "the accelerated uptake of these technologies . . . constitutes the key to achieving the SDGs by their target date of 2030". Schor similarly noted, "Advocates of technological solutions argue that more intelligent design and technological innovation can dramatically reduce or even stop the depletion of ecological resources, as well as eliminate toxic chemicals and ecosystem disruption" (Schor, 2005: 310). For example, the applications of digital technology in the mining and minerals extraction industries "include building a more comprehensive understanding of the resource base, optimizing material and equipment flow, improving anticipation of failures, increasing mechanization through automation, and monitoring performance in real time" (Durrant-Whyte et al., 2015: webpage). However, Schor also points out that such approaches "fail to address increases in the scale of production and consumption" (Schor, 2005: 310).

On a more positive note, the unprecedented nature and pace of technology development within the ICT industry may provide sustainable solutions to seemingly elusive environmental and social challenges and thus allow the ICT industry to make a major and lasting contribution to the SDGs. Heeks (2014: 2), for example, noted that ICT products and services that are currently to the fore for use in developing countries are "near-ubiquity of mobile, spread of broadband, more big/open/real-time data, use of field sensors/embedded computing, more social media, more crowd-sourcing models, more cloud, more smartphones, and 3D printing" and that the scope, reach and depth of ICTs in developing countries is changing apace. Heeks (2017: webpage) noted, "The relationship between digital ICTs and international development can be divided into three paradigms – pre-digital, ICT4D, and digital development". The digital paradigm is now on the ascent and will overtake the ICT4D paradigm by 2030. Heeks (2016: 1) concludes, "We can foresee a 'digital development' paradigm in which ICTs are no longer just tools to enable particular aspects of development, but the platform that mediates development". Continued research on the successive phases of technology development should clarify relative costs and benefits. However, Easterly (2007) argues that large-scale scientific programmes do nothing to solve the problems of poor contract enforcement, corruption and extortion and the ineffective government services that plague so many aid initiatives in developing countries.

Continued economic growth

Ericsson (2016) explicitly links rapid economic growth with SDG success and, in addressing SDG #7 (decent work and economic growth), GSMA (2016: 165) looked to "sustain per capita economic growth in accordance with national circumstances and, in particular, at least seven per cent gross domestic product growth per annum in the least developed countries". Many critics argue that such growth will make increasing demands on Earth's finite natural resources, which will ultimately prove unsustainable. Higgins (2013: webpage) maintains, "The economic growth we know today is diametrically opposed to the sustainability of our planet". The counter argument builds upon the notion of "decoupling economic growth from environmental degradation" (GSMA, 2016: 20), but this concept remains poorly defined.

It thus appears that the term "sustained economic growth" refers – within the ICT industry – to the perceived importance of securing continuing economic growth rather than to explaining how such growth is to be achieved within finite environmental limits. At the same time, some critics see decoupling as an elusive goal. Jackson (2009: 8) highlighted the distinction between "relative" and "absolute" decoupling. The former refers to the decline of resource impacts relative to growth, and the latter signifies an absolute decline in such impacts. Although some large corporations might claim to support relative decoupling through their commitments to efficiency, they currently show little enthusiasm for absolute decoupling, which Jackson (2009: 48) believed "is essential if economic activity is to remain within ecological limits".

Castro (2004) has questioned the very possibility of sustainable development under capitalism and argued that economic growth relies upon the continuing and inevitable exploitation of both natural and social capital, and Mingers (2001) has insisted that future research in this area must adopt a transdisciplinary and multi-methodological approach. Raiti (2006: 1) has viewed the need for a multi-disciplinary approach as "a piece of the development puzzle", but it is evident that the various disciplines contributing to the field, "such as anthropology, computer science, geography, development studies, and IS" cannot easily "be brought together under one methodological or theoretical umbrella" (Walsham, 2017: 34).

Conclusions

The realisation of the wide-ranging global vision for a sustainable future embodied in the SDGs will require commitment from a range of public and private sector entities, not least national governments. The UN has called upon all businesses to play a central role in achieving the SDGs, but monitoring and evaluating the role of the ICT industry in advancing the SDGs seems likely to be a complex and contested process. Current research initiatives in the ICT4D field offer an initial framework for tracking and evaluating the key issues discussed in this chapter, even if the ICT industry and the ICT4D research community often take different philosophical (and at times, political) standpoints. It is to be hoped that ICT4D researchers can play a valuable role in what Unwin (2017: 61) has called "a flexible and effective multi-sector partnership (governments, private sector, civil society, and citizens) approach", which is important "for implementing ICT initiatives that contribute to sustainability".

The advent of SDGs constitutes a very significant business opportunity for the ICT industry, which would involve what GSMA (2016: 98) describe as the "co-ordination and standardisation of the industry's messages globally", which is "critical to achieve optimal results for all stakeholders". The ICT industry emphasised the vital importance of the role of governments in creating a more liberal market environment and in funding many of the necessary improvements in connectivity, but the role of governments, particularly in less developed economies, in effectively addressing these challenges may prove problematic. The rapid pace of technological development may revolutionise how the SDGs can be achieved; but for some critics the fundamental problem will be the tension between the SDGs and continuing commitments to production and consumption in advancing economic growth.

Ultimately, it is important to recognise that in some ways the SDGs may be unattainable and that while they can be seen to be laudable and universally agreed upon aspirations, they face testing challenges against a background of continuing world population growth. A number of factors might be seen to contribute to such a pessimistic potential scenario. The SDGs look to build on the UN's arguably less ambitious Millennium Development Goals (MDGs) established in 2001. However, the failure to meet many of the MDGs, perhaps most notably demonstrated by overall increases in carbon dioxide emissions, in water scarcity, and in the uneven progress across the globe, do not provide universal grounds for optimism.

That said, the ICT industry has certainly identified the SDGs as a massive and geographically wide–ranging business opportunity, and continuing corporate and government investment will undoubtedly support progress in helping to meet the SDG goals and more specifically in improving access, connectivity and efficiency. Looking to the future, the ICT industry will want to monitor how a range of ICT initiatives is contributing to the SDGs and in publicly reporting on progress, they will help to maintain momentum both within the industry and in the wider business community. At the same time, the academic community also has an important role to play in working with business leaders and in supporting national and international policy makers in addressing the opportunities and the challenges presented by the UN's commitment to the SDGs.

References

Castro, C. "Sustainable Development: Mainstream and Critical Perspectives." *Organization and Environment*, 17(2), 2004: 195–225.

Clark, W. C. and Dickson, N. M. "Sustainability Science: The Emerging Research Program." *Proceedings of the National Academy of Sciences in the United States of America*, 14(4), 2003: 8059–8061.

Crane, A., Palazzo, G., Spence, L. J. and Matten, D. "Contesting the Value of Creating Shared Value." *California Management Review*, 56(2), 2014: 130–154.

Durrant-Whyte, H., Geraghty, R., Pujol, F. and Sellschop, R. "How Digital Innovation Can Improve Mining Productivity." *Metals and Mining*. McKinsey & Company. September 2015. Accessed February 8, 2018. www.mckinsey.com/industries/metals-and-mining/our-insights/how-digital-innovation-can-improve-mining-productivity.

Easterly, W. *The White Man's Burden: Why the West's Efforts to Aid the Rest Have Done So Much Ill and So Little Good.* London: Penguin, 2007.

Ericsson. *ICT and SDGs: How ICT Can Accelerate Action on the SDGs: Final Report.* Ericsson and the Earth Institute Columbia University. 2016. Accessed February 1, 2018. www.ericsson.com/assets/local/news/2016/05/ict-sdg.pdf.

French, D. A. "The Role of the State and International Organizations in Reconciling Sustainable Development and Globalization." *International Environmental Agreements: Politics, Law and Economics*, 2, 2002: 135–150.

GeSI (Global e-Sustainability Initiative). "Global e-Sustainability Initiative and Accenture Strategy: System Transformation: How Digital Solutions Will Drive Progress towards the Sustainable Development Goals." 2016. Accessed January 23, 2017. http://system transformation-sdg.gesi.org/160608_GeSI_SystemTransformation.pdf.

GSMA (Groupe Spécial Mobile Association). *2016 Mobile Industry Impact Report: Sustainable Development Goals.* 2016. Accessed January 23, 2017. www.gsma.com/betterfuture/wp-content/uploads/2016/09/_UN_SDG_Report_FULL_R1_WEB_Singles_LOW.pdf

Harris, R. W. "How ICT4D Research Fails the Poor." *Information Technology for Development*, 22(1), 2016: 177–192.

Heeks, R. "ICT4D 2016: New Priorities for ICT4D Policy, Practice and WSIS in a Post-2015 World." *Development Informatics*, Working Paper Series, No. 59. 2014. Accessed March 23, 2017. http://hummedia.manchester.ac.uk/institutes/gdi/publications/workingpapers/di/di_wp59.pdf.

Heeks, R. "Examining 'Digital Development': The Shape of Things to Come?" *Development Informatics*, Working Paper Series, No. 64. 2016. Accessed July 20, 2018. http://humme-dia.manchester.ac.uk/institutes/gdi/publications/workingpapers/di/di_wp64.pdf.

Heeks, R. "An Emerging Digital Development Paradigm." 2017. Accessed March 21, 2017. http://blog.gdi.manchester.ac.uk/emerging-digital-development-paradigm/.

Higgins, K. L. "Economic Growth and Sustainability: Are They Mutually Exclusive?" 2013. Accessed May 28, 2017. www.elsevier.com/connect/economic-growth-and-sustainability-are-they-mutually-exclusive.

Jackson, T. "Prosperity without Growth?" *Sustainability Development Commission*. 2009. Accessed December 4, 2009. www.sd-commission.org.uk/data/files/publications/prosperity_without_growth_report.pdf.

Microsoft. "Microsoft and the UN Sustainable Development Goals." 2016. Accessed January 23, 2017. www.microsoft.com.

Mingers, J. "Combining IS Research Methods: Towards a Pluralist Methodology." *Information Systems Research*, 12(3), 2001: 240–259.

OECD (Organisation for Economic Co-Operation and Development). *OECD Environmental Outlook to 2030.* Paris: OECD, 2009.

Porter. M. E. and Kramer, M. R. "Strategy and Society: The Link between Competitive Advantage and Corporate Social Responsibility." *Harvard Business Review*, 87, 2011: 78–92.

Qureshi, S. "The Forgotten Awaken: ICT's Evolving Role in the Roots of Mass Discontent." *Information Technology for Development*, 23(1), 2017: 1–17.

Raiti, G. C. "The Lost Sheep of ICT4D Research." *Information Technologies and International Development*, 3(4), 2006: 1–7.

Sachs, J. "Sustainable Development: A New Kind of Globalization." www.bostonglobe.com/opinion/2016/07/18/sustainable-development-new-kind-globalization/8n33gJU KfUVDyMUD3J5iJK/story.html.

Schor, J. B. "Prices and Quantities: Unsustainable Consumption and the Global Economy." *Ecological Economics*, 55, 2005: 309–320.

Sein, M. K. and Harindranath, G. "Conceptualizing the ICT Artifact: Toward Understanding the Role of ICT in National Development." *The Information Society: An International Journal*, 20(1), 2004: 15–24.

Shared Value Initiative. *The Unexpected Market Potential in the SDGs*. 2015. Accessed July 4, 2017. https://sharedvalue.org/groups/unexpected-market-potential-sdgs.

Souter, D., Maclean, D., Akoh, B. and Creech, H. "ICTs, the Internet and Sustainable Development: Towards a New Paradigm." 2010. Accessed Jane 23, 2017. www.iisd.org/sites/default/files/publications/icts_internet_sd_new_paradigm.pdf.

United Nations. "Transforming Our World: The 2030 Agenda for Sustainable Development." 2015. Accessed July 20, 2018. https://sustainabledevelopment.un.org/post2015/transformingourworld.

Unwin, T. "ICTs and the Failure of the Sustainable Development Goals." 2015. Accessed January 23, 2017. https://unwin.wordpress.com/2015/08/05/icts-and-the-failure-of-the-sustainable-development-goals/.

Unwin, T. "ICTs, Sustainability and Development: Critical Elements." In A. Sharafat and W. Lehr (eds.), *ICT-Centric Economic Growth, Innovation and Job Creation*. Geneva: ITU, 2017.

Van Biljon, J. and Alexander, T. "Information and Communication Technology for Development (ICT4D) Research: The Quest for a Shared Conceptual Framework Continues." *Proceedings of the 8th International Development Informatics Conference* (IDIA2013). Port Elizabeth, South Africa, November 3–4, 2014: 361–371.

Walsham, G. "ICT4D Research: Reflections on History and Future Agenda." *Information Technology for Development*, 23(1), 2017: 18–41.

8

CREATIVE INDUSTRIES AS A TOOL FOR POVERTY ALLEVIATION IN PIROT, SERBIA

Hristina Mikić

Abstract

The chapter is focused on the potential of sustainable socioeconomic development in a rural part of Serbia through creative industries entrepreneurship. It provides for a better understanding of the creative industries' contribution to the advancement of the Sustainable Development Goals (SDGs). Through data, results and lessons learned from two projects in Pirot, Serbia, in the period 2015–2017, the chapter provides insights into how creative industries entrepreneurship could advance the SDGs. Special attention is paid to the issues, challenges and recommendations related to the actions that should be taken in implementing SDGs in rural and less developed areas.

Introduction

The end of 1980s was marked by the rising interest of theoreticians and practitioners in topics related to the role of creative industries in fostering economic development. The United Nations (UN) dealt with this topic through issues such as the rights to freedom of expression and creativity and intercultural dialogue. The discussion about culture, cultural industries and development came to the fore by the nineties with several UNESCO's reports such as "Our Creative Diversity" (UNESCO, 1996), "Creativity and Markets" (UNESCO, 1998) and "Cultural Diversity, Conflicts and Pluralism" (UNESCO, 2000). Since that time, the global developmental agenda has gradually started its reshaping. The Millennium Development Goals (MDGs) for the period up to 2015, adopted by the UN, addressed creative industries in a very modest way. They were discussed mainly by exploring their potential for contributing to employment and poverty reduction (see: Mikić, 2018b: 5). With the aim of bringing up the issue of culture and creative industries, the UN adopted three resolutions on culture and development (UN, 2003, 2010, 2013) that invited all member states to rethink the role of culture and creative industries in development policies and strategies.

The UN Sustainable Development Solutions Network (SDSN) was established in 2012. The network brings together global experts and development leaders to propose practical solutions for sustainable development and a preliminary list of sustainable development goals. The process of defining the SDGs was of a participatory nature, and it included more than three years of consultations and intergovernmental negotiations. Public consultation meetings involved the participation of citizens, and five countries (Serbia, Bosnia and Herzegovina, Ecuador, Mali and Morocco) were selected for national consultations on culture and development.

Before the final SDGs were proposed, several international conferences and meetings were held. The two of them (in Hangzhou and Florence) have given special attention to culture as a pillar of future policies for sustainable development. "The Hangzhou Declaration Placing Culture at the Heart of Sustainable Development Policies" proposed more explicit involvement of culture in development processes and a better understanding of the power of culture and creative industries in addressing the global developmental challenges (UNESCO, 2013). Participants of the Third UNESCO World Forum on Cultural and Creative Industries adopted the Florence Declaration, which called key stakeholders to integrate culture into sustainable development, to strengthen the legal and political environment and to enhance new partnership and investment strategies for culture and creative industries (UNESCO, 2014).

The international nongovernmental organizations (NGOs) gathered around the platform #culture2015goal and also made efforts by advocating and lobbying the explicit involvement of culture into the SDGs (United Cities and Local Governments, 2014), but their vision related to culture and sustainable development was not included in Agenda 2030. Therefore, it was adopted without any explicit goal dedicated to culture and creative industries. Those areas are treated in Agenda 2030 as cross-sectoral ones and a cross-cutting issue of public policies. Thus, mainstreaming culture and creative industries was of a horizontal nature, covering issues related to the entire Agenda 2030 development process and relevant for all the SDGs and their implementation (Mikić, 2018b).

This chapter is focused on the potential of the creative industry entrepreneurship for sustainable socioeconomic development in rural parts of Serbia. There is a strong connection between culture and creative industries entrepreneurship. Creative industries entrepreneurship enables creation, production and commercialization of creative content that is intangible and cultural in nature (Mikić, 2012). It includes a set of activities, knowledge and skills that produce creative goods and services embodying or convening cultural expressions. Thus, creative industries entrepreneurship is very important for promotion and protection of the diversity of cultural expressions and human-centered development. Adequately nurtured, creative industries fuel culture, create jobs and stimulate innovation and trade, while contributing to social inclusion, cultural diversity and environmental sustainability (UNCTAD, 2010: XIX).

The objective of this chapter is to provide evidence, analysis and better understanding of creative industries entrepreneurship as a tool for poverty reduction (SDG #1) as well as its impact on advancing sustainable development of rural areas. It is primarily based on data collected during a mapping exercise and investigation of creative entrepreneurs in Pirot and stakeholder workshops on group and individual consultations with members of the local community as well as the evaluation of two projects for developing creative industries in this area. These two projects, "Strengthening local and regional institutional capacities for the support to creative industries in Serbia" and "Rural creative economy: Economic strengthening of rural creative industries" were implemented by the Creative Economy Group Foundation in the period 2015–2017.

In addition, the chapter provides an overview of poverty and creative industries entrepreneurship in Serbia. This is followed by an analysis of the two creative industries projects, their contribution to achieving the SDGs and the testimonies and personal impressions of some beneficiaries. The last section contains lessons learned and recommendations on which kind of action needs to be taken, particularly in rural and less developed areas such as the region of Pirot.

Poverty and creative industries entrepreneurship

The concept of poverty in Serbia includes persons who cannot meet basic needs and whose income is below the poverty line. However, income is not the only criterion for determining poverty in Serbia. Poverty is also considered to include people lacking the resources necessary for decent life. Poverty mostly affects socially vulnerable groups – Roma (Gypsies) communities, elderly women, people with special needs, rural population and so on. In Serbia, there were about 600,000 recorded poor persons in 2017 with a monthly income of less than 100. About 25.5 percent of the total population (1.8 million inhabitants) are under the risk of poverty (Office of Statistics Serbia, 2016). Based on the poverty map data (Office of Statistics Serbia, 2016), persons belonging to the group of poor or at risk of poverty originate from rural multimember households, live in the southern parts of Serbia and are mostly unemployed.

Pirot is a municipality in Southeast Serbia where the poverty rate goes up to 28.5 percent, and the poverty gap is 9.4 (Office of Statistics Serbia, 2016). This mean that 28.5 percent of Pirot citizens have an income that is 9.4 percent below the line of poverty – 60 percent of average income at the national level.

This area with average density of inhabitants less than 47 square kilometers is dominantly categorized as a rural region. A great majority of the population in the area primarily works in agriculture. Poverty mainly affects rural women and persons from marginalized groups (Roma, for example). A considerable number of people live in poverty's risk as a consequence of the ownership transformations in large state-owned companies. Due to privatization, many industrial facilities closed down, making local inhabitants of Pirot jobless and without a stable source of livelihood. Many of them turned their creative hobbies into a small entrepreneurship businesses.

Pirot has a long tradition in several creative entrepreneurship activities. Jovanović (2012) describes Pirot as a well-known crafts and trading place. He reported the existence of more than 3,600 crafts in the period between the liberation from the Ottoman Empire and World War II. The rapid industrialization of rural areas during the Communist era transformed Pirot's economy in many ways, especially in causing the loss of many creative entrepreneurship activities.

There are 355 different firms, entrepreneurs, organizations and individuals that work in creative industries entrepreneurship in Pirot. Some of them are doing business in the formal creative economy (68%); others work in the informal sector. Traditional creative entrepreneurship (knitting, sewing, crocheting, traditional rug making, etc.) accounts for 82 percent of the total number of (formal and informal) creative businesses. A smaller number of activities can be found in contemporary creative domains such as web design, multimedia, design and publishing. Crafts and cultural and natural heritage represent more than 50 percent of creative entrepreneurs (Creative Economy Group, 2017a).

A creative industries mapping exercise done in Pirot (Mikić, 2018a) has shown notable gender differentiation in entrepreneurial cultural activities, where men make up around 62 percent of the entrepreneurs. The same research also identified several characteristics of entrepreneurial activities: domination of micro firms that have less than five employees; seasonality of creative business, the simple supply chains with one or two activities that are coved by cultural entrepreneurs and their family members.

Due to business barriers related to the high level of taxation, economic uncertainty and limited and unstable market, the majority of creative entrepreneurs started with these activities as a hobby, and after achieving a certain stability, they decide to register their creative business (for more see: Mikić, 2018a: 256). Most of these individuals (94%) have reduced the risk of poverty by engaging in creative entrepreneurship. They saw this business as the main exit from poverty, because in a very short time they could acquire creative skills, procure materials and resources and start up a business.

Annual revenues from creative industries range between €5,000 and 25,000. They are commonly unstable since most products are sold in local markets or in neighboring municipalities. More than 70 percent of creative industries entrepreneurs sell their products through local stores or own workshops. For around 85 percent of these entrepreneurs, creative industries are their main occupation, and revenues gained from this business are the main source of their household income.

Because of the importance that creative entrepreneurship has for their quality of life, most entrepreneurs are dedicated to developing and improving their creative businesses. Very often, however, some tailor-made mentorship, education and additional professional development programs are unavailable. About 40 percent of creative entrepreneurs have not taken any training to increase business or their managerial skills. Neither do they use social and web networks to promote their business. Their economic strength is low. Limited too is their capacity to run a business and overcome barriers to financial viability and growth, such as in the areas of product placement, access to finance and the sourcing of new consumers.

Impacts of creative industries projects in Pirot in achieving SDGs

To strengthen the creative industries entrepreneurship in rural parts of Serbia, two projects were implemented in the period 2015–2017: "Strengthening local and regional institutional capacities for the support to creative industries in Serbia" (supported by the UNESCO International Fund for Cultural Diversity and the Ministry of Culture of Serbia) and "Rural creative economy: Economic strengthening of rural creative industries" (supported by the US Embassy in Serbia). The first project was focused on improving local and regional capacities for enacting a strategic approach, cross-sectoral and innovative partnership in creative industries through reinforcing existing institutional infrastructure and creating a network of local and regional creative industries stakeholders. The second project had the aim to promote a sustainable market economy and poverty reduction of rural people through enhancing rural creative industries entrepreneurship and public-private partnership.

The projects have the overall goal to reduce poverty of rural population and to improve their economic and cultural position, the first one at the policy level (so-called policy component) while the second one at the entrepreneurship level (so-called entrepreneurial component). This was done through capacity building (Laboratory for Creative Entrepreneurship, Creative Economy School); sustainable creative industries policy (Creative Industries Mapping Studies, Agenda for Creative Industries Development); networking and visibility of creative entrepreneurs (Rural Creative Industries Fair) and creating web platforms for promotion, branding and selling products of rural creative industries (Creative Economy Expo Platform) as well as raising the awareness of local governments about the developmental impact of rural creative entrepreneurship and strengthening the partnership for sustainable development (Creative Economy Forum).

While creating conditions for poverty reduction of rural population (SDG #1), these projects indirectly contributed to the advancement of the following goals as well:

  SDG #4 – Ensure inclusive and equitable quality of education and promote lifelong learning opportunities for all
  SDG #6 – Achieve gender equality and empower all women and girls
  SDG #8 – Promote sustained, inclusive and sustainable economic growth
  SDG #17 – Strengthen the partnership for sustainable development

The projects were created based on the idea that high poverty rates in rural areas had been caused mainly by low economic development and insufficient diversification of the rural economy. The diversification of the rural economy through creative industries good governance and increasing number of creative entrepreneurs can generate pathways for reducing the risk of vulnerability of the rural population, especially for women and youth.

Project activities

The entrepreneurial component of these two projects started with the mapping of creative entrepreneurs and the assessment of their capacities and needs. This data was used by the municipal government, task forces for creative industries and a project team to define an action plan within the project with the consultation of creative entrepreneurs. The aim of the action plan was to define a road map for the creation of a better environment for the development of rural creative entrepreneurship.

This was followed by organizing the Laboratory of Creative Entrepreneurship, attended by 86 entrepreneurs. This specific open-innovation and knowledge-sharing laboratory served as a capacity building for rural creative entrepreneurs by which they obtained and improved the skills, knowledge and other resources needed to do business in creative industries. The participants gained knowledge about legal aspects of their business, marketing through social networks, photographing their products, intellectual property protection and possible funding. They were also trained on how to become creative business mentors in their respective communities, who could support other entrepreneurs in improving their creative activities or in motivating other community members to start their own creative industries entrepreneurship.

The selected 42 entrepreneurs were visited by creative industries business coaches, who helped them to improve their products, sales methods, promotion and visibility. Their products were photographed, and business coaches helped them present their businesses better on a digital platform created within the project and establish better communication with their clients. The closing events for the Laboratory of Creative Entrepreneurship, called Creative Economy Forum and the Rural Creative Industries Fair, helped project participants to network, get business contacts and create new partnerships and joint projects with other creative entrepreneurs as well as with the government and municipality representatives.

Project results and their link to the SDGs

In order to achieve their objectives, the entrepreneurial component of the projects provide assistance to a number of creative entrepreneurs regarding strengthening their business and personal capacities as well as creating conditions for poverty alleviation in rural places. Achieved results address more than one of the SDGs, highlighting their interconnectedness and interrelationships.

SDG #1 (**Poverty reduction**). Digital platforms and better visibility through creative industries mapping studies, forums, fairs, round tables, conferences and other public events enabled project participants to increase their revenues by about 20 percent. Through the platforms, many buyers not living in Pirot contacted the creative entrepreneurs and bought their products. Cooperation between the entrepreneur and the buyer is direct, without any intermediaries or additional costs. Seventeen entrepreneurs and nongovernmental organizations took part in different interregional projects such as Instrument for Pre-Accession for Cross Border Cooperation Bulgaria-Serbia or activities implemented by local tourist organizations and local municipalities, which increased their revenues by about 35 percent.

SDG #4 (**Ensure inclusive and equitable quality of education and promote lifelong learning opportunities for all**). The Laboratory of Creative Entrepreneurship offered training to 86 rural people (64 of whom were unemployed) on doing business in creative industries. Due to the projects, rural people (especially youth) went from being unemployed to becoming entrepreneurs, starting up various nongovernmental organizations (NGOs) and organizations like DekuPi.

WORKSHOP DEKUPI, BILJANA MARINKOV

Ms. Biljana Marinkov used to work as a journalist but left the position in 2015 due to poor working conditions. She took up decoupage technique and started making usable creative objects as a hobby. "Participation in projects of the Creative Economy Group has motivated me to think about economic aspects of my hobby, and to become a creative entrepreneur", Biljana said.

> In the meantime, I was thinking about the development of my creative skills. Participating in the Creative Entrepreneurship Laboratory on packaging, markets for creative products and local cultural motifs, made me significantly change my approach towards product making. My husband and sons acquired skills of graphic design for my creative products. In the selection of Pirot rug motifs that would apply to my products, I had consulted a local historian from Pirot, Ms. Radmila Vlatkovic´. The knowledge acquired in these workshops and support received from the mentors of the Creative Economy Group gave me guidelines on how to register my workshop DekuPi, prepare a business plan and improve my business activities as well increase my household budget.

By registering the DekuPi workshop, we have expanded our market, because now I can sell my products to legal entities, companies and tourist organisations. Since I went into the creative entrepreneurship, my family and I have been living much better, and we can afford to buy many things now. Our family budget has increased. Finally, creative entrepreneurship linked us better, and made us spend our time together in a better way – we travel together to fairs and other events, and we deal with promotion and sales of creative products as a family. I have also started to hold workshops for young entrepreneurs, to teach them creative skills and to encourage them to promote diversity of local cultural expressions. In personal terms, creative entrepreneurship has made me more self-confident, helped me spend my time in better quality, and make social contacts with different people.

PHOTO 8.1 Biljana and Igor Marinkov, DekuPi Workshop Pirot

Source: Photo taken by Biljana Marinkov, Pirot & Institute for creative entrepreneurship and innovations ©Biljana Marinkov & Institute for creative entrepreneurship and innovations

SDG #6 (Achieve gender equality and empower all women and girls).
Of the total number of participants in "Rural creative economy: Economic strengthening of rural creative industries", around 85 percent were women. These projects helped and encouraged them to get into creative entrepreneurship and gain new knowledge and information needed for running a business. They gained more courage through the projects and found new ideas on how to improve their products' design, packaging and marketing. They also learned how to engage in the digital sales function.

PLETISANKA MILIJANA BY MILIJANA PETROV

Ms. Milijana Petrov has been in different creative hobbies since early childhood. A foreign correspondent by vocation, she could not find a job in the Pirot region for a long time. Milijana says: "The most important milestone in my work was when I met the Creative Economy Group. Participating in their Creative Entrepreneurship Laboratory made me change my view of entrepreneurship, I have learned about new possibilities of promoting creative products, and how to improve the production process. New knowledge helped me also in terms of legal and financial improvement of my business, and making my manufacturing more productive and cost-effective."

PHOTO 8.2 Milijana Petrov at the laboratory for creative entrepreneurship in nis and her knitting works

Milijana's progress in creative entrepreneurship was mostly attributed to open support from the mentors of the Creative Economy Group, who taught her how to correct mistakes in her work. She also benefitted from digital promotion through the expo.kreativnaekonomija.com platform, where one can find main details about her work and contact her for ordering the products. Thanks to her involvement in the project, Milijana Petrov is now a proud creative entrepreneur, who believes that without the support she received from the Creative Economy Group, she would be still dealing with this as a hobby, not a real business.

SDG #8 (Promote sustained, inclusive and sustainable economic growth). Project "Rural creative economy: Economic strengthening of rural creative industries" has created better access of rural creative industries to new markets and consumers. This was mostly archived by creating the digital platform Creative Economy Expo (www.expo. kreativnakonomija.com). Many entrepreneurs use this platform as their ID card when they want to present themselves to new clients. Many of them do not have webpages, and thus it is very difficult for potential buyers to reach them. A digital profile of creative entrepreneurs can also serve as some kind of validation of the quality of rural products and the creative business that protects and promotes the diversity of local cultural expressions. The platform is free of charge for users. Photos and profiles uploaded on this website are created by a professional team of photographers and experts.

PRALIPE, PIROT

"Pralipe" is an NGO in Pirot, dealing with the promotion of Roma culture and improvement of the lives of the Roma people. The founder of the NGO is Mr. Radovan Asković. Together with the Creative Economy Group, this NGO has been working on mapping the Roma creative entrepreneurship in Pirot, working conditions, and barriers that the Roma people face dealing with creative entrepreneurship. Mr. Asković stresses, "The project has contributed to the improvement of social position of Roma, through publication of research on Roma creative entrepreneurship where the Roma people are observed in a positive light, and the diversity of Roma cultural expressions is perceived in a positive way".

The selected Roma creative entrepreneurs can be found at www.expo. kreativnaekonomija.com, which helps them reach their buyers better. The ID cards on this platform are also a kind of quality assurance, since this confirms that Roma creative entrepreneurs protect through their work a diversity of cultural expressions.

PHOTO 8.3 Kaja Redzic, a weaver in CIC Pralipe, Pirot

Source: Photo taken by A. Ciric © Institute for Creative Entrepreneurship and Innovation

SDG #17 (Strengthen the partnership for sustainable development).
The events such as the Creative Economy Forum and Rural Creative Industries Fair (implemented through the project "Strengthening local and regional institutional capacities for the support to creative industries in Serbia") were dedicated to establishing communication and networking between creative entrepreneurs and other participants and to creating new contacts and new forms of cooperation. A total of 192 participants took part in the Forum and Fair, where 46 new cooperative partnerships were established. These included partnerships between NGO members and individuals, between government bodies and creative entrepreneurs and between tourist organizations and creative entrepreneurs. As a result of these partnerships, 24 new joint local projects were created and implemented, starting in 2017.

HERITAG – CENTRE FOR RESEARCH AND PROMOTION OF CULTURAL HERITAGE

HeriTag is an organization founded by young historians Ms. Dušanka Gojić and Ms. Gordana Milanović. When they completed their masters' degrees, they faced difficulties in finding jobs in their profession. Participating in project activities of the Creative Economy Group enabled them to become

PHOTO 8.4 Dušanka Gojić, the cofounder of HeriTag, with young participants of the project

Source: Photo taken by ©HeriTag

motivated and obtain the necessary advice and instructions on how to create their own organization and establish its main activities.

The Centre for Research and Promotion of Cultural Heritage implements projects that involve the local community and young people in conserving the local cultural heritage. One of their projects is a virtual community museum, where they, together with members of the local community, document the nontangible and tangible heritage of Stara Pazova.

Ms. Dušanka Gojić emphasizes, "In the workshops within the Creative Economy Laboratory and Forum, I have seen numerous novelties that helped me in my work and inspired me for new project ideas. Also, those events created possibilities to meet new people and make new partnerships with different NGOs and creative entrepreneurs". She particularly values the cooperation with the Creative Economy Group, which has extended beyond the project completion. "I received so many useful instructions on how to run my organisation, without which I don't believe I could so easily have established and run my project activities", Dušanka said.

Lessons learned and looking ahead

The development of creative industries in rural areas can contribute to diversification of the rural economy and to poverty reduction among the population. In Serbia, about 25.5 percent of the population is at risk of poverty. Most of them live in rural areas in the south of Serbia and are active predominantly in agriculture. Their income is low, and they have limited access to education and training.

The projects described in this chapter show how creative industries can help the rural population improve its economic position and quality of life. The results of the two projects addressed several SDGs, implying how interrelated and interconnected creative entrepreneurship and sustainable development can advance SDG #4 (ensure inclusive and equitable quality of education and promote lifelong learning opportunities for all), SDG #6 (achieve gender equality and empower all women and girls), SDG #8 (promote sustained, inclusive and sustainable economic growth) and SDG #17 (strengthen the partnership for sustainable development).

However, it is not always easy to motivate rural entrepreneurs to get involved in such projects. The projects' experience has shown that projects for developing rural creative entrepreneurship must be mobile and easily accessible to the rural population. They must include a personalized component, such as mentoring and business coaching, so as to establish a closer and more open contact with creative entrepreneurs. In this way, it is possible to provide incentives for the development of creative entrepreneurship tailored to the individual needs of rural creative entrepreneurs.

Lessons learned also show that a cascading-down approach enables the transfer of knowledge and skills, as well as the motivation and enthusiasm, acquired through the two projects from the projects participants to other active or emerging entrepreneurs in the creative industry entrepreneurship.

The challenges of such projects are that they cannot be of a large scale. Experience has shown that to ensure high-quality work by the entrepreneurs, the Creative Entrepreneurship Laboratory could only include a small number of participants. The future of such projects should be enhanced by their institutionalization through a partnership with state institutions (e.g., regional development agencies or local economic development offices). Only in this way, conditions can be created for the continuous and sustainable development of rural creative entrepreneurship in a region like Pirot.

Bibliography

Creative Economy Group. *Beneficiary's Testimonials* (Project documentation). Belgrade: Creative Economy Group, 2016a.

Creative Economy Group. *Project Report: Strengthening Local and Regional Institutional Capacities for the Support to Creative Industries in Serbia* (Project documentation). Belgrade: Creative Economy Group, 2016b.

Creative Economy Group. *Database on Creative Industries*. Pirot, Belgrade: Creative Economy Group, 2017a.

Creative Economy Group. *Project Report Rural Creative Economy: Economic Strengthening of Rural Creative Industries*. Belgrade: Creative Economy Group, 2017b.

Jovanović, B. *Old Crafts in Pirot and Neighbourhood*. Pirot: National Library, 2012.

Mikić, H. *Measuring Economic Contribution of Cultural Industries: Review and Assessment of Methodological Approaches*. Montreal: UNESCO-Institute for Statistics, 2012.

Mikić, H. "Cultural Entrepreneurship and Rural Development: Case Study of Pirot, Serbia." In E. Innerhofer, H. Pechlaner and E. Borin (eds.), *Entrepreneurship in Culture and Creative Industries: Perspectives from Companies and Regions*. Cham, Switzerland: Springer, 2018a: 245–263.

Mikić, H. "Culture and Sustainable Development Agenda 2030." *Čitalište: The Scientific Journal on Theory and Practice of Librarianship*, (33), 2018b: 3–15.

Office of Statistics Serbia. "Poverty Map in Serbia." Belgrade. 2016.

United Cities and Local Governments. "Culture: Fourth Pillar of Sustainable Development: Committee on Culture for 2011–2013." 2014. www.agen-da21culture.net/docs_circulars/ECOSOC2013-Committeeonculture-ENG.pdf.

United Nations Conference on Trade and Development. "Creative Economy Report 2010: Creative Economy: A Feasible Development Option." New York. 2010.

United Nations Educational, Scientific and Cultural Organization. "Our Creative Diversity." Paris. 1996. http://unesdoc.unesco.org/images/0010/001055/105586e.pdf.

United Nations Educational, Scientific and Cultural Organization. "Culture, Creativity and Markets." Paris. 1998.

United Nations Educational, Scientific and Cultural Organization. "Cultural Diversity, Conflicts and Pluralism." Paris. 2000.

United Nations Educational, Scientific and Cultural Organization. "Hangzhou Declaration Placing Culture at the Heart of Sustainable Development Policies." Paris. 2013.

United Nations Educational, Scientific and Cultural Organization. "Florence Declaration Outlines Recommendations on Culture for Post: 2015 Agenda: Culture, Creativity and Sustainable Development: Research, Innovation, Opportunities." Florence. 2014.

United Nations (UN) General Assembly. "Resolution Adopted by the General Assembly: 57/249." In *Culture and Development* 57/249. New York: UN, 2003.

United Nations General Assembly. "Resolution on Culture and Development A/C.2/65/ L.50." New York, NY. 2010.

United Nations General Assembly. "Resolution on Culture and Sustainable Development A/C8/440/add.4." New York, NY. 2013.

PART III

Gender equality, women's empowerment and social inclusion

9

WOMEN'S EMPOWERMENT THROUGH INDIGENOUS SOCIAL ENTERPRISES IN LATIN AMERICA

Mario Vázquez-Maguirre

Abstract

This chapter explores innovative enabler mechanisms for women's empowerment in social enterprises and how they promote gender equality and community well-being. For this purpose, three social enterprises located in indigenous rural communities in Mexico, Peru and Guatemala are analyzed following an inductive approach and qualitative methods. With the use of in-depth interviews, observation and analysis of secondary data, the three cases show different levels of women's empowerment and gender equality, probably as a result of the particular mechanisms each has designed to achieve this purpose. The male-dominated culture in each community has partially prevented women's participation in productive entities and decision-making. However, empowerment mechanisms such as access to decent job opportunities, gender equality policies, training and promotion and governance based on local values have had a dignifying effect on indigenous women, establishing a sense of self-worth and self-respect in them. This has also reduced structural discrimination against indigenous women in terms of education, decision-making and access to employment. The three cases also represent examples of how various Sustainable Development Goals (SDGs), such as no poverty (SDG #1), well-being (SDG #3), gender equality (SDG #5), decent work (SDG #8), reduced inequalities (SDG #10) and sustainable communities (SDG #11), are interrelated and interconnected.

Introduction

Most countries in Latin America have policies and strategies to promote gender equality; however, women in this region still struggle to have access to the opportunities that most men have. The resulting gap is more notorious in indigenous communities, where male-dominated patterns are deeply embedded in their culture. Although public policies and developmental activities have intended to target women in order to have a stronger impact in the household (women usually spend a higher percentage of their income on their children's well-being), the results have been, in most cases, limited or even discouraging (Collier, 2007).

Even more, the budget restrictions that governments in the region are currently facing sometimes end up defunding these programs. Under such a scenario, entrepreneurship presents itself as a sustainable alternative to promote women's well-being and one of the best strategies to empower women and elevate them to equal status with men (Coughlin and Thomas, 2002). Although female participation in the workplace contributes to a more egalitarian society, barriers still prevent women from participating in commercial entities (Avolio and Di Laura, 2017). These barriers include lack of flexible work arrangements, limited access to resources, lack of training and experience, cultural patterns and personal barriers regarding family and children care (e.g., Mattis, 2004; Lockyer and George, 2012; Nguyen et al., 2014).

The objective of the chapter is to explore innovative enabler mechanisms for women's empowerment in social enterprises and how they promote gender equality and community well-being. For this purpose, three social enterprises located in indigenous rural communities in Mexico, Peru and Guatemala are analyzed using an inductive approach and qualitative methods.

Social entrepreneurship and women's empowerment

Entrepreneurship has many forms and objectives from profit-maximizing entities to social-purpose enterprises that seek to solve a social need. In this sense, social enterprises, which usually emerge from local contexts, can be created for the specific purpose of promoting women's well-being or achieving this as a result of the empowering mechanisms they create (Yunus, 2010). Social enterprises "can sustain the empowerment of the weakest social sectors like Indigenous women, who suffer a condition of double discrimination [being a woman, and being an Indigenous person]" (Giovannini, 2012: 292).

Women's empowerment means creating the conditions for women to be able to make choices, which implies that women may not only have different preferences than men but also different abilities to make choices due to gender inequalities in bargaining power and access to resources (Independent Evaluation Group, 2016). In this sense, the empowerment of marginalized individuals or disadvantaged groups outside and inside the organizational boundaries seems to be one of the main characteristics of social entrepreneurship, which differentiates it from other fields (Levander, 2010; Vázquez-Maguirre et al., 2018). This implies that social enterprises usually create mechanisms and tools that both reduce the stakeholders' dependencies on the organization and increase the stakeholders' abilities to contribute to the solution and to their own welfare (Santos, 2012), which includes the creation of novel organizational arrangements (Jensen, 2017).

The context

Latin America is the world's most unequal region. Measured by the Gini coefficient, countries in this region are 30 percent more unequal than the world average (Lustig, 2015). Unequal levels of income and wealth inequality have prevented sustainable growth and social inclusion. In 2014, the richest 10 percent of the population had amassed 71 percent of the region's wealth (Bárcena and Byanyima, 2016). At the bottom of the pyramid, the indigenous population is one of the most vulnerable groups. Forty-two million indigenous people live in Latin America; Mexico, Guatemala, Peru and Bolivia had the largest populations, accounting for more than 80 percent of the total (The World Bank, 2018). While indigenous peoples make up 8 percent of the population in the region, they represent 14 percent of the poor and 17 percent of the extremely poor. Half of Latin America's indigenous population still lives in rural areas (The World Bank, 2018). According to a study from the Economic Commission for Latin America and the Caribbean (2013), there is structural discrimination against indigenous communities, but especially indigenous women in terms of education systems and access to employment. Another challenge faced by indigenous communities in Latin America is their cultural survival. The pressure posed by modern capitalism sometimes favors their disappearance or marginalization.

Indigenous people tend to hold different values than the mainstream culture. They believe in unity between the person and the environment; therefore they preserve their resources as a form of preserving themselves. Their culture privileges equality and a sense of community over individual interest. In addition, they live in deeply religious communities that often mix pre-colonial beliefs and the Catholic religion in a unique form. Also, they emphasize democratic decision-making, community work, and accountability (Vázquez-Maguirre, 2018).

The three social enterprises

This chapter highlights three social enterprises in Latin America: Ixtlán Group, Wakami and Granja Porcon. The first case, Ixtlán Group, involves a social enterprise that was established in 1988 with the mission to create decent jobs for the community (approximately 3,000 inhabitants) and to reduce the migration of its inhabitants to the United States and northern Mexico. It was created by people from the community that used to work under precarious conditions for an international corporation that was granted permission to exploit the forest in the region. People from Ixtlán and neighboring communities boycotted this entity until the government returned ownership of these resources to the communities. Ixtlán Group is located in southern Mexico, in the second poorest state in the country: Oaxaca. This enterprise, composed mainly of indigenous people from the Zapotec ethnic group, is vertically integrated from timber extraction and forest management to furniture manufacturing and retail. Ixtlán Group has the Forest Stewardship Council (FSC) certification for sustainable forest management. The group has also opened new businesses to generate more jobs and meet the needs of the community. It has a gas station, a hardware store, a microcredit lending institution and an eco-tourism park. Ixtlán Group generates around 250 jobs; a third of them are held by women.

The second case is Wakami, a social enterprise created ten years ago with the mission of empowering indigenous women (from Mayan origin) in Guatemala by providing decent jobs, access to markets and other mechanisms. It was created by Maria Pacheco, a social entrepreneur who wanted to improve the living conditions of rural women in her country. Women have specially suffered decades of violence (due to guerrilla warfare in the region) that have displaced thousands of them from their communities. Wakami designs, produces and exports fashion accessories (neck-laces, bracelets, handbags) to Mexico, the United States, some European countries and Japan. Those accessories are manufactured by groups of indigenous women directly in their homes. There are around 17 groups that manufacture Wakami's products throughout Guatemala, directly benefiting more than 500 families.

The third case is Granja Porcón, a social enterprise located in a community with the same name where some 1,200 people live. Its inhabitants are mainly descen-dants of the Canari-Cajamarca ethnic group. It is located in the northern state of Cajamarca, the poorest in Perú, with an incidence of 50 percent poverty (Instituto Nacional de Estadística e Informática, 2016). Granja Porcón was formed in the early 1980s by people from the community with the objective of generating decent jobs and improving living conditions. In order to have forest resources, the commu-nity planted about 9,000 hectares of forest through community work and alliances with international organizations. Forestry, agriculture and livestock were the main activities of the entity, but in the 1990s, Granja Porcón began to diversify into other industries including tourism (zoos, cabins, restaurants and horseback riding), dairy products, fish farming and handicrafts. In 2014, Granja Porcón had 200 permanent jobs and the same number of temporary jobs.

Empowerment mechanisms

Access to decent job opportunities

The first empowerment mechanism is the ability of these three enterprises to pro-vide decent jobs for both men and women. This is not common in indigenous communities in Latin America, where jobs are usually taken by men while women have a role at home raising their children. These entities have managed to break this cultural barrier by allowing and encouraging women in the workplace. Internal policies allow female employees to care for their children and other needs (such as compliance with government social programs that require women to attend talks during working hours).

Wakami, in particular, seeks to employ women and organize them into formal productive groups. The main challenge, as described by a company trainer, is to convince a small group of women to learn how to produce the wristbands. These women face greater social pressure to quit the activity and continue with their traditional duties. One of the women explains how she dealt with her husband: "At first I had to hide, I worked when he went to work as a bricklayer, until, I thank God, the demand increased so much he found out. . . . But his attitude changed little by little, he no longer gets angry when I leave the house [to deliver the products or to receive the inputs to make them], or sometimes he helps me with the housework". Men also started to manufacture products when they found out their wives made more money than they did; 5 percent of the employees are men. Once women in the community realized this small group of women was generating an income and improving their homes, they also sought to join Wakami.

Managers at Ixtlán and Granja Porcón comment that men were initially dissatisfied with women working with them. In the 1990s, both entities designed schemes where teams of men and women worked separately while doing similar activities. At the end of the day, the managers compared the outputs and realized women usually outperformed men, so men ended up accepting women as their coworkers. A 68-year-old former worker at Ixtlán Group remembers participating in these work schemes. He is glad the circumstances are now different for women because "women are smarter than men in many jobs". Now, the culture has changed, and it is natural for men and women to work together. There are even entities where female employees are preferred because of their skilled work. Women having an income directly benefits the quality of life of the household, especially children's education. One of the group leaders describes how women of her group spend their income: "They are using it with their families . . . to buy corn . . . to improve their homes . . . there are some who are already saving money because they will need it if there is a problem".

A decent job also includes social benefits, which these entities provide to every employee. Generally, indigenous communities are immersed in the informal economy, and jobs have no social benefits. However, the enterprises in these three cases generate jobs that usually comply with the benefits mandated by law for every commercial organization (medical insurance for the family, paid vacations, payment of overtime, savings for retirement, Christmas bonus, etc.). They also grant additional benefits (interest-free loans, punctuality bonuses, uniforms, flexible work hours, activities for the family, donations of construction materials, etc.) A female worker at Ixtlán's furniture factory explains: "Our salary is low, although everywhere is also low, but I have benefits, 14 days off every year, uniforms. I am close to getting my house. Employees in the formal sector can access a credit system to buy a house at preferential interest rates".

Granja Porcón and Ixtlán Group have developed organizational arrangements that resemble the governance structures of each community. The highest governance body of both enterprises is the general assembly, which makes decisions democratically under the one-person, one-vote scheme. Both communities elect their governors through this method, and this practice has been transferred to each social enterprise to choose not only the general manager but to approve future projects, annual reports, new policies, broad strategies, and so on. These mechanisms contribute to legitimize the actions of the entity through accountability and transparency.

Also, the general assembly provides valuable feedback that helps to analyze a situation from different perspectives before making a decision. In this sense, each project is evaluated in its social, economic and environmental dimensions. One of the managers at Ixtlán Group comments that, while other enterprises consider only financial indicators like return on investment (ROI) or net present value (NPV) when evaluating a project, the managers and the general assembly analyze the different social and environmental outcomes the project may have: "The first question we ask when someone presents a project is how many jobs it will generate".

The hierarchical structure in each of the three cases tends to be horizontal and generally consists of three levels: general manager, head of department or team and operative workers. This structure allows closeness among every employee, a better dialogue and more participatory decision-making, which are part of the values of these indigenous communities. This also translates into low CEO-worker pay ratios. Both Granja Porcón and Ixtlán Group (there is no data from Wakami) have pay ratios that range from 3 to 1 and 5 to 1, respectively. Most people in these communities consider it unethical if someone earns considerably more money than other individuals working the same amount of time. (According to the Economic Policy Institute (2018), CEOs earn 312 times the average worker's wage in the United States). Lower ratios also contribute to a more equal society but still provide the economic incentives to seek a promotion within the enterprise.

Participation in decision-making

The three cases also promote a more participatory environment for women, who traditionally have not been involved in decision-making. The first woman that took a managerial position at Ixtlán Group narrates that: "The workers did not accept my orders at first: 'How could a woman lead us?' they said. Little by little, a few years later more women took managerial positions". Today, three out of the eight entities that constitute Ixtlán Group are led by women under 40 years old. Women at Ixtlán Group are also active in general assemblies and lead many initiatives to improve their community. Participation in decision-making was also a cultural struggle for women in the 1990s; this would not have been successful if the entity had not established the internal policies that promoted women's participation in decision-making. Neighboring communities acknowledge today that women still do not participate in general assemblies or have managerial positions in any local enterprise, so Ixtlán Group is an exception rather than a generalized phenomenon in the region.

Wakami's beneficiaries have become more proactive in their communities and homes. They have bank accounts, administer their own time and money, have access to microcredits, have the means to send their children to school, decide how to balance work and family and allocate their income in their best interest. One of the trainers recalls: "Women also feel useful, because maybe since childhood they were told by their parents that they were not good for anything . . . now they send their daughters to school, because men only gave education to their sons, and think women should stay at home". In this case, the economic empowerment derived from having an income has increased decision-making and the influence of women in their homes and the community.

Gender equality policies, training and promotion

The salary gap between men and women in these communities tends to be significant, so gender equality policies in the workplace have also empowered women. In the three cases, men and women are paid by the position regardless of the gender of the employee. Also, women have equal access to training and promotions. One female manager at Ixtlán Group believes there is fair access to managerial positions within the social enterprise. Women are given the confidence and are allowed to make decisions, which is somewhat challenging for the manager because she leads a microcredit entity with a lot of growth potential. While there is a higher percentage of male managers in Ixtlán Group, she believes the reason for this gap is that such positions usually require an extra amount of work (also traveling), and many women prefer to spend more time with their family.

Wakami also seeks to have indigenous women become group leaders and trainers of their groups, the two highest positions in each productive entity. Moreover, Wakami's headquarters in Guatemala City employs more women than men. Some of these women were part of a production group but were given the opportunity to take a managerial or operative position that impacts every group of women. One of them remembers that she joined a productive group at age 14; then she became a trainer and a group leader. A year ago she was offered a position at the headquarters. She is happy because at Wakami: "Women can accomplish their dreams: someone just told me that her daughter just finished high school and is starting a professional degree, and there is Santa, who finally has built her home".

Gender equality policies have also had a dignifying effect on women, establishing a sense of self-worth and self-respect. Women have gained employment in areas that have traditionally been closed to them, like the labor market, entrepreneurship and decision-making. As a result, these communities have improved their general well-being. When compared with neighboring communities, Granja Porcón, Ixtlán and villages where Wakami has a presence have better living standards. People from neighboring communities come to Ixtlán and Granja Porcón to seek jobs, better salaries and benefits that they cannot find in their own communities.

Concluding remarks and implications for management education

Indigenous communities in Latin America account for 8 percent of the population but 14 percent of the poor (The World Bank, 2018). To reduce their vulnerabilities more successfully, institutions like The World Bank (2018) suggest looking at indigenous issues through a different lens that takes into account the voices, cultures and identities of these indigenous people. In this sense, this chapter shows how communities can incorporate their values in the creation and management of socially productive enterprises that aim to generate greater social and economic well-being.

In these three cases, women, in particular, have benefited from these social enterprises, as they have been traditionally excluded from the labor market in indigenous communities in Latin America. The empowerment mechanisms described in this chapter have restored the dignity of women and reconfigured their role in the community. Evidence suggests this new role reinforces their sense of self-worth and self-respect, which ultimately translates into a better quality of life for their household and the community. The three cases also represent examples of how various SDGs, such as no poverty (SDG #1), well-being (SDG #3), gender equality (SDG #5), decent work (SDG #8), reduced inequalities (SDG #10) and sustainable communities (SDG #11), are interrelated and interconnected. Thus, promoting women's empowerment through social enterprises has a multiplier effect on achieving the SDGs holistically and successfully.

Evidence from this work suggests that investment in women's employment opportunities can have great impact on the well-being of families and the community. In this sense, Avolio and Di Laura (2017) found that promoting female employment in Latin America can contribute to poverty eradication and the economic empowerment of women. It also changes spending in ways that benefit children (The World Bank, 2012) and is related with faster economic growth (OECD, 2012). Decent work opportunities for women also contribute to changing the prevailing culture toward a more egalitarian society, increasing community well-being and the women's willingness to participate in political and managerial decision-making (Vázquez-Maguirre et al., 2016). Therefore, public and private efforts to promote decent employment for women are useful in fostering community well-being.

Walsh et al. (2003) and Pirson (2017) note a sizeable deficit in management research concerning social outcomes. This chapter helps to fill this gap by describing economic, social and environmental outcomes that derive from the empowering mechanisms these social enterprises generate to achieve their purpose. The cases also show different managerial elements and principles, which naturally emerged from indigenous values (unity with the environment, sense of community, democratic decision-making, accountability, dignity protection, promotion, etc.). These elements can contribute to a reconceptualization of existing paradigms in management theories that could provide better managerial solutions to environmental degradation, poverty and social inequities.

These cases are also valuable examples that can be best used in academic courses that analyze issues related to social entrepreneurship, sustainability, empowerment of indigenous people, dignity at work and gender equality. Moreover, management education should consider including such cases to describe alternative management practices that generate sustainable value for the whole community, not just some stakeholders.

References

Avolio, B. E. and Di Laura, G. F. "The Progress and Evolution of Women's Participation in Production and Business Activities in South America." *CEPAL Review [Economic Commission for Latin America and the Caribbean]*, 122, 2017: 32–55.

Bárcena, A. and Byanyima, W. "Latin America Is the World's Most Unequal Region: Here's How to Fix It." 2016. Accessed April 15, 2018. www.weforum.org/agenda/2016/01/inequality-is-getting-worse-in-latin-america-here-s-how-to-fix-it/.

Collier, P. *The Bottom Billion: Why the Poorest Countries are Failing and What Can Be Done About It.* New York, NY: Oxford University Press, 2007.

Coughlin, J. H. and Thomas, A. R. *The Rise of Women Entrepreneurs: People, Processes and Global Trends.* Westport: Quorum Books, 2002.

Economic Commission for Latin America and the Caribbean. "Mujeres indígenas en América Latina, dinámicas demográficas y sociales en el marco de los derechos humanos [Indigenous Women in Latin America, Demographic and Social Dynamics within the Framework of Human Rights]." 2013. Accessed September 21, 2018. https://repositorio.cepal.org/bitstream/handle/11362/4100/1/S2013792_es.pdf.

Economic Policy Institute. *CEO Compensation Surged in 2017.* 2018. Accessed November 21, 2018. www.epi.org/publication/ceo-compensation-surged-in-2017/.

Giovannini, M. "Social Enterprises for Development as Buen Vivir." *Journal of Enterprising Communities: People and Places in the Global Economy*, 6(3), 2012: 284–299.

Independent Evaluation Group. "Women's Empowerment in Rural Community Driven Development Projects." 2016. Accessed March 14, 2018. http://ieg.worldbankgroup.org/sites/default/files/Data/Evaluation/files/lp_genderincdd_01272017.pdf.

Instituto Nacional de Estadística e Informática. "Pobreza y gasto social [Poverty and Social Spending]." 2016. Accessed May 13, 2018. www.inei.gob.pe/estadisticas/indice-tematico/sociales/.

Jensen, P. R. "People Can't Believe We Exist!: Social Sustainability and Alternative Nonprofit Organizing." *Critical Sociology*, 44(2), 2017: 1–14.

Levander, U. "Social Enterprise: Implications of Emerging Institutionalized Constructions." *Journal of Social Entrepreneurship*, 1(2), 2010: 213–230.

Lockyer, J. and George, S. "What Women Want: Barriers to Female Entrepreneurship in the West Midlands." *International Journal of Gender and Entrepreneurship*, 4(2), 2012: 179–195.

Lustig, N. *Most Unequal on Earth.* International Monetary Fund. 2015. Accessed February 12, 2019. www.imf.org/external/pubs/ft/fandd/2015/09/lustig.htm.

Mattis, M. C. "Women Entrepreneurs: Out from under the Glass Ceiling." *Women in Management Review*, 19(3), 2004: 154–163.

Nguyen, C., Frederick, H. and Nguyen, H. "Female Entrepreneurship in Rural Vietnam: An Exploratory Study." *International Journal of Gender and Entrepreneurship*, 4(2), 2014: 179–195.

Organization for Economic Cooperation and Development (OECD). "Gender Equality in Education, Employment and Entrepreneurship: Final Report to the MCM [Ministerial Council Meeting]." 2012. Accessed December 17, 2018. www.oecd.org/employment/50423364.pdf.

Pirson, M. "A Humanistic Perspective for Management Theory: Protecting Dignity and Promoting Well-Being." *Journal of Business Ethics*, 2017: 1–19. Doi.org/10.1007/s10551-017-3755-4.

Santos, F. M. "A Positive Theory of Social Entrepreneurship." *Journal of Business Ethics*, 11(3), 2012: 335–351.

Vázquez-Maguirre, M. "Sustainable Ecosystems through Indigenous Social Enterprises." In J. Leitão, H. Alves, N. Krueger and J. Park (eds.), *Entrepreneurial, Innovative and Sustainable*

Ecosystems: Applying Quality of Life Research (Best Practices). Cham, Switzerland: Springer, 2018: 173–189.

Vázquez-Maguirre, M., Camacho, G. and García de la Torre, C. "Women Empowerment through Social Innovation in Indigenous Social Enterprises." *Revista de Administração Mackenzie [Mackenzie Administration Journal]*, 17(6), 2016: 164–190. http://dx.doi.org/10.1590/1678-69712016/administracao.v17n6p164-190.

Vázquez-Maguirre, M., Portales, L. and Velásquez, I. "Indigenous Social Enterprises as Drivers of Sustainable Development: Insights from Mexico and Peru." *Critical Sociology*, 44(2), 2018: 323–340.

Walsh, J. P., Weber, K. and Margolis, J. D. "Social Issues and Management: Our Lost Cause Found." *Journal of Management*, 29(6), 2003: 859–881.

The World Bank. *Indigenous Latin America in the Twenty-First Century*. 2018. Accessed July 17, 2018. www.worldbank.org/en/region/lac/brief/indigenous-latin-america-in-the-twenty-first-century-brief-report-page.

The World Bank. *World Development Report: Gender Equality and Development*. 2012. Accessed December 17, 2018. http://siteresources.worldbank.org/INTWDR2012/Resources/7778105-1299699968583/7786210-1315936222006/Complete-Report.pdf.

Yunus, M. *Building Social Business: The New Kind of Capitalism That Serves Humanity's Most Pressing Needs*. New York: Public Affairs, 2010.

10

STRUGGLES TO BREAK THE CORPORATE BOARD CEILING

The case of women in North Africa

Jalila El Jadidi, Sonia Arsi and Hebatallah Ghoneim

Abstract

After the political and social actions taken place through the Arab Spring in late 2010, North African countries have witnessed major revisions of their constitutions, which have heavily supported gender equality and women's empowerment in all activities and sectors. Along the same line, many countries adopted the 2030 Agenda for Sustainable Development Goals (SDG), and particularly the fifth goal, denoted SDG #5, that aims to "ensure women's full and effective participation and equal opportunities". Within this framework, this chapter addresses the situation of women on corporate boards based on a comparative analysis of Egypt, Morocco and Tunisia. It investigates the women directors' profile of the 440 listed companies in the Egyptian, Casablanca and Tunisian stock exchanges, covering 285, 82 and 73 companies, respectively in 2018. The chapter provides quantitative and qualitative information on these directors to draw a comprehensive picture. The findings document gender inequality on the corporate boards in these countries. The chapter highlights the relevant implications for politicians, practitioners and advocates of gender parity. It concludes with lessons and recommendations to promote change and inspire gender equality in the boardroom.

Introduction

Women empowerment is not just about adjusting the biases of male dominance in the workplace compared to women; it is about the process of bringing women into the decision-making arena. Women empowerment is also about giving women the support and conditions they need to maximize their potential without constraints. Empowerment success can be evaluated through three dimensions: personal, relational and collective. *Personal* means developing self-confidence and skills; *relational* includes the ability to build relationships and influence others; *collective* embraces the ability to work within the frame of collective action and teams (Rowlands, 1997).

In the goals progress report of the United Nations (UN) Sustainable Development Knowledge Platform of 2018, women in managerial positions are earmarked as an important indicator of attaining or reaching the SDG #5 in order to "achieve gender equality and empower all women and girls". Today, women are still underrepresented in managerial and leadership positions. This would bring into question how the SDG #8 that seeks to "promote sustained, inclusive and sustainable economic growth, full and productive employment and decent work for all" could be achieved. In the light of this position, women empowerment could be considered as a method not only to reduce poverty (SDG #1) but also to promote equality (SDG #10).

This raised the interest to explore and describe the situation of gender equality within the corporate boards of directors of publicly traded companies in the North African countries of Egypt, Morocco and Tunisia, where the authors have lived and worked. Like many Arabic and North African women, they are eager to highlight progress in their respective countries and, at the same time, identify areas for improvement.

Gender bias in North Africa

Women are increasingly integrating the political, social and economic fields, representing 50 percent of the workforce (McKinsey Global Institute, 2017). However, gender parity is still a worldwide issue for investors, researchers and legislators. Gender biases have long been present in the Middle East and North Africa (MENA) region (Chapman, 2015; Karshenas et al., 2016; Radwan et al., 1994; Roudi-Fahmi and Moghadam, 2006). Women in this region have always been facing the glass ceiling, encompassing hidden barriers that impede women's ability to progress in their careers. Parents have traditionally promoted and supported males in terms of educational investments and social progress, while restricting women's role to family and household responsibilities. In addition, the MENA region tends to be more of a male-dominant society that sets the male as the decision maker, whose role is to support the family financially and to protect it, while the woman is considered to be the homemaker, who is responsible for carrying out the household duties. This has made it difficult for women to find job opportunities and progress professionally in the private sector (Assaad and El-Badawy, 2004; Behery et al., 2017; Metcalfe, 2011).

The role of women in society has long been debated especially in Muslim-majority countries (Metcalfe, 2011; Metcalfe and Rees, 2010; Ramadan, 2009). Moreover, globalization, along with the rise of social media use, has demonstrated that women's role in Islamic-dominant societies varies from one country to another and cannot be studied in isolation from the political system (Mernissi, 2001; Metcalfe, 2010, 2011). In 2011, women along with men were marching in unity, demanding political rights and justice. This was seen particularly in Egypt and Tunisia and is known as the Arab Spring movement. It was a movement of youth who were refuting the long-standing failures in promoting economic development and in abolishing patterns of human rights violations and social injustice (Aras and Falk,

TABLE 10.1 Gender overview in Egypt, Tunisia and Morocco

Percentage of Female	Egypt	Morocco	Tunisia
Labor force, 2018	23.1	26.0	26.5
Survival to age 65, 2016	80.7	87.8	87.4
Progression to secondary school[1]	95.6	87.0	92.6

Source: World Development Indicators

2016). The waves of the Arab Spring started in Tunisia in 2010, portaged to Egypt in 2011 and then to Libya and Bahrain (Saidin, 2018). It was an alert for the whole region to pay attention to the calling for freedom, dignity and good governance.

Based on the World Bank data (see Table 10.1), women now represent just a little more than 25 percent of the labor force in these three countries, which is still below the average rate of 39 percent for the low- and middle-income countries. However, the Arab Spring has contributed to notable structural and legislative reforms that target gender diversity in countries like Egypt, Morocco and Tunisia.

In Egypt, for example, the government designated 2017 as the "Year of the Egyptian Woman" as part of the "Government National 2030 Strategy" to allow more power to women in the economic, political and social arenas and in accordance to the Egyptian Constitution. As a result, the first female governor was appointed that year. Following this progressive path, six females were selected for the first time as ministers for the Egyptian Government in January 2018. Women ministers in Egypt currently fill 20 percent of the cabinet seats and play strategic roles in the health and tourism government ministries. This is viewed as a sign of modernization and an attempt to break the glass ceiling that hinders women from moving up toward higher levels on the career ladder.

In Tunisia, the Constitution of 2014 consolidated the "gender equality" principles and encouraged women's empowerment. According to the World Economic Forum (2017: 21), Tunisia is ranked as the first Arabic country, and the second one in the MENA area, in terms of gender equality, particularly in "ministerial positions and basic literacy". In August 2017, the Commission for Individual Freedoms and Equality (COLIBE) was established with its primary goal to meet "perfect" gender equality. One month after its establishment, the Assembly of the Representatives of the People declared that the marriage between a Tunisian woman and a non-Muslim man is no longer prohibited. Within this context, Tunisia is studying a draft law that will incorporate equality in inheritance rights.

Morocco, sharing cultural, religious and location similarities with Tunisia and Egypt, weathered the Arab Spring mainly due to the swift actions taken by the King of Morocco. Unlike presidential republics such as Egypt and Tunisia, protestors in the Arab monarchies called for reforms instead of abolishing the existing royal regime (Barany, 2012). King Mohamed VI acknowledged and strategically responded to activists' demands (Maghraoui, 2011) and proceeded with instituting his own initiative measures. He ordered an expedited parliamentary election and launched a media campaign to urge people to vote for the new constitution. Spearheaded by the king, women's empowerment initiatives were strongly encouraged and promoted *via* the improvement of constitutional rights, specifically related to gender equality, which states that women and men should have equal access to administrative, political and economic decision-making roles. In 2016, Morocco's efforts to boost gender parity were addressed through the addition of new seats in the parliament reserved only for women.

This chapter focuses on how these improvements have affected gender equality in corporate boardrooms.

Prior studies on women on corporate boards in North Africa

Gender diversity on corporate boards had been appraised by regulatory, economic and political structures worldwide. As noted in Women on Boards (2018), particular attention was paid to gender equality with the desirable target of 20 percent of corporate board seats filled by women in the United States by the year 2020. A number of developed and developing countries have established voluntary or compulsory women director quotas for corporate boards (Howaidy, 2016; Kim and Starks, 2016). These regulations are often based on arguments claiming that gender-diverse boards improve the firm's value. It is believed that women on boards expand corporate strategy to include more social responsibility involvement, since women are more prone to addressing social issues (Amorelli and Garcia Sanchez, 2019; Cook and Glass, 2017; Cruz et al., 2019; Hyun et al., 2016). Nevertheless, Huse et al. (2009: 592) found that "the contribution of women to creative discussion only existed when the women had a different background from the men". Huse et al. (2009: 593) pointed out an insignificant relation between diversity on the board and budget control, which suggested that "women directors are more likely to contribute to board tasks of qualitative rather than quantitative nature". In addition, Dankwano and Hassan (2018: 332) indicated that Indian "firms with more than 10% female recorded higher financial performance". The authors explained that a "firm's performance is highly influenced by the board of directors and it has been evident that women directors exhibit very high professional experiences as compared to male directors". They also added that diversity in the boardroom enhances creativity and innovation.

UN Women (2018) highlighted that the MENA area has achieved some progress toward reducing gender inequality, in general; nevertheless, the gap is still prominent in the workplace. The report stated that the widest gender gap in Labor Force Participation Rate (LFPR) was detected within the Northern Africa and Western Asia regions; where LFPR was nearly 60 percent and the female LFPRs were less than 35 percent. Additionally, data showed that women's participation had increased only slightly in the last 20 years, from 29 percent in 1997 to 34 percent in 2017. Respectively, the pursuit of gender parity in publicly traded companies would give insights not only into the women's participation in the workplace but also into the decision-making process.

Few studies have addressed women's underrepresentation on boards in North Africa. For Egypt, Agag and El-Ansary (2011: 12) could not prove a statistical impact between the number of women and company profits, but they justified the selection of women on boards by "record of accomplishments, variety of work experiences, advanced education, membership in/certification from professional organizations, rights' connections, and ability to devote sufficient time". Howaidy (2016) showed that women held 8.7 percent of corporate board seats in Egypt in 2013. The author also stressed the importance of changing legislation and adding a specific quota for women on boards to overcome the male bias. Ararat et al. (2017) demonstrated that diversity in Egyptian boardrooms improved the company's performance under complex environments and shocks. Abdelzaher and Abdelzaher (2019) underlined a positive and significant relation between the percentage of Egyptian women board members and the firm's value.

For Tunisia, M'hamid et al. (2011) investigated 34 publicly traded companies for the period 2000–2007. The results pointed out that gender diversity contributed to increases in the firm's value as long as the women board members followed "the masculine conventions". In other words, women directors complied with the current rules and standards set forth by men. In later research, Aliani et al. (2011) used the same sample and period to show that women on boards played an effective role and participate in the tax optimization process, as they improved the discussions' quality and ensured a better supervision of the firm's reports and tax payments. Indeed, the authors demonstrated that women on boards were risk averse and tended to comply with tax regulations. This fact was confirmed by the investigation of Loukil and Yousfi (2015) on 30 firms from the period 1997–2007, where the authors found that including women in boardrooms led to invaluable decisions. These studies tackled a pre–Arab Spring period; thus, it seems important to review the presence of Tunisian women directors, as long as the Article 46 of the Tunisian Constitution requires gender equality within corporate boards.

In 2007 and before the Arab Spring hit the region, Morocco initiated corporate governance practice guidelines, inspired by international practices and the Organization for Economic Co-operation and Development (OECD) directives. The report titled "Moroccan Code for Best Practices in Corporate Governance" emphasized the inclusion of ethical, qualified, informed and involved board members, with a mixture of expertise; professional experience and diversity of gender, age and nationality. The Moroccan Institute for Directors (2016) highlighted that gender diversity was still very limited. It noted that only 3 percent of the 29 publicly traded companies had at least three women on their boards in 2012, which increased to 11 percent by 2015.

Women on boards in Egypt, Morocco and Tunisia in 2018

This chapter focuses on women on corporate boards in these three countries in 2018. The data are for the listed companies on the Egyptian Stock Exchange (285 companies), the Casablanca Stock Exchange (73 companies) and the Tunisian Stock Exchange (82 companies).[2]

Women directors

Table 10.2 highlights the status of women on corporate boards in these three countries in 2018. Morocco accounts for the greatest percentage of women directors with 11.7 percent, followed by Tunisia with 11 percent and Egypt with 9.9 percent. In terms of trends, Deloitte Global Corporate Center (2017) reported the share of women corporate directors for publicly traded companies in 2014 as 11 percent for Morocco and 8 percent for both Tunisia and Egypt. Thus, Tunisia has had the largest gain during this period, followed by Egypt and Morocco. The McKinsey Global Institute (2017) released 9 percent as the North African average for 2017.

The percentage of companies by the number of women on boards is illustrated in Table 10.3. In Egypt, 59.2 percent of the boards had no women directors in

TABLE 10.2 Gender and corporate boards, 2018

	Egypt	Morocco	Tunisia
Number of listed companies	285	73	82
Number of women board members	201	66	79
Number of men board members	1826	499	641
Number of women board chairs	12	6	7
Women as % of all board members	9.9%	11.7%	11.0%

Source: Constructed by authors and retrieved from different sources; Mubasher and Decypha websites for Egypt, the Moroccan Authority of Capital Markets' website for Morocco and annual reports directly accessible from the Council of Financial Market for Tunisia.

TABLE 10.3 Corporate boards by number of women directors, 2018

Number of Women Directors	Percentage of Companies		
	Egypt (n = 285)	Morocco (n = 73)	Tunisia (n = 82)
0	59.2%	42.5%	42.7%
1	22.8%	30.1%	30.5%
2	10.5%	24.7%	17.1%
3	5.0%	1.4%	7.3%
4 or more	2.5%	1.4%	2.4%

Source: Constructed by authors and retrieved from different sources; Mubasher and Decypha websites for Egypt, the Moroccan Authority of Capital Markets' website for Morocco and annual reports directly accessible from the Council of Financial Market for Tunisia.

2018. In Tunisia and Morocco, 42.7 percent and 42.5 percent, respectively, had all male boards. Howaidy (2016) reported that 48.4 percent of the companies listed on the Egyptian Stock Exchange in 2013 had no women on their boards; thus gender equality had diminished in that regard. In 2018, 52 more companies were listed on the Egyptian Exchange than in 2013, so the trend could reflect companies joining the exchange in recent years with no women directors. Alternatively, some of the companies listed over that period could have replaced women directors with men. The net result displays minor features of board diversity on exchange-listed companies in Egypt.

Gender patterns by industrial sector

Investigations, including those of Baez et al. (2018) and Brieger et al. (2017), highlighted that women's share of corporate directors varies by industrial sector. Table 10.4 exhibits the percentages of women directors by industrial sector, by country, in 2018.

In Egypt, women have the greatest representation on the corporate boards of financial and insurance (26.4%) and basic materials companies (21.4%). The health sector follows with 15.9 percent women directors. The energy and mining (5.5%), technology (4%) and consumer services (1%) sectors have the fewest women directors.

Moroccan women directors have their greatest share of seats on financial and insurance boards with 27.3 percent. Equally, they represent more than 20 percent of the directors in the manufacturing sector, capital goods and real

TABLE 10.4 Percent women corporate board members, by industry sector, 2018

	Egypt	Morocco	Tunisia
Financial and insurance companies and banks	26.4%	27.3%	12.5%
Telecommunications	2.5%	0.0%	12.5%
Consumer services	1.0%	7.6%	8.5%
Health, medical and pharmaceutical industries	15.9%	3.0%	19.0%
Consumer goods	13.4%	13.6%	9.4%
Industry, capital goods and real estate investment	10.0%	21.2%	6.7%
Basic materials	21.4%	13.6%	2.5%
Energy and mining	4.0%	3.0%	33.3%
Technology	5.5%	10.6%	25.0%
Total	11.1%	11.1%	14.4%

Source: Constructed by authors and retrieved from different sources; Mubasher and Decypha websites for Egypt, the Moroccan Authority of Capital Markets' website for Morocco and annual reports directly accessible from the Council of Financial Market for Tunisia.

TABLE 10.5 All-male boards by industry sector, 2018

	Percentage of Companies with No Women Directors		
	Egypt	*Morocco*	*Tunisia*
Financial and insurance companies and banks	55.9%	42.9%	29.6%
Telecommunications	60.0%	100.0%	50.0%
Consumer services	48.3%	50.0%	55.6%
Health, medical and pharmaceutical industries	52.4%	50.0%	0.0%
Consumer goods	65.2%	60.0%	47.1%
Industry, capital goods and real estate investment	60.3%	71.4%	53.8%
Basic materials	72.7%	33.3%	80.0%
Energy and mining	50.0%	33.3%	0.0%
Technology	75.0%	42.9%	33.3%
Total	60.0%	53.8%	38.8%

Source: Constructed by authors and retrieved from different sources; Mubasher and Decypha websites for Egypt, the Moroccan Authority of Capital Markets' website for Morocco and annual reports directly accessible from the Council of Financial Market for Tunisia.

estate investment sector. In contrast, there are no women directors in the tele-communications sector and represent only 3 percent in the health and energy sectors.

Tunisia has a much higher percentage of women directors in the energy and mining (33.3%) and the technology (25%) sectors than the other two countries. Women directors account for 19 percent of directors on health, medical and pharmaceutical company boards and 12.5 percent in the financial and insurance sector.

The pattern of all male boards by industry sector across the three countries is shown in Table 10.5. Egypt has the highest percentage of all-male boards (60%), in comparison to Morocco (53.8%) and Tunisia (38%). Not one woman serves on a board of a telecommunications publicly held company in Morocco, in contrast to Egypt and Tunisia.

Gender patterns by firm size

The percentage of women on corporate boards by board size in 2018 is shown in Table 10.6. The majority of the companies in each country have between six and ten directors. For these companies, women directors account for 34.6, 62.1 and 58.2 percent of the board members in Egypt, Morocco and Tunisia, respectively. For smaller-sized boards, women account for 9, 19.7 and 5.1 percent of the directors in

TABLE 10.6 Women on corporate boards, by board size, 2018

Number of Board's Members	Percentage of Companies			Percentage of Women Directors		
	Egypt	Morocco	Tunisia	Egypt	Morocco	Tunisia
Less than 5	22.5%	28.8%	9.8%	9.0%	19.7%	5.1%
Between 6 and 10	52.2%	53.4%	72.0%	34.6%	62.1%	58.2%
Between 11 and 15	11.3%	17.8%	18.3%	28.0%	18.2%	36.7%
More than 15	14.0%	–[3]	–[4]	28.4%	–	–

Source: Constructed by authors and retrieved from different sources; Mubasher and Decypha websites for Egypt, the Moroccan Authority of Capital Markets' website for Morocco and annual reports directly accessible from the Council of Financial Market for Tunisia.

Egypt, Morocco and Tunisia, compared to 28, 18.2 and 36.7 percent of the directors, respectively, for larger (more than ten members) boards. Aliani et al. (2011) and M'hamid et al. (2011) found that large-size boards of Tunisian listed companies are dominated by men, and those companies are reluctant to integrate women into their boardrooms.

Education levels and family linkages of women directors

Hodigere and Bilimoria (2015:543) stressed out the importance of education since it is of "overwhelming importance of a woman's profession for her appointment on a corporate board". Agag and El-Ansary (2011) emphasized that advanced education, as well as diversified and strong work experiences, is a key attribute of the women selected for corporate directors in Egypt. Table 10.7 provides data on the education level of women directors in Egypt, Morocco and Tunisia. All the women directors on these boards in the three countries have at least a four-year college degree. This is line with the highlights related to the significant educational attainment levels reached in the region (Assaad et al., 2018; Karshenas et al., 2016; Majbouri, 2018; Moghadam, 2018a, 2018b). A further noteworthy point is that the vast majority of women directors in Morocco and Tunisia have a master's degree as their highest educational level, with 82.6 and 77.2 percent, respectively. Moghadam (2018b, 2018a) underlined the fact that highly educated women are less likely to work for government entities, while Assaad et al. (2018) emphasized that customs, traditions and social background play a major role in the workplace of educated women. In Morocco, 8.7 percent of these directors have a PhD, as do 19 percent in Tunisia. In Egypt, 5.5 and 6 percent, respectively, have a master's or a PhD degree.

Data on family connections and board memberships are provided in Table 10.8. In particular, family linkages between the owners or shareholders of the company

TABLE 10.7 Women on corporate boards, by educational level, 2018

Highest Educational Level	Percentage of Women Directors		
	Egypt (n = 285)	Morocco (n = 23)	Tunisia (n = 82)
BA degree	88.5%	8.7%	4.0%
Master's degree	5.5%	82.6%	77.2%
PhD	6.0%	8.7%	19.0%

Source: Constructed by authors and retrieved from different sources; Mubasher and Decypha websites for Egypt, the Moroccan Authority of Capital Markets' website for Morocco and annual reports directly accessible from the Council of Financial Market for Tunisia.

TABLE 10.8 Women on corporate boards, by family linkages, 2018

	Egypt	Morocco	Tunisia
Existence of family linkages with owners or shareholders	22.5%	15.2%	35.4%

Source: Constructed by authors and retrieved from different sources; Mubasher and Decypha websites for Egypt, the Moroccan Authority of Capital Markets' website for Morocco and annual reports directly accessible from the Council of Financial Market for Tunisia.

on whose board the women serve exist for 22.5, 15.2 and 35.4 percent in Egypt, Morocco and Tunisia, respectively.

This result contradicts the comments of Abdelsalam et al. (2008: 955), who reported that "one of the main features of the ownership structure in Egypt involves considerable controlling stakes of some families, financial and industrial institutions, and the government". Rather, the 2018 data suggest that most women corporate directors are elected without having had family connections. The authors also touched upon another assumption stated by Galbreath (2011) that business and economic relations play important roles in electing the corporate boards' members, as they will impact the firm's profitability in the near future.

Women board chairs

Table 10.9 presents data on women board chairs for the three countries in 2018. Overall, women serve as board chair at only 2.6, 5.8 and 4.8 percent of listed companies in Egypt, Morocco and Tunisia, respectively. In all three countries, women are most likely to be board chair in the financial and insurance and consumer services sectors. No women serve as board chairs in the three countries within the telecommunication, energy and mining and technology sectors; Brieger et al.

TABLE 10.9 Women board chairs by industry sector, 2018

	Percentage of Companies with Women Chairs		
	Egypt	Morocco	Tunisia
Financial and insurance companies and banks	10.3%	14.3%	14.8%
Telecommunications	0.0%	0.0%	0.0%
Consumer services	6.9%	16.7%	22.2%
Health, medical and pharmaceutical industries	4.8%	0.0%	0.0%
Consumer goods	0.0%	10.0%	5.9%
Industry, capital goods and real estate investment	1.3%	0.0%	0.0%
Basic materials	0.0%	11.1%	0.0%
Energy and mining	0.0%	0.0%	0.0%
Technology	0.0%	0.0%	0.0%
Total	2.6%	5.8%	4.8%

Source: Constructed by authors and retrieved from different sources; Mubasher and Decypha websites for Egypt, the Moroccan Authority of Capital Markets' website for Morocco and annual reports directly accessible from the Council of Financial Market for Tunisia.

(2017) and Raghuram (2008) underlined that these sectors are known to be male dominated.

Glances at the future

Diversity in the board of directors is a *must* for ensuring a variety of thoughts and backgrounds, which is increasingly associated with effective corporate governance (Geletkanycz et al., 2018; Huse et al., 2009; Kim and Starks, 2016). Having women on boards denotes that women's voice is not only represented at the highest levels of management decisions but will also significantly contribute to changing gender biases in the workplace and, in return, might provide more equality. It is expected that having women on board will decrease the possibility of practices based on stereotyping and social segregation that might act against women recognition and success (Bilimoria, 2006).

Howaidy (2016) highlighted the importance of legislative changes requiring a minimum number of women in corporate boardrooms. The problem is that setting quotas is not a guarantee for providing opportunities for hardworking and competent women looking for leadership. A case could be made for the owners' relatives who may take advantage of the situation and thus undermine the quotas and degree of diversity being represented on the board. It is rather preferred to follow the Moroccan Institute for Directors' (2016: 13) suggestion that a quota of independent women members without family ties should be set. Smith (2018: 2) highlighted that this approach would increase the female share on boardrooms, promote gender diversity and "improve the quality of the decision-making process compared with a more homogeneous board". Also, board diversity provides training and coaching (Kakabadse et al., 2015). Such programs help ensure that women gain leadership positions, are creative and share a vision. In fact, ambitious women willing to hold top managerial positions should actively participate in training programs that will enable them to bravely project their feminine skills and at the same time be decisive. Also, Smith (2018: 1) reported that "having female top executives may have positive effects on the career development of women at lower levels of an organization".

Lately, women in North African countries have started to chip away male dominance and social biases in major issues, such as education and earnings (Assaad et al., 2018; Karshenas et al., 2016; Moghadam, 2018a, 2018b; Radwan et al., 1994; Roudi-Fahmi and Moghadam, 2006). However, this was accompanied with an overwhelming increase in women's duties in order to build a career while meeting their family needs. Respectively, Arab countries should consider adding legislation that involves males in parenting and, for example, considers annual leaves for family care. This would help balance the female's workload and provide her with additional time to build more qualifications. In 1985, Germany issued a law providing parental leaves, where the leave is transferable between both wife and husband. Such a law gives a chance for both mother and father to share in career and family duties together (Schiek, 2002).

Conclusion

This chapter analyzes women on corporate boards in three North African countries: Egypt, Morocco and Tunisia, to assess the achievements made related to gender equality in the region. In this regard, the SDG #5 is set as a guiding principle and takes on the task to "ensure women's full and effective participation and equal opportunities for leadership at all levels of decision-making in political, economic and public life". The findings display that the percentages of women directors in the three countries are around 11 percent in 2018, which is below the desirable target of 20 percent. In addition, the share of companies with no women on their corporate boards that year was 38.8 percent in Tunisia, 53.8 percent in Morocco and 60 percent in Egypt.

Putting statistics aside, it cannot be denied that women are gaining more rights in comparison to previous decades in the MENA region. However, it is still no secret that women face obstacles while progressing in their careers. These obstacles could be due to social presumptions and perceptions, family obligations and male biases in the workplace. Reaching the corporate boardroom is a sign that women are able to pass the traditional barriers and break the glass ceiling, especially in the North African region. Moreover, it puts women in a position to vote on including more women directors on their boards. In fact, women directors should become members of their companies' board nominating committee and make sure that qualified female candidates are in the pool for new directors.

Notes

1 For Egypt and Morocco, the given data are related to the year 2016, while it is of 2014 for Tunisia.
2 The data are from different sources: Mubasher and Decypha websites for Egypt, the Moroccan Authority of Capital Markets' website for Morocco and annual reports directly accessible from the Council of Financial Market for Tunisia.
3 The Moroccan law 17–95, Article 39, related to public limited companies imposes a minimum of three members on the corporate board and a maximum of 12 members that can be extended to 15 if the company is publicly listed (*Cf.* Moroccan Institute for Directors, 2016: 13).
4 The Tunisian Companies Code indicates that the corporate boards have to include at least three members and 12 members at the most.

References

Abdelsalam, O. H., El-Masry, A. A. and Elsegini, S. A. "Board Composition, Ownership Structure and Dividend Policies in an Emerging Market: Further Evidence from CASE 50." *Managerial Finance*, 34(12), 2008: 953–964.

Abdelzaher, A. and Abdelzaher, D. "Women on Boards and Firm Performance in Egypt: Post the Arab Spring." *The Journal of Developing Areas*, 53(1), 2019: 225–241.

Agag, A. E.-S. and El-Ansary, O. "Exploring the Impact of Board Gender Diversity on Profitability for Egyptian Corporations." *18th International DAVO Congress of Contemporary Research on the Middle East.* Berlin, 2011.

Aliani, K., M'hamid, I. and Zarai, M. A. "Diversité en Genre dans le Conseil d'Administration et Optimisation Fiscale: Validation dans le Contexte Tunisien [Gender Diversity on Corporate Board and Fiscal Optimization: Validation in the Tunisian Context]." *Global Journal of Management and Business Research*, 11(8), 2011: 40–49.

Amorelli, M. F. and Garcia Sanchez, I. M. "Critical Mass of Female Directors, Human Capital, and Stakeholder Engagement by Corporate Social Reporting." *Corporate Social Responsibility and Environmental Management*, June 2019: 1–18.

Ararat, M., El-Helaly, M. and Shehata, N. F. "Boards's Gender Diversity and Firm Performance before and after the Egyptian Revolution." *SSRN Electronic Journal*, 2017: 1–45. https://doi.org/http://dx.doi.org/10.2139/ssrn.3063867.

Aras, B. and Falk, R. "Five Years after the Arab Spring: A Critical Evaluation." *Third World Quarterly*, 37(12), 2016: 2252–2258.

Assaad, R. and El-Badawy, A. "Private and Group Tutoring in Egypt: Where Is the Gender Inequality." *Economic Research Forum 11th Annual Conference: Post Conflict Reconstruction*, Beirut: Lebanon 2004: 14–16.

Assaad, R., Hendy, R., Lassassi, M. and Yassin, S. "Explaining the MENA Paradox: Rising Educational Attainment, Yet Stagnant Female Labor Force Participation." *Working Paper, IZA Institute of Labor Economics*, 11385, 2018: 1–46.

Baez, A. B., Baez-Garcia, A. J., Flores-Munoz, F. and Gutiérrez-Barroso, J. "Gender Diversity, Corporate Governance and Firm Behavior: The Challenge of Emotional Management." *European Research on Management and Business Economics*, 24(3), 2018: 121–129.

Barany, Z. "After the Arab Spring: Revolt and Resilience in the Arab Kingdoms." *Parameters*, 43(2), 2012: 89–101.

Behery, M., Al-Nasser, A. and Parakandani, M. "Examining the Effect of Leadership on Women Career Paths in the Middle-East: A Mediation Effect of Glass Ceiling." *Journal of Competitiveness Studies*, 25(3/4), 2017: 266–286.

Bilimoria, D. "The Relationship between Women Corporate Directors and Women Corporate Officers." *Journal of Managerial Issues*, 2006: 47–61.

Brieger, S. A., Francoeur, C., Welzel, C. and Ben-Amar, W. "Empowering Women: The Role of Emancipative Forces in Board Gender Diversity." *Journal of Business Ethics*, March 2017: 459–511.

Chapman, K. A. "Economic Development and Female Labor Force Participation in the Middle East and North Africa: A Test of the U-Shape Hypothesis." *Gettysburg Economic Review*, 8(1), 2015: 5–22.

Cook, A. and Glass, C. "Women on Corporate Boards: Do They Advance Corporate Social Responsibility?" *Entrepreneurship Theory and Practice*, 71(7), 2017: 897–924.

Cruz, C., Justo, R. and Larraza-Kintana, M. "When Do Women Make a Better Table? Examining the Influence of Women Directors on Family Firm's Corporate Social Performance." *Entrepreneurship Theory and Practice*, 43(2), 2019: 282–301.

Dankwano, R. N. and Hassan, Z. "Impact of Gender Diversity on Indian Firm's Financial Performance." *Journal of Management, Accounting & Economics*, 5(5), 2018: 319–341.

Deloitte Global Center for Corporate Governance. "Women in the Boardroom: A Global Perspective." Deloitte Perspective Report 5th edition, *Deloitte Touche Tohmatsu Limited*, 2017: 1–84. www2.deloitte.com/content/dam/Deloitte/cn/Documents/risk/deloitte-cn-ra-ccg-e1-women-in-the-boardroom-a-global-perspective-fifth-edition.pdf.

Galbreath, J. "Are There Gender-Related Influences on Corporate Sustainability? A Study of Women on Boards of Directors." *Journal of Management and Organization*, 17, 2011: 17–38.

Geletkanycz, M., Clark, C. and Gabaldon, P. "When Boards Broaden Their Definition of Diversity, Women and People of Color Lose Out." *Harvard Business Review*, 2018. Accessed November 28, 2018. https://hbr.org/2018/10/research-when-boards-broaden-their-definition-of-diversity-women-and-people-of-color-lose-out.

Hodigere, R. and Bilimoria, D. "Human Capital and Professional Network Effects on Women's Odds of Corporate Board Directorships." *Gender in Management: An International Journal*, 30(7), 2015: 523–550.

Howaidy, G. "Women on Corporate Boards in Egypt: Time for Change." *Overcoming Challenges to Gender Equality in the Workplace*, (Greenleaf Publishing/PRME Book Series, London, 2016): 178–188.

Huse, M., Nielsen, S. T. and Hagen, I. M. "Women and Employee-Elected Board Members, and Their Contributions to Board Control Tasks." *Journal of Business Ethics*, 89(4), 2009: 581–597.

Hyun, E., Yang, D., Jung, H. and Hong, K. "Women on Boards and Corporate Social Responsibility." *Sustainability*, 8(300), 2016: 1–26.

Kakabadse, N. K., Figueira, C., Nicolopoulou, K., Hong Yang, J., Kakabadse, A. P. and Ozbilgin, M. F. "Gender Diversity and Board Performance: Women's Experiences and Perspectives." *Human Resource Management*, 54(2), 2015: 265–281.

Karshenas, M., Moghadam, V. M. and Chamlou, N. "Women, Work, and Welfare in the Middle East and North Africa: Introduction and Overview." In *Women, Work and Welfare in the Middle East and North Africa: The Role of Socio-Demographics, Entrepreneurship and Public Policies*. London: Imperial College Press, 2016: 1–30.

Kim, D. and Starks, L. T. "Gender Diversity on Corporate Boards: Do Women Contribute Unique Skills?" *American Economic Review*, 106(5), 2016: 267–271.

Loukil, N. and Yousfi, O. "Does Gender Diversity on Corporate Boards Increase Risk-Taking?" *Canadian Journal of Administrative Sciences*, 33(1), 2015: 66–81.

Maghraoui, D. "Constitutional Reforms in Morocco: Between Consensus and Subaltern Politics." *Journal of North African Studies*, 16(4), 2011: 679–699.

Majbouri, M. "Fertility and the Puzzle of Female Employment in the Middle East." *Working Paper*, IZA Institute of Labor Economics. 2018: 1–34.

McKinsey Global Institute. "Women Matter: Time to Accelerate, Ten Years of Insights into Gender Diversity." *Working Paper*. 2017.

Mernissi, F. "Le Harem et l'Occident." *Paris: Albin Michel Eds*, 231, 2001.

Metcalfe, B. D. "Reflecting on Difference: Women, Islamic Feminism and Development in the Middle East." In J. M. Syed and M. Ozgilbin (eds.), *Gender and Diversity Management in Asia*. Cheltenham: Edward Elgar Publishing, 2010: 40–160.

Metcalfe, B. D. "Women, Empowerment and Development in Arab Gulf States: A Critical Appraisal of Governance, Culture and National Human Resource Development (HRD) Frameworks." *Human Resource Development International*, 14(2), 2011: 131–148.

Metcalfe, B. D. and Rees, C. J. "Gender, Globalization and Organization: Exploring Power, Relations and Intersections." *An International Journal*, 29(1), 2010: 5–22.

M'hamid, I., Hachana, R. and Abdelwahed, O. "Diversité Genre dans le Conseil d'Administration et Performance des Entreprises Tunisiennes Cotées[Gender Diversity in the Board of Directors and Performance of Tunisian Publicly Listed Companies]." *Global Journal of Management and Business Research*, 11(4), 2011: 164–174.

Moghadam, V. M. "Gender Inequality and Economic Inclusion in Tunisia: Key Policy Issues." Issue Brief, Rice University's Baker Institute for Public Policy. 2018a: 1–8.

Moghadam, V. M. "The State and the Women's Movement in Tunisia: Mobilization, Institutionalization, and Inclusion." Working Paper, Rice University's Baker Institute for Public Policy. 2018b: 1–22.

Moroccan Institute for Directors. "Enquête sur les Pratiques de Gouvernance des Sociétés Cotées [Survey on Corporate Governance Practices of Publicly Listed Companies]." Working Paper. 2016: 1–36.

Radwan, A., Assaad, R. and Al-Qudsi, S. "Employment Experience in the Middle East and North Africa." *Economic Research Forum*, Working Paper. 1994: 1–56.

Raghuram, P. "Migrant Women in Male-Dominated Sectors of the Labour Market: A Research Agenda." *Population, Space and Place*, 14(1), 2008: 43–57.

Ramadan, T. *Islamic Ethics*. Cambridge, MA: Harvard University Press, 2009.

Roudi-Fahmi, F. and Moghadam, V. M. "Empowering Women, Developing Society: Female Education in the Middle East and North Africa." *Al-Raida Journal*, 2006: 4–11.

Rowlands, J. *Questioning Empowerment: Working with Women in Honduras*. Dublin: Oxfam GB, 1997.

Saidin, M. "Rethinking the 'Arab Spring': The Root Causes of the Tunisian Jasmine Revolution and Egyptian January 25 Revolution." *International Journal of Islamic Thought*, 13, 2018: 69–79.

Schiek, D. "From Parental Leave to Parental Time: German Labour Law and EU Law." *Industrial Law Journal*, 31(4), 2002: 361–369.

Smith, N. "Gender Quotas on Boards of Directors." *IZA World of Labor* (No. 7). 2018. https://wol.iza.org/articles/gender-quotas-on-boards-of-directors/long.

United Nations Women. "Gender Equality and Women's Empowerment." Working Paper, 52. 2018. www.un.org/sustainabledevelopment/gender-equality/.

Women on Boards. "2020 Women on Boards: Gender Diversity Index: Progress of Women Corporate Directors by Company Size, State and Industry Sector." Working Paper. 2018: 1–8.

World Economic Forum. "The Global Gender Gap Report 2017." Working Paper. 2017. www3.weforum.org/docs/WEF_GGGR_2017.pdf.

11

THE RENAISSANCE OF GENDER EQUALITY RESEARCH AND SUSTAINABLE DEVELOPMENT IN THE ACADEMIC CONTEXT OF MARKETING

Championing paths forward

Linda Tuncay Zayer, Wendy Hein, Jan Brace-Govan, Catherine A. Coleman, Robert L. Harrison, Nacima Ourahmoune, Minita Sanghvi and Laurel Steinfield

Abstract

The United Nations (UN) Sustainable Development Goal (SDG) of gender equality and the empowerment of all women and girls (SDG #5) is cited as interlinked with other SDGs. One often hears that "Global Goals cannot be achieved without ensuring gender equality and women's empowerment" (UN, 2015) and that "gender equality is critical to all areas of a healthy society, from reducing poverty (SDG #1) to promoting health (SDG #3) and education (SDG #4), and to the protection of the well-being of girls and boys" (UN, 2016). Despite its importance, business academics have been slow to acknowledge issues surrounding gender equality among other SDGs. This chapter argues that despite these challenges, gender research in the wider field of marketing is experiencing a renaissance, fueled in part by global, political and social movements and by the persistence of academics studying these connections. Three research areas for championing a path forward – gender violence, intersectionality and local and global perspectives in marketing – are presented. The translation of this research to inquiry based and transformative learning is particularly emphasized. Lastly, the chapter calls for and advocates ongoing and future efforts to keep the momentum of gender and sustainability issues at the forefront of the marketing field. Using marketing as an illustration for wider business disciplines, it is their role to recognize and become key drivers in shaping sustainable development.

Introduction

The sustainable development goal (SDG) of gender equality and the empowerment of all women and girls (SDG #5) has been cited as strongly interlinked with other SDGs. It is often the case that "Global Goals cannot be achieved without ensuring gender equality and women's empowerment" (UN, 2015), and "gender equality is critical to all areas of a healthy society, from reducing poverty to promoting health, education, protection and the well-being of girls and boys" (UN, 2016). Despite its importance, business academics have been slow to acknowledge issues surrounding gender equality. Yet, inequalities form part of the fabric of everyday life. Globally, at this point in time, no country has achieved gender equality (OECD, 2012). Nowhere in the world do women and men equally benefit from rights, resources and recognition, nor do women and men equally occupy decision-making positions to change these conditions. Additionally, gender equality does not just relate to women but encompasses a wider range of intersecting identities: sex, age, ethnicity, social stratum, non-religion, sexuality and rural and urban geographies.

Beyond gender equality, economics, business and management, both in theory and practice, play key roles in the SDGs, ranging from no poverty (SDG #1), to responsible consumption and production (SDG #12) and the development of partnerships for the goals (SDG #17). It may therefore be surprising to learn that gender equality and other SDGs are not always central to business research and practice. Examining a specific subject discipline – the authors' discipline of marketing – shows a lack of progress toward the study of gender equality. Although a range of research in marketing has contributed to critical gender perspectives, (e.g., Maclaran et al., 2009; Ourahmoune et al., 2014), some mainstream research still overlooks differences between gender and sex, disconnects gender from sustainable and responsible marketing and instead focuses on the use of gender as a variable to document differences between men and women. However, critical and cultural gender scholarship in marketing is vast and growing (see Arsel et al., 2015; Bettany et al., 2010; Dobscha, 2019; Otnes and Zayer, 2012). For example, a range of research has explored gender identities as constructed through consumption (Hein and O'Donohoe, 2014; Kates, 2003; Thompson and Üstüner, 2015) and the role of advertising and media in portraying or shaping gender ideals (Gurrieri et al., 2013; Schroeder and Zwick, 2004; Zayer and Coleman, 2015), often via feminist perspectives (Borgerson, 2007; Dobscha and Ozanne, 2001; Dobscha and Prothero, 2012; Hearn and Hein, 2015). What is lacking, however, is a more consistent focus by the marketing field on gender inequalities (Fischer, 2015) and broader social divisions in which markets, marketing and consumption play significant roles (Hein et al., 2016; Steinfield et al., 2019a; Zayer et al., 2017).

Indeed, some scholars note that gender research is predominantly welcomed in the business academy if it remains apolitical (Hearn and Hein, 2015). Academics who seek to introduce more critical and political perspectives may face obstacles or become discouraged, as many journals in the field emphasize managerial or theoretical contributions over research that prioritizes consumer welfare and broader issues of sustainability. This may create an environment where incentive structures are lacking for academics to research social issues, such as gender (in)equality. Indeed, a recent review by McDonagh and Prothero (2018) of gender research published in top journals in marketing from 1993 to 2016 reveals that just 2 percent of the 17,525 papers focused on gender (and the majority of this research approached gender as a binary category rather than pursuing gender equality or a gender justice perspective). Moreover, a closer look at the composition of leadership positions in the leading journals reveals that only 18.5 percent of editors-in-chief, 38.9 percent of co-editors, 28 percent of associate editors and 28.3 percent of editorial review board members were female (McDonagh and Prothero, 2018).

Despite these imbalances, gender research in the wider field of marketing is experiencing a renaissance, fueled in part by global, political and social conversations – for example, those surrounding the #MeToo and #TimesUp movements – in addition to the persistence of a minority of scholars. Academics are in a unique position to capture these cultural conversations both in terms of building an agenda of advancing knowledge through research and action and also in classrooms in preparing the next generation of business professionals.

Championing transformative gender justice research

A growing community of researchers and changing social conditions are facilitating efforts to engage in research with an activist or action stance (Frisby et al., 2009; Hein et al., 2016). This chapter highlights ways of addressing or overcoming the many obstacles raised above, including: finding and giving a voice, building foundations and embracing conditions conducive to change and attempting to make impact beyond the academy. As Fischer (2015: 1721) notes, progress on market-level research with regard to gender inequality is, "limited in many geographic regions, and often stalls or reverses even in those jurisdictions and institutions where we most expect it to flourish."

Topics particularly important yet neglected in the field of marketing in relation to gender equality are, therefore, highlighted in the chapter. These are as follows:

1 Gender violence in the market

Gender violence is a major injustice and sadly a regular, even normalized, occurrence in contemporary markets, marketing and consumers' lives. Images of violence against women in advertising and media, in general, including social media and gaming are pervasive. In advertising, shockingly violent images are used to gain attention, often breaching regulations, and, when challenged, advertisers were identified as denying responsibility or claiming the images were "art" (Gurrieri et al., 2016). Further research should address the myriad of representational violence (and misrepresentations) and move toward positive, affirmative gender depictions that can transform women's and men's lives.

So far, very little research has investigated the pervasiveness of physical and sexual violence in markets. Human and sex trafficking, for example, are firmly based on unjust, often global, gender relations that remain muted or sidelined in marketing literature, despite exceptions, such as Pennington et al. (2009), Varman et al. (2018) and a recent special issue on "Violence, Markets and Marketing" in the *Journal of Marketing Management* (Varman, 2018). Similarly, domestic violence or cultural practices, ranging from the high price of idealized beauty to female genital mutilation, are significant issues affecting many women's lives, often underpinned by unequal power relations in families or households, and affecting fundamental access to consumption decisions. Women's bodies are commoditized and objectified, in a myriad of ways. Practices and systems ranging from forms of prostitution, sex trafficking, pornography, plastic surgery to domestic labor (e.g., Filipino maids in Europe) and surrogacy or contract pregnancy (e.g., surrogates in Gujarat, India, that service international clients) have been argued as examples of this commoditization (see, for example, Sharp, 2000; Yee, 2018). Marketing and consumer research have a responsibility to highlight market(ing) dynamics that contribute to unsustainable, unjust consumption and production (SDG #12) while offering potential resolutions. If gender inequality becomes acknowledged as a root problem, it is these areas, among others, that require significant research attention and action in the wider field of marketing.

2 Intersectionality, markets and marketing

Markets and marketing are complicit in gender exclusion, discrimination and oppression as much as they are powerful in giving people voices. Yet power and discrimination are rarely a research focus in marketing. Crenshaw (1991) introduced the concept of intersectionality as a metaphor for the complexity that lies in the experience of discrimination on the basis of several different oppressions concurrently, such as gender/sex, race, sexuality, religion, class and age (to name a few identity markers). Intersectionality thus seeks to address the rights and voices of those who are currently invisible.

Although originally applied to explore multiple discriminations in legal contexts, the chapter argues that there is a need to translate this feminist critical perspective to our contexts of (unequal) markets, marketing and consumption. Indeed, early research has conceptualized intersectionality as it relates to marketing as, "the interactivity of social identity structures such as race, class, and gender in fostering life experiences, especially experiences of privilege and oppression" (Gopaldas, 2013: 90). However, much marketing scholarship overlooks the intersection of multiple sources of oppression — for example, racism, classism and sexism (i.e., women of color) — wherein one or the other is given more attention, and the comprehensive context is not accounted for. Harnessing the transformative potential of intersectionality, a marketing research focus could shift from studying gender categories toward the study of sexism and gender discrimination at the intersection of other forms of discrimination (Steinfield et al., 2019b) and as a result study root causes of inequalities (SDG #10) and gender inequalities (SDG #5). Scholars and practitioners are urged to build and expand on existing research in this area (e.g., Corus et al., 2016; Crockett et al., 2011; Gopaldas and Fischer, 2012; Gopaldas and Siebert, 2018; Harrison et al., 2017; Zayer et al., 2017). Indeed, as a recent review by Ger (2018) highlights, intersectionality is often treated implicitly in existing marketing scholarship. In the pursuit of sustainability, scholars are encouraged to focus on revealing and countering sources of systemic oppression, which can emerge in business and marketing – issues that are often linked together with critical gender injustice topics.

3 Widening local and global research perspectives and replacing an overemphasis on traditionally Western communities

Lastly, and related to the first two issues above, critical scholars highlight gender as studied from a Western and privileged perspective. Although it is important to differentiate meanings of "Western" or "whiteness," relative privilege becomes evident in relation to women and men in developing countries and of diverse ethnic backgrounds. Studying the overlooked, invisible and silenced communities thus also requires critical, transnational perspectives of local, national, regional and global market relations (i.e., how they are experienced, socioculturally ingrained, structured and institutionalized). A nuanced look at the various levels of gender and global market relations can further highlight links across SDGs with a view toward transformations.

Scholars in marketing have called for more research on consumption phenomena within non-Western contexts (Jafari et al., 2012), and indeed, there is evidence of research that tackles the intersection between gender and consumption issues outside the Western world (e.g., Ourahmoune and Özça lar-Toulouse, 2012; Sredl, 2018; Steinfield et al., 2019a; Varman et al., 2018). However, scholars need to question the meanings of center and periphery and move toward transdisciplinary approaches. For example, the growing marketing and consumption of skin-lightening products across Africa, Asia and Latin America need to be contextualized within the global legacy of colonialism that is wielded by transnational companies that profit from linking social and global capital to skin color (Glenn, 2008). Postcolonial and decolonial paradigms in marketing can emphasize the "coloniality" of power and knowledge of the present time (Appadurai, 1996; Bhabha, 1994; Spivak, 1988). These paradigms offer important conceptual and methodological insights to advance understandings of the mechanisms of marketplace (re)production of gender inequities.

It is important to note that one cannot laud differences and diverse voices (in marketing), while disregarding the historical conditions and processes that reproduce complex social inequalities (Chaudhuri, 2004). A decolonial approach is particularly salient in Latin American contexts, where it valorizes and builds from the lived realities of indigenous and black populations, inseparable from the colonial legacy. As Escobar notes (2010: 43), "decolonial feminism, while questioning

Enlightenment-derived modern/colonial feminist discourses, also unveils patriar-
chal constructions of womanhood harbored within appeals to tradition and cultural
difference."

Decolonial perspectives are global, based on a logic of protests made by scholars
located in the Global North or South regardless of their background (colonial or
otherwise), who are committed to understanding and changing the relations of
dominance and oppression through new social movements. These are elements of
a process of decolonization of thought, which merit close attention by marketing
scholars to enrich current conceptualizations of (gendered) transnational market
phenomena. More broadly, it is time for researchers in marketing to engage with
plural, alternative non-Western-centric approaches to better capture the logics of
domination and levers of emancipation at the heart of emerging economies and
their specific challenges to meet gender equality and sustainable development.

Championing inquiry-based and transformative learning and teaching

Marketing academics are increasingly poised to translate research on gender equality and justice into pedagogies (Gelles and Miller, 2017). Attempting to make an
impact with inquiry-based, transformative learning at higher education institutions
relies on the premise that students leave the institution better equipped to deal
with a dynamic and challenging global business world (Thomas and Brown, 2011).
Inquiry-based learning is an approach to teaching that gives students ownership of
their learning, while also attending to diversity in classrooms in terms of attitudes
and interests. Oriented around higher-order thinking as per Bloom's taxonomy and
Kolb's experiential learning, inquiry-based learning encourages students to engage
with authentic investigations and become an "active participant in the learning
process" (Blessinger and Carfora, 2015: 6). In this approach, the instructor provides
theoretical frames, which can be multidisciplinary, that are purposefully designed
to open up areas to student knowledge creation and exploration. There are clear
opportunities to introduce the juxtaposition of surprising and interesting contexts
and questions for learners to investigate either individually or in groups. Designing
group work and other forms of student interaction and sharing (whether in the
classroom or online) opens up avenues for "learning new meaning schemes and
learning through meaning transformation" (Kitchenham, 2008: 110).

The inquiry-based approach matches well with Mezirow's (2000) transformative learning, incorporating social and emotional development as well as critical
self-reflection and competence evaluation. Critical reflection and questioning of
assumptions were key developments in Mezirow's transformative learning theory
(Kitchenham, 2008: 116) along with his recognition of the significance of "affec-
tive, emotional and social aspects" of adult transformative learning.

Challenging taken-for-granted ideas through learning has a long history (Freire,
1973). However, there is a timely opportunity not only to engage students more
deeply in their own learning but also to be sensitive to their diverse starting points

on challenging issues while concurrently introducing them to meaningful frameworks that allow them to critically reflect on complex and important contemporary topics, especially as they relate to gender equality and marketing. The previously mentioned SDG that resonates with adjusting perspectives on violence, intersectionality and globalism is SDG #5 "Achieve gender equality and empower all women and girls," with the target to end all forms of discrimination against all women and girls everywhere (UN Women). Rising concerns around various social issues, in tandem with the increasing involvement of consumers in digital media protests, has gradually generated a shift in organizational engagement with policy and change. For example, in the United States, *Harvard Business Review* reports on the "New CEO Activists" (Chatterji and Toffel, 2018), identifying business leaders not only as advocates for change around issues that are unrelated to their business but also, importantly, using the economic significance of their businesses to support their views, such as threatening to move away from states that pass controversial laws. This kind of leadership activity has real consequences in terms of generating change, potentially an exciting and hopeful space for students to investigate. In addition, such public stances also require that marketing activities are flexible and adaptive, driving the curriculum into new and dynamic learning spaces.

In Australia, leadership around SDG #5 was given impetus in 2010 when the Sex Discrimination Commissioner established Male Champions for Change. Male Champions for Change (MCC) is "a disruptive strategy to accelerate the advancement of women in leadership and achieve gender equality" that works with, and learns from, many organizations, including UN Women (MCC, 2018: 7). The signatories are male CEOs who commit their enterprises to deliver change for women and gender equity across a range of issues. The 2018 Impact Report noted that there were 12 groups comprising more than 200 leaders of 600,000 employees globally (MCC, 2018). These activities and their increasingly impactful presence are sufficiently diverse to appeal to a broad range of marketing students and their interests. The accessible reporting and transparency also allows in-depth discussion from a substantiated position, which is essential around gender as a topic and, importantly, offers a window into the marketing world that students are likely to enter. Thus, an inquiry-based approach can be particularly useful for marketing academics to apply in teaching a range of core marketing topics, such as segmentation, product development and advertising messaging.

The chapter concludes by providing recommendations for other academics who seek to champion gender equality research and teaching in their field, particularly as they contribute to the SDGs put forth by the UN. By providing a framework for conducting research focused on gender justice as well as highlighting recent efforts in gender scholarship, this chapter hopes to celebrate the inroads scholars have made in bringing gender scholarship to the forefront in marketing.

Conclusions and recommendations

This chapter has sought to document the struggles and successes of a group of marketing scholars in their efforts to center gender equality in research, teaching and action toward sustainability. The many obstacles relate to how gender is currently theorized and how research findings are put into practice.

The chapter points toward a current dominance of studying gender as reduced to variables, essentialized in biology and reproduced in stereotypes. Links to sustainable development are neglected as is research that seeks to transform pervasive inequalities and injustices. Gender is complex, transnational and deeply entrenched in systems and practices that drive sustainability. In other words, sustainable futures are those that focus on gender equality. Important foundations are being built, for example, in frameworks that propose solutions for addressing these complexities, such as the Transformative Gender Justice Framework (TGJF) (see Hein et al., 2016).

The TGJF approaches gender from perspectives of material *distributive justice*, sociocultural *recognition theory* and the empowerment of individuals via *capabilities approach*. It is imperative that these, and other approaches, are embraced and conversations facilitated in wider sustainability scholarship to ensure gender equality gains further prominence. Importantly, the chapter repeatedly emphasizes that gender equality, as represented in theories and important topics raised above, deserves more prominence in marketing and business academia. Issues of gender justice, sustainability and responsibility are at times secondary to profitable, efficiency-driven managerial implications.

However, increasingly there are groups of like-minded scholars and journal editors who actively pursue topics and theories proposed above as well as other areas of importance. Part of the struggle is thus to enhance the momentum of these groups and convince more scholars, senior academics and changemakers to acknowledge the importance and impact of such work. In such a way, a point where these voices are brought to the fore and scholarship that moves beyond solely improving the bottom line can be widely celebrated.

Looking ahead to the future of marketing and gender research, it appears likely that the impact that marketing academics, business professionals and students can have on championing a path forward that is commensurate with the SDGs is increasing. In particular, in this year alone, several dedicated special issues of marketing journals related to gender (SDG #5 on gender equality and SDG #10 on reduced inequalities) including issues in the *Journal of the Association for Consumer Research*, *Journal of Macromarketing*, *Journal of Marketing Management*, *Consumption Markets & Culture*, and *Journal of Advertising Research* have been published or are forthcoming. Moreover, gender scholarship in marketing continues to be highlighted in marketing and consumer behavior edited volumes (see, for example, *Handbook of Research on Gender and Marketing*, Dobscha, 2019) and various recent book chapters such as Maclaran et al. (2017) in the *Routledge Handbook on Consumption*, Zayer et al. (2017) in *The Routledge Companion to Consumer Behavior* and Visconti et al. (2017) in *Consumer Culture Theory*. In addition to an increasing voice in journal publications, edited books and book chapters, the tradition of the Association for Consumer Research Gender, Marketing and Consumer Behavior biennial conferences has continued (since its inception in 1991) where gender scholars from around the globe gathered in Dallas,

Texas, in October 2018 with a focus on social change. Events included a roundtable highlighting transformative gender issues as well as the first meeting of the GEN-MAC advisory board, a group of scholars dedicated to advancing social change and building knowledge on gender, marketing and consumer behavior (www.genmac. co). This momentum is expected to continue in the years to come, as these efforts translate to the pursuit of gender and social justice within marketing as one of many disciplines from the wider field of business and management.

Beyond the struggles and steps that some scholars have taken to ensure continued efforts to direct marketing research and practice to the areas defined above, this chapter has sought to inspire and encourage other disciplines, particularly relating to business and economics, to recognize their roles and responsibilities in addressing the most pressing issues of our time. Given the complexity and interlinkages between the SDGs, academies and industries, it is vital that research, education and practices join forces to champion a shared path into the future, with sustainability at its core.

References

Appadurai, A. *Modernity at Large: Cultural Dimensions of Globalization.* Minneapolis: University of Minnesota Press, 1996.

Arsel, Z., Eräranta, K. and Moisander, J. "Introduction: Theorising Gender and Gendering Theory in Marketing and Consumer Research." *Journal of Marketing Management,* 31(15–16), 2015: 1553–1558.

Bettany, S., Dobscha, S., O'Malley, L. and Prothero, A. "Moving beyond Binary Opposition: Exploring the Tapestry of Gender in Consumer Research and Marketing." *Marketing Theory,* 10(1), 2010: 3–28.

Bhabha, H. *The Location of Culture.* New York: Routledge, 1994.

Blessinger, P. and Carfora, J. M. "Innovative Approaches in Teaching and Learning: An Introduction to Inquiry-Based Learning for Multidisciplinary Programs." In P. Blessinger and J. M. Carfora (eds.), *Inquiry-Based Learning for Multidisciplinary Programs: A Conceptual and Practical Resource for Educators* (Innovations in Higher Education Teaching and Learning, Volume 3). Bingley, UK: Emerald Group Publishing Limited, 2015: 3–22.

Borgerson, J. L. "On the Harmony of Feminist Ethics and Business Ethics." *Business and Society Review,* 112(4), 2007: 477–509.

Chatterji, A. and Toffel, M. "The New CEO Activists." *Harvard Business Review,* January–February, 2018: 78–89.

Chaudhuri, M. *Feminism in India: Issues in Contemporary Feminism.* New Delhi: Kali for Women, 2004.

Corus, C., Saatcioglu, B., Kaufman-Scarborough, C., Blocker, C. P., Upadhyaya, S. and Samuelson, A. "Transforming Poverty-Related Policy with Intersectionality." *Journal of Public Policy & Marketing,* 35(2), 2016: 211–222.

Crenshaw, K. "Mapping the Margins: Intersectionality, Identity Politics, and Violence against Women of Color." *Stanford Law Review,* 43(6), 1991: 1241–1299.

Crockett, D., Anderson, L., Bone, S. A., Roy, A., Wang, J. J. and Coble, G. "Immigration, Culture, and Ethnicity in Transformative Consumer Research." *Journal of Public Policy & Marketing,* 30(1), 2011: 47–54.

Dobscha, S. (ed.). *Handbook of Research on Gender and Marketing.* Cheltenham, UK: Edward Elgar Publishing, 2019.

Dobscha, S. and Ozanne, J. L. "An Ecofeminist Analysis of Environmentally Sensitive Women Using Qualitative Methodology: The Emancipatory Potential of an Ecological Life." *Journal of Public Policy & Marketing*, 20(2), 2001: 201–214.

Dobscha, S. and Prothero, A. "(Re)igniting Sustainable Consumption and Production Research through Feminist Connections." In C. C. Otnes and L. T. Zayer (eds.), *Gender, Culture and Consumer Behavior*. London, UK: Routledge Academic, 2012: 331–392.

Escobar, A. *Globalization and the Decolonial Option*. London: Routledge, 2010.

Fischer, E. "Towards More Marketing Research on Gender Inequality." *Journal of Marketing Management*, 31(15–16), 2015: 1718–722.

Freire, P. *Education for Critical Consciousness*. New York: Continuum, 1973.

Frisby, W., Maguire, P. and Reid, C. The 'f' Word Has Everything to Do with It: How Feminist Theories Inform Action Research." *Action Research*, 7(1), 2009: 13–29.

Gelles, D. and Miller, C. C. "Business Schools Now Teaching #MeToo, N.F.L. Protests and Trump." *The New York Times*, December 25, 2017. www.nytimes.com/2017/12/25/business/mba-business-school-ethics.html.

Ger, G. "Intersectional Structuring of Consumption." *Journal of Consumer Research* (Curation Introduction), Spring 2018.

Glenn, E. N. "Yearning for Lightness: Transnational Circuits in the Marketing and Consumption of Skin Lighteners." *Gender & Society*, 22(3), 2008: 281–302.

Gopaldas, A. "Intersectionality 101." *Journal of Public Policy & Marketing*, 32(special issue), 2013: 90–94.

Gopaldas, A. and Fischer, E. "Beyond Gender: Intersectionality, Culture, and Consumer Behavior." In C. C. Otnes and L. T. Zayer (eds.), *Gender, Culture, and Consumer Behavior*. New York: Routledge, 2012: 393–410.

Gopaldas, A. and Siebert, A. "Women over 40, Foreigners of Color, and Other Missing Persons in Globalizing Mediascapes: Understanding Marketing Images as Mirrors of Intersectionality." *Consumption Markets & Culture*, 21(4), 2018: 323–346.

Gurrieri, L., Brace-Govan, J. and Cherrier, H. "Controversial Advertising: Transgressing the Taboo of Gender-Based Violence." *European Journal of Marketing*, 50(7/8), 2016: 1448–1469.

Gurrieri, L., Previte, J. and Brace-Govan, J. "Women's Bodies as Sites of Control: Inadvertent Stigma and Exclusion in Social Marketing." *Journal of Macromarketing*, 33(2), 2013: 128–143.

Harrison, R. L., Thomas, K. D. and Cross, S. N. "Restricted Visions of Multiracial Identity in Advertising." *Journal of Advertising*, 46(4), 2017: 503–520.

Hearn, J. and Hein, W. "Reframing Gender and Feminist Knowledge Construction in Marketing and Consumer Research: Missing Feminisms and the Case of Men and Masculinities." *Journal of Marketing Management*, 31(15–16), 2015: 1626–1651.

Hein, W. and O'Donohoe, S. "Practising Gender: The Role of Banter in Young Men's Improvisations of Masculine Consumer Identities." *Journal of Marketing Management*, 30(13–14), 2014: 1293–1319.

Hein, W., Steinfield, L., Ourahmoune, N., Coleman, C. A., Zayer, L. T. and Littlefield, J. "Gender Justice and the Market: A Transformative Consumer Research Perspective." *Journal of Public Policy & Marketing*, 35(2), 2016: 223–236.

Jafari, A., Fuat, F., Süerdem, A., Askegaard, S. and Dalli, D. "Non-Western Contexts: The Invisible Half." *Marketing Theory*, 12(1), 2012: 3–12.

Kates, S. M. "Producing and Consuming Gendered Representations: An Interpretation of the Sydney Gay and Lesbian Mardi Gras." *Consumption, Markets and Culture*, 6(1), 2003: 5–22.

Kitchenham, Andrew. "The Evolution of John Mezirow's Transformative Learning Theory." *Journal of Transformative Education*, 6(2), 2008: 104–123.

Maclaran, P., Miller, C., Parsons, E. and Surman, E. "Praxis or Performance: Does Critical Marketing Have a Gender Blind-Spot?" *Journal of Marketing Management*, 25(7–8), 2009: 713–728.

Maclaran, P., Otnes, C. and Zayer, L. T. "Gender, Sexuality and Consumption." In M. Keller, B. Halkier, T.-A. Wilska and M. Truninger (eds.), Abingdon: *Routledge Handbook on Consumption*, 2017: 292–302.

Male Champions of Change. *Impact Report 2018*. Accessed January 22, 2019. http://malechampionsofchange.com/wp-content/uploads/2018/12/MCC-Impact-Report-2018-1.pdf. @ http://malechampionsofchange.com/.

McDonagh, P. and Prothero, A. "An Assessment of the Gender Discourse and Gender Representation in Marketing's Journals: 1993–2016." *14th ACR Gender, Marketing and Consumer Behavior Conference*. Dallas, TX. 2018.

Mezirow, John. *Learning as Transformation: Critical Perspectives on a Theory in Progress*. San Francisco: Jossey-Bass, 2000.

OECD. "Closing the Gender Gap." Paris: Organisation for Economic Co-Operation and Development. 2012. Accessed October 16, 2017. www.oecd-ilibrary.org/content/book/9789264179370-en.

Otnes, C. C. and Zayer, L. T. (eds.). *Gender, Culture, and Consumer Behavior*. New York, NY: Taylor & Francis, 2012.

Ourahmoune, N., Binninger, A. S. and Robert, I. "Brand Narratives, Sustainability, and Gender: A Socio-Semiotic Approach." *Journal of Macromarketing*, 34(3), 2104: 313–331.

Ourahmoune, N. and Özça lar-Toulouse, N. "Exogamous Weddings and Fashion in a Rising Consumer Culture: Kabyle Minority Dynamics of Structure and Agency." *Marketing Theory*, 12(1), 2012: 81–99.

Pennington, J. R., Ball, A. D., Hampton, R. D. and Soulakova, J. N. "The Cross-National Market in Human Beings." *Journal of Macromarketing*, 29(2), 2009: 119–134.

Schroeder, J. E. and Zwick, D. "Mirrors of Masculinity: Representation and Identity in Advertising Images." *Consumption Markets & Culture*, 7(1), 2004: 21–52.

Sharp, L. A. "The Commodification of the Body and Its Parts." *Annual Review of Anthropology*, 29, 2000: 287–328.

Spivak, G. C. "Can the Subaltern Speak?" In C. Nelson and L. Grossberg (eds.), *Marxism and the Interpretation of Culture*. Chicago: University of Illinois Press, 1988: 271–313.

Sredl, K. C. "Gendered Market Subjectivity: Autonomy, Privilege, and Emotional Subjectivity in Normalizing Post-Socialist Neoliberal Ideology." *Consumption Markets & Culture*, 21(6), 2018: 532–553.

Steinfield, L., Coleman, C., Zayer, L. T., Ourahmoune, N. and Hein, W. "Power Logics of Consumers' Gendered (In)Justices: Reading Reproductive Health Interventions through the Transformative Gender Justice Framework." *Consumption Markets & Culture*, (4), 2019a: 406–429.

Steinfield, L., Sanghvi, M., Zayer, L. T., Coleman, C., Ourahmoune, N., Harrison, R., Hein, W. and Brace-Govan, J. "Transformative Intersectionality: Moving Business towards a Critical Praxis." *Journal of Business Research*, 100(July), 2019b: 366–375.

Thomas, D. and Brown, J. S. *A New Culture of Learning: Cultivating the Imagination for a World of Constant Change*. Lexington, KY: CreateSpace, 2011.

Thompson, C. and Üstüner, T. "Women Skating on the Edge: Marketplace Performances as Ideological Edgework." *Journal of Consumer Research*, 42(2), 2015: 235–265.

United Nations (UN). "Global Goals Cannot Be Achieved without Ensuring Gender Equality and Women's Empowerment: UN Chief." 2015. Accessed October 16, 2017. www.un.org/sustainabledevelopment/blog/2015/09/global-goals-cannot-be-achieved-without-ensuring-gender-equality-and-womens-empowerment-un-chief/.

United Nations (UN). "Gender Equality: Why It Matters." 2016. Accessed October 16, 2017. www.un.org/sustainabledevelopment/wp-content/uploads/2016/08/5_Why-it-Matters_GenderEquality_2p.pdf.

Varman, R. (ed.). "Violence, Markets, and Marketing." Special issue of *Journal of Marketing Management*, 34, 2018: 11–12.

Varman, R., Goswami, P. and Vijay, D. "The Precarity of Respectable Consumption: Normalising Sexual Violence against Women." *Journal of Marketing Management* 34(11–12), 2018: 1–33.

Visconti, L., Bettany, S. and Maclaran, P. "Gender(s), Consumption and Markets." In E. Anould and C. Thompson (eds.), *Consumer Culture Theory*. London: Sage Publications, 2017: 180–206.

Yee, S. W. "The Female Body as a Commodity." Distinction Paper, 64. 2018. https://digitalcommons.otterbein.edu/cgi/viewcontent.cgi?article=1067&context=stu_dist.

Zayer, L. T. and Coleman, C. A. "Advertising Professionals' Perceptions of the Impact of Gender Portrayals on Men and Women: A Question of Ethics?" *Journal of Advertising*, 44(3), 2015: 1–12.

Zayer, L. T., Coleman, C. A., Hein, W., Littlefield, J. and Steinfield, L. "Gender and the Self: Traversing Feminisms, Masculinities, and Intersectionality towards Transformative Perspectives." In M. R. Solomon and T. M. Lowrey (eds.), *The Routledge Companion to Consumer Behavior*. London: Routledge, 2017: 147–162.

12

CANADA'S FEMINIST FOREIGN POLICY AND THE SDGS

Working with business to address gender inequality

Maureen A. Kilgour

Abstract

Gender equality and the empowerment of women and girls are critical elements in the achievement of the Sustainable Development Goals (SDGs). State governments, businesses and civil society have all been asked to work toward the achievement of the SDGs. Given the complexity of the current global governance regime and the overlapping interests among the various actors, collaboration and innovation are required to move toward the achievement of these goals. The Canadian government (Canada) has historically been a strong advocate for international action on gender inequality. This engagement was formalized in 2017, when the Canadian government committed to a "feminist" foreign policy. The goal of this chapter is to discuss the early successes and challenges in the implementation of a "feminist" approach to the attainment of the SDGs with a focus on Canada's relationship with business. It examines areas of interaction between Canada's feminist policy in support of the SDGs and business and identifies both strengths and weaknesses. A review of Canada's SDG initiatives in support of gender equality provides insights into the ways in which governments intersect with business on sustainability issues and highlights areas of interrogation for responsible management education, especially in the area of gender equality.

Introduction

Two weeks after the adoption of the Sustainable Development Goals (SDGs) in September 2015, a self-declared feminist became the prime minister of Canada (Trudeau, 2015). When asked why he had strived for gender parity in his first cabinet, Prime Minister Trudeau responded, "because it is 2015" (Ditchburn, 2015). Two years later, gender equality was cited as a top priority in the Canadian government's strategy for the SDGs: "Achieving gender equality and the empower-ment of all women and girls at home and around the world . . . is at the heart of the Government of Canada's approach to implementing the 2030 Agenda" (Global Affairs Canada, 2018b). In September 2018, Canada's Minister of Foreign Affairs Chrystia Freeland hosted the first ever meeting of women foreign ministers in Montreal, Canada, and stated that "[a]s minister of foreign affairs and as a commit-ted feminist, I know that all of our efforts to advance our diplomatic, trade, security and development priorities must fully take into account the needs of women and girls" (Global Affairs Canada, 2018c). Partnerships with business are also at the heart of the strategy. A review of Canada's SDG initiatives in support of gender equality provides insights into the ways in which governments intersect with business on sustainability issues and highlights areas of interrogation for responsible manage-ment education (RME), especially in the area of gender equality, which has been lacking (Haynes and Murray, 2015).

Gender equality and the SDGs

Gender equality and the empowerment of women and girls have been deemed to be critical elements in the overall achievement of the SDGs. Gender equality (SDG #5) is both a stand-alone goal (to "achieve gender equality and empower all women and girls") and a cross-cutting goal. SDG #5 targets economic equality, gender-based violence, decision-making, workplace discrimination and reproduc-tive health and rights. As a cross-cutting goal, all other SDGs must be viewed from a gender-aware perspective in order to "draw . . . attention to the gender dimensions of poverty, hunger, health, education, water and sanitation, employment, climate change, environmental degradation, urbanization, conflict and peace, and financing for development" (UN Women, 2018). This has significant implications for both governments and businesses as they develop strategies for the attainment of all of the goals.

Governments and partnerships with business

Although UN member states are committed to the SDGs, there is a recognition that many actors must work in partnership to achieve them (*Transforming Our World: The 2030 Agenda for Sustainable Development*, 2015). Scholars have stressed the importance of interrogating the government and business nexus in relation to sus-tainability and to gender equality (Kourula et al., 2019; Piscopo, 2015). Responsible management education also needs to pay attention to the ways in which govern-ments interact with businesses under the guise of action on sustainability. These partnerships can be risky due to the inherent conflict between the profit-seeking behaviour of firms and some of the social goals enumerated in the SDGs (Abshagen et al., 2018). In addition, foreign policy can be fraught with contradictions as gov-ernments try to create enabling market environments for businesses to thrive while trying to accomplish social goals such as the SDGs (Aggestam et al., 2019).

The goal of this chapter is to discuss some of Canada's SDG initiatives focussed on gender equality and suggest themes that should be considered in RME. The next section identifies criticisms of Canada on the issue of responsible business and gender when the SDGs where adopted in 2015. This sets the scene for a review of a series of initiatives that Canada launched as part of its SDG commitment. The chapter concludes by identifying key themes for responsible management education.

Canada's reputation

While Canada has a relatively positive reputation on issues of human rights and gender equality, concerns have been raised about the harm caused by Canadian businesses in the extractive sector, particularly in Latin America, where they dominate. One 2012 publication was titled "Imperial Canada Inc: Legal haven of choice for the world's mining industries" (Deneault and Sacher, 2012). Another study, named "The Canada Brand", claimed that "[t]he world is taking notice of Canadian companies – for the wrong reasons", and referred to demands from "five UN bodies. . . . The Inter-American Commission on Human Rights . . . and 180 organizations from Latin America" to prevent human rights abuses arising out of the operations of Canadian companies abroad (Imai et al., 2017: 5). Numerous critiques involved concerns about gender inequality, especially for indigenous women ("Creating an International Gender and Peace Agenda: Impact of Canadian Mines in Latin America", 2016). The World Bank, Oxfam and others point out the gendered impact of the extractive industry where women are adversely affected, including by discrimination, disruption to family structures in communities, environmental degradation and by gender-based violence (Ward et al., 2011; Parks and Orozco, 2018; Hill et al., 2016). A high-profile court case in Canada (*Choc v. Hudbay Minerals*) is testing the responsibilities of Canadian companies when operating internationally: Eleven women have alleged they were gang-raped and evicted from homes by personnel associated with a Canadian-owned mine in Guatemala (Eulich and Llana, 2019).

Although Canadian companies may be no worse than those in other countries (Haslam et al., 2018), significant national and international pressure on Canada appears to have motivated it to address the concerns. Critiques of the Canadian extractive industry led to the creation of Canada's CSR policy in the 2000s, and observers have suggested that Canada's foreign policy is designed in part around protecting the Canadian extractive companies operating abroad (Marques, 2016). Given this background, it is important to assess the steps Canada is taking as part of its commitment to the SDGs to understand if it is still business as usual with regard to its business practices around the globe.

Canada's SDG actions for gender equality

In order to better understand how governments and business interact under the SDG framework, this section discusses seven initiatives that illustrate Canada's attempt to engage business, either directly or indirectly, with the SDGs relating to gender equality.

1 Canada's feminist foreign policy (2017)

In 2017, the Canadian government announced its "feminist" foreign policy and the adoption of a feminist approach and gender-based analyses in its international endeavours (Chapnick, 2019). While Canada has had public policy influenced by feminism decades prior to this announcement, the explicit labelling of the foreign policy as feminist arose as a constellation of factors, including, importantly, the appointment of a feminist as Minister of Foreign Policy, Chrystia Freeland, in January 2017. It was Freeland who began discussing the importance of a feminist foreign policy shortly after taking on the portfolio, and these references appeared to influence the Prime Minister, who subsequently adopted her approach (Chapnick, 2019). The formal adoption of this type of approach to policy helps focus on the gender-based discrimination, exclusion and violence, among other issues, that impede progress on gender equality (Aggestam et al., 2019). However, the policy has been labelled "highly ideological" and "aspirational" (Courtney, 2018), leading to suggestions to ensure that the policy has impact, for example, by requiring Canadian firms operating abroad to report on gender issues (Kenny, 2018). These feminist declarations by states have been lauded but have also been criticized (for example, in Percival, 2017; Srdjan, 2017). Critics were quick to allege hypocrisy, given Canada's arms sales to Saudi Arabia (Vucetic, 2017). Despite the lack of concrete commitments, the impact of the policy statement is symbolic, and the policy may signal to Canadian businesses, international agencies and other stakeholders that gender equality is a legitimate focus of foreign policy initiatives including development assistance, trade agreements and humanitarian aid, among other areas.

2 Canada's Feminist International Assistance Policy (2017)

The first announcement connected to the feminist foreign policy was that Canada would have a "Feminist International Assistance Policy". Although the budget for development assistance did not increase, 15 per cent of aid investments "would specifically target gender equality and the empowerment of women and girls", and gender would be a consideration in at least 80 per cent of all foreign aid initiatives by 2021–2022 (meaning most of the aid would not have gender equality as the primary goal) (Asquith, 2018). Critics have noted that the concept of feminist aid may be too vague to have any real meaning, suggesting the announcement could be perceived as a "PR stunt" (Pittman, 2017).

In keeping with the financing approach advocated by the UN, the policy does emphasize the importance of engaging the private sector in development work with some of the aid in the form of both repayable and nonrepayable contributions to businesses that contribute to the government's goals on the SDGs (Global Affairs Canada, 2017a). However, funding the private sector to do development work does raise issues of accountability, impact and transparency, which may work counter to the aspirations of the SDGs (Mawdsley, 2018). The confidential and proprietary nature of most businesses may make it difficult to assess the impact of such funding on gender equality and women's empowerment.

3 Gender Chapters in trade agreements (2017)

The governments of Canada and Chile agreed to a "Gender Chapter" in their 2017 trade agreement, in line with Canada's commitment to incorporate gender equality provisions into trade agreements (Global Affairs Canada, 2019a). The *Trade and Gender Chapter* makes explicit reference to SDG #5 and commits both countries to consult, gather data and cooperate in a number of different areas relating to gender equality. Cooperation activities between businesses and governments include:

- programmes on skills and capacity building for women in businesses, at work and on corporate boards;
- improving women's access to, and participation and leadership in . . . business;
- developing better practices to promote gender equality within enterprises; and
- fostering women's participation in decision-making positions in the . . . private sector.

(Global Affairs Canada, 2017b)

Despite the broad principles and enumeration of specific areas of cooperation, there is no dispute resolution mechanism for the Gender Chapter (Global Affairs Canada, 2017b). The Israeli-Canada Trade Agreement, negotiated the following year, contains a Gender Chapter with a dispute resolution process, although there are few commitments to enforce (Global Affairs Canada, 2018e). One pro-business policy organization characterized the chapter as "[a]t best . . . an aspirational first step to recognizing issues of gender discrimination in trade; at worst, it is a hollow declaration since it has no teeth" (Stephens, 2018: 4). Despite the Prime Minister's 2017 announcement that he hoped to obtain a Gender Chapter in a renegotiated North American Free Trade Agreement (as reported in McFarland, 2017), this did not transpire. However, Canada did commit in 2018 to ensuring that gender-based analyses accompany all trade negotiations, and its Trade Policy and Negotiations Branch has developed a Gender Pledge for staff who work on future negotiations (Global Affairs Canada, 2019b).

Despite the slow progress, support for addressing gender in trade agreements is building, with increased focus on how to make them more effective (Larouche-Maltais and MacLaren, 2019). There are suggestions that trade agreements incorporate protections and redress for human rights defenders (Barcia, 2017) and explicitly prohibit countries from allowing discrimination on the grounds of sex, among other grounds (Kenny, 2018). While unlikely that certain countries will accept these provisions, the gender chapters highlight the roles of businesses and governments in promoting gender equality in the international trade arena.

4 Supporting the Global Compact Network Canada (2018)

The Global Compact Network Canada (GCNC) has been slow to attract members compared to some other global compact country networks; less than 100 Canadian companies signed on to the UN Global Compact. The extractive industry (mining, oil and gas) forms the largest sector within the network, disproportionate to its status in the Canadian business community ("UN Global Compact", 2019). Canada has been a strong supporter of the GCNC, contributing financially, providing grants and endorsing the activities and positions of the GCNC. Although the GC country network's function is to bring businesses together in support of the UN Global Compact's Ten Principles, Canada has joined the GCNC as a "visionary supporter" (the highest membership level), which requires a CAD 25,000 annual fee (Status of Women Canada, 2018). One of the other four visionary supporters is Barrack Gold, which has received significant negative attention on the issue of gender equality (Hill et al., 2016)

On International Women's Day in 2018, Canada announced a CAD 858,500 grant to the GCNC for a three-year project to study "women's economic empowerment" (Status of Women Canada, 2019a). The GCNC, which promotes this project under SDG #5, received funds to "Defin[e] what Gender Equality at the workplace looks like" to explore "How will we recognize a company where Gender Equality exists? And to "Identify . . . and address . . . the wicked challenges and barriers that we, as companies and as a society, face in making this vision a reality". The GCNC is developing a gender certification programme for companies as part of this project (Status of Women Canada, 2018). Although Canada is one of the most advanced countries in the world in terms of gender equality laws, most of Canada's private sector is not covered by pay equity legislation. In addition, Canada has balked at taking legislative action to address the dearth of women on corporate boards. The results of this study have yet to be released, but it remains to be seen whether a business organization will recommend the government take concrete steps through regulation and legislation to advance gender equality as envisioned in the SDGs.

5 Gender-aware corruption (2018)

Canada has made efforts to link gender inequality and corruption, which are intimately connected (Kilgour, 2018). In 2018, Canada hosted a conference on corruption and human rights with a focus on gender in preparation of the meetings of the Organization of American States. Women activists from Latin America and the Caribbean were invited to share their experiences with corruption and showcase their work combatting it (Global Affairs Canada, 2018d). In addition, the 2018 Report to Parliament on Corruption addresses links between gender and corruption (Global Affairs Canada, 2018a).

In 2018, Canada endorsed the GCNC's efforts on anti-corruption, through encouraging Canadian businesses to participate in its fee-based webinars and indicating its support of the GCNC in the Report to Parliament on Corruption as evidence of Canada's progress on this issue (Global Affairs Canada, 2018a). Unfortunately, the GCNC's training on corruption does not address the gendered nature of corruption, and the GCNC's 140-page e-book on corruption does not mention women, gender or the gendered impacts of corruption (Global Compact Network Canada, 2017). This illustrates one of the pitfalls that can occur when governments endorse or recommend anti-corruption efforts led by the private sector – there is no guarantee that a feminist or gender-aware view on corruption will be addressed, despite endorsement from a feminist government.

6 Equality Fund (2018)

In 2018, Canada announced the Equality Fund and reallocated CAD 300 million in aid money to it the following year (Global Affairs Canada, 2019c). The Fund is designed to mobilize funds from philanthropic organizations and the private sector in support of gender equality and women's organizations (Equality Fund, 2019). This initiative aligns with the UN's acknowledgement that private sector funds are required to meet the SDGs:

> The finance needs for SDG investments are vast and urgent . . . the public sources of funding in all countries, rich and poor alike, clearly do not suffice to fund the SDGs. Hence, private finance is an essential component of the financing of the 2030 Agenda.
> *("SG-Financing-Strategy_Sep2018.Pdf", 2018)*

It has been suggested that governments may find it easier to raise money from the private sector in support of the SDGs rather than to implement policy and regulatory changes that challenge the status quo (Abshagen et al., 2018).

Despite some concerns about the details of the government's funding, one organization views it as "a game changer, a disruptor . . . to generate new money and assets to fund permanent change led by and for women around the world" (McLeod Group, 2019). One of the key recommendations of the *2019 Equal Measures 2030 SDG Gender Index* (where Canada scored 85%) is to "[p]rioritize funding and support for girls' and women's movements, advocates and champions from across sectors and at every level, from political leaders, to girl- and women-led movements in the smallest villages" (Equal Measures 2030, 2019). Many women's organizations, especially in the Global South, struggle with a lack of funding, which impacts negatively on their roles as essential partners in development and the attainment of the SDGs (Siyanga, 2016). Unless the funds are available to grassroots women's organizations in the Global South (which may be challenging the status quo in their countries), this type of fund could fail to change current economic and political structures that have often created and/perpetuated women's inequality.

7 Canadian Ombudsperson for Responsible Enterprise (2019)

In January 2018, Canada announced that it would establish an "independent Canadian Ombudsperson for Responsible Enterprise (CORE)", and linked this to its feminist foreign policy and the SDGs. In contrast to the previous CSR counsellor's limited advisory role, the "multisectoral" CORE would have a mandate to "investigate allegations of human rights abuses linked to Canadian corporate activity abroad . . . [and] will be empowered to independently investigate, report, recommend remedy and monitor its implementation". The Ombudsperson (CORE) was appointed in April 2019 but without the promised mandate, scope and independence (Status of Women Canada, 2019b).

The appointment announcement was met with criticism from civil society groups who had long campaigned for a stronger, independent role (Detloff, 2019; Kairos Canada, 2019; Swan, 2019). The promised independence did not materialize and few of the promised powers were given to the CORE, including the power to investigate and compel witnesses and documents. However, the CORE was given the power to investigate people who submit allegations about a company's misconduct, raising concern among human rights defenders (Simons, 2019). Advocates for gender equality have stressed the importance of having protections for human rights defenders: "[an] approach . . . based on feminist principles would pay particular attention to the impact of corporate activity on women's ability to exercise their rights . . . [and] would also seek to protect women's rights defenders, who organize against corporate abuses" (Rhodes, 2017: 11). There is concern that the CORE's powers to investigate complainants could result in retaliation or a censoring on the part of those who would otherwise make allegations of corporate abuses.

In July 2019, labour and civil society members resigned *en masse* from Canada's Advisory Body on Responsible Business Conduct Abroad (Maquila Solidarity Network, 2019), accusing Canada of "having bowed to industry pressure and reneged on concrete commitments" (CNCA, 2019). The responsible minister responded to the critics with a promise to clarify the CORE's roles in the summer of 2019, but this did not happen. There is speculation the government was "lobbied to death" to renege on its promises (Friedman, 2019). From January 2018 when the CORE policy was announced to when the appointment was made in April 2019, the two main lobby groups in the mining/extractive sector met with key decision makers and politicians on the CORE file over 500 times, with at least approximately 20 per cent of those meetings listed as international subject matter (Connolly, 2019; Friedman, 2019). The policy that was to have been critical to the rehabilitation of Canada's reputation abroad and to the commitment of a feminist foreign policy in support of the SDGs has garnered much criticism and little support and has highlighted key issues in the area of agenda setting, lobbying and the divergent interests and roles of government and business.

This brief discussion of some of the more high-profile Canadian government actions in support of the SDGs draws attention to a number of themes that should be considered essential elements in responsible management education. The next section identifies some of these themes.

Key themes for responsible management education

The complexity and multifaceted nature of the SDGs (especially of gender equality and women's empowerment) makes it difficult to identify successes and failures. However, an audit of Canada's SDG efforts found that Canada was using a "[n]arrow interpretation of sustainable development", had "[n]o national implementation plan and few national targets" and had "[n]o analysis of the extent to which individual policies and programs could contribute to achieving the 2030 Agenda targets and goals" (Office of the Auditor General Canada, 2018). In addition to these concerns, there are certain themes that are worthy of reflection arising out this brief survey of Canada's SDG actions.

The role of government

All parties need to acknowledge that the SDGs were adopted by governments, and the latter have the primary responsibility in working towards their achievement. Observers note that "more, not less, governance will be required to achieve the SDGs" (Agarwal et al., 2017: 2). Even though partnerships with business are essential, government's role is to lead, adopt policies and regulations and prioritize the SDGs. Voluntary actions on the part of businesses are not substitutes for lawmaking and government regulation (Ruggie, 2017). Canada has taken a backseat on some issues and let other actors set the agenda (Maher et al., 2019: 1170). As discussed in this chapter, some critics have suggested that Canada's backtracking on the promised powers of the CORE was a result of extensive lobbying. Governments need to be aware of the double-hatted role of private-sector companies combining their "public" pro-SDG roles with lobbying interests and practices that may run counter to sustainable development principles (Kamphof and Melissen, 2018).

The role of business

Businesses are being asked to become nonaccountable partners in the delivery of public policy goals. Businesses do not have the same mandates and responsibilities as governments with regard to SDG implementation (Kamphof and Melissen, 2018). Identifying that governments and businesses wear different hats does not mean there are no shared interests; for example, mining companies need a healthy workforce and a clean, sustainable and peaceful environment in order to optimize their investment (Fraser, 2019). It is also important to recognize that businesses are not homogeneous (Marques, 2016). While there are some exemplary business contributions to the SDGs, others could and should be more supportive of government actions on the SDGs (Agarwal et al., 2017). There is an assumption that businesses have the capacity and the will to work towards the SDGs, but in reality the characteristics of those businesses may be constraining.

Diversity of stakeholders needed

Multi-stakeholder engagement in monitoring and in keeping parties accountable is important, especially by civil society groups (Fukuda-Parr, 2016; Winkler and Williams, 2017). The resignation of the civil society representatives of the Advisory Body on Responsible Business Conduct Abroad, leaving only business representatives, means that important perspectives will be missing. It is also critical that voices, including women's voices, from the Global South are listened to (Musindarwezo, 2018). The Equality Fund and the Feminist Foreign Policy Assistance could play pivotal roles in ensuring this happens.

Risk of SDG washing

SDG washing – "positively contributing to some of the SDGs while ignoring the negative impact of others" – is a risk (Eccles and Karbassi, 2019). Because SDG #5 is a cross-cutting goal, there is a danger "that governments may choose to neglect issues that are contentious or challenge underlying power relations" (UN Women, 2018). With the SDGs there are so many goals, targets and indicators that there is a risk that companies and governments only pick and choose rights that are palatable or market friendly. This can be a problem for gender equality, given the power shift that is required to achieve it.

Mythmaking

Progress towards the SDGs must be measured against the goals, indicators and targets themselves, not just to the commitments made by governments and businesses. The concept of mythmaking can be useful to understand the harm of empty commitments to sustainability (Ferns et al., 2019). Some governments and businesses have strategies that undermine sustainable development despite public commitments to the contrary (Kamphof and Melissen, 2018). It is thus important to have concrete commitments where progress can be measured.

Integration of gender equality

It is essential to address gender equality and women's empowerment as stand-alone subjects in RME but also, as with the SDGs, view them as cross-cutting issues and adopt a gender-based approach to other topics in management education, such as finance or accounting (Flynn et al., 2015).

Concluding comments

In sum, each initiative discussed in this chapter raises questions about the multi-stakeholder path to the attainment of the SDGs and provides significant opportunities for further interrogation in both management education and policy settings. The SDG framework arose out of the consensus of the international community. Despite numerous critiques, the SDGs provide a set of ideas and aspirations that can help mobilize governments and nongovernmental actors such as businesses, civil society and students. Getting gender equality as a stand-alone goal with an acknowledgement that all other goals have gender dimensions was an important achievement.

Despite the projected utility of the SDGs, there is concern that the enthusiasm for the SDGs is waning already (Winkler and Williams, 2017). Canada's embrace of feminism in connection with the SDG commitments could perhaps best be understood in reference to the concept of "market feminism", which results in "public policy agendas [which] are increasingly mediated via private sector organizations according to the logic of the market" (Kantola and Squires, 2012: 383). Critics of Canada's path to the attainment of SDG #5 suggest that despite a feminist foreign policy, it seems to be "business as usual":

> it does little for the . . . government to tout a foreign policy that purports to promote the rights of women. . . . As long as the government continues to agree to "business as usual", the world's women . . . hardly stand a chance.
>
> *(Woodley, 2019)*

However, "business as usual" cannot continue (Winkler and Williams, 2017: 1025). Responsible management education has a role to play in ensuring it does not.

References

Abshagen, M., Cavazzini, A., Graen, L. and Obenland, W. "Hijacking the SDGs: The Private Sector and the Sustainable Development Goals." Berlin: German NGO Forum on Environment and Development, 2018. www.brot-fuer-die-welt.de/fileadmin/mediapool/2_Downloads/Fachinformationen/Analyse/Analyse78-en-v08.pdf.

Agarwal, Namit, Gneiting, Uwe and Mhlanga, Ruth. "Raising the Bar: Rethinking the Role of Business in the Sustainable Development Goals." *Oxfam*, 2017. www.oxfam.org/en/research/raising-bar-rethinking-role-business-sustainable-development-goals.

Aggestam, Karin, Bergman Rosamond, Annika and Kronsell, Annica. "Theorising Feminist Foreign Policy." *International Relations*, 33(1), 2019: 23–39. https://doi.org/10.1177/0047117818811892.

Asquith, Lyric Thompson, Christina. "One Small Step for Feminist Foreign Policy." *Foreign Policy* (blog), 2018. https://foreignpolicy.com/2018/09/20/one-small-step-for-feminist-foreign-policy-women-canada/.

Barcia, Immaculada. "Women Human Rights Defenders Confronting Extractive Industries an Overview of Critical Risks and Human Rights Obligations." *AWID, WHRDIC*, 2017. www.awid.org/sites/default/files/atoms/files/whrds-confronting_extractive_industries_report-eng.pdf.

Chapnick, Adam. "The Origins of Canada's Feminist Foreign Policy." *International Journal*, 74(2), 2019: 191–205. https://doi.org/10.1177/0020702019850827.

CNCA. "News Release: Government of Canada Turns Back on Communities Harmed by Canadian Mining Overseas, Loses Trust of Canadian Civil Society." *CNCA*, July 11, 2019. http://cnca-rcrce.ca/recent-works/news-release-government-of-canada-turns-back-on-communities-harmed-by-canadian-mining-overseas-loses-trust-of-canadian-civil-society/.

Connolly, Charlotte. "Report on Lobbying by Mining Industry." *Justice and Corporate Accountability Project*, Osgoode Hall Law School, 2019. https://justice-project.org/wp-content/uploads/2019/07/2.-Report-on-Lobbying-by-Mining-Industry-july-24-fin.pdf.

Courtney, Suzanne. "Canada's Foreign Aid Policy Isn't Making Much Progress on a Gender Equal World." *National Post*, October 30, 2018. www.nationalpost.com.

"Creating an International Gender and Peace Agenda: Impact of Canadian Mines in Latin America." 2016. www.wilpf.org/wilpf-publications/.

Deneault, A. and Sacher, W. *Imperial Canada Inc: Legal Haven of Choice for the World's Mining Industries.* Vancouver: Talon Books, 2012.

Detloff, Dean. "Canadian Catholics Skeptical New Oversight Office Will Stop Mining Exploitation Abroad." *America Magazine*, April 29, 2019. www.americamagazine.org/politics-society/2019/04/29/canadian-catholics-skeptical-new-oversight-office-will-stop-mining.

Ditchburn, Jennifer. "Women No Longer a 'Curiosity' in Cabinet | CBC News." *CBC*, November 4, 2015. www.cbc.ca/news/politics/canada-trudeau-liberal-government-cabinet-1.3304590.

Eccles, Robert G. and Karbassi, Lila. "The Right Way to Support the Sustainable Development Goals." *MIT Sloan Management Review* (blog), 2019. https://sloanreview.mit.edu/article/the-right-way-to-support-the-uns-sustainable-development-goals/.

Equality Fund. "Innovative New Canadian Initiative Will Mobilize Unprecedented Funds towards Gender Equality." *Equality Fund*, 2019. https://equalityfund.ca/news/partnership-for-gender-equality.

Equal Measures 2030. "Harnessing the Power of Data for Gender Equality: Introducing the 2019 EM2030 SDG Gender Index." 2019. https://data.em2030.org/wp-content/uploads/2019/05/EM2030_2019_Global_Report_ENG.pdf.

Eulich, Whitney and Llana, Sara Miller. "When Mining Companies Work Abroad, Should Justice Follow Them Home?" *Christian Science Monitor*, April 9, 2019. www.csmonitor.com/World/Americas/2019/0409/When-mining-companies-work-abroad-should-justice-follow-them-home.

Ferns, George, Amaeshi, Kenneth and Lambert, Aliette. "Drilling Their Own Graves: How the European Oil and Gas Supermajors Avoid Sustainability Tensions Through Myth-making." *Journal of Business Ethics*, 158(1), 2019: 201–231. https://doi.org/10.1007/s10551-017-3733-x.

Flynn, Patricia M., Haynes, Kathryn and Kilgour, Maureen A. *Integrating Gender Equality into Business and Management Education: Lessons Learned and Challenges Remaining.* Sheffield, UK: Greenleaf Publishing Limited, 2015.

Fraser, Jocelyn. "Creating Shared Value as a Business Strategy for Mining to Advance the United Nations Sustainable Development Goals." *The Extractive Industries and Society*, May 2019. https://doi.org/10.1016/j.exis.2019.05.011.

Friedman, Gabriel. "'Lobbied to Death': Liberals Face Backlash over Corporate Responsibility Ombudsman." *The Telegram*, 2019. www.thetelegram.com/news/canada/lobbied-to-death-liberals-face-backlash-over-corporate-responsibility-ombudsman-299368/.

Fukuda-Parr, Sakiko. "From the Millennium Development Goals to the Sustainable Development Goals: Shifts in Purpose, Concept, and Politics of Global Goal Setting for Development." *Gender & Development*, 24(1), 2016: 43–52. https://doi.org/10.1080/13552074.2016.1145895.

Global Affairs Canada. "Canada's Feminist International Assistance Policy." February 21, 2017. 2017a. www.international.gc.ca/world-monde/issues_development-enjeux_developpement/priorities-priorites/policy-politique.aspx?lang=eng#4.

Global Affairs Canada. "Appendix II: Chapter N Bis: Trade and Gender." June 5, 2017. 2017b. www.international.gc.ca/trade-commerce/trade-agreements-accords-commerciaux/agr-acc/chile-chili/fta-ale/2017_Amend_Modif-App2-Chap-N.aspx?lang=eng.

Global Affairs Canada. "Canada's Fight against Foreign Bribery: Nineteenth Annual Report to Parliament." Government of Canada. 2018a. www.international.gc.ca.

Global Affairs Canada. "Canada's Implementation of the 2030 Agenda for Sustainable Development: Voluntary National Review." Global Affairs Canada. 2018b. https://sustainabledevelopment.un.org/content/documents/20033CanadasVoluntaryNationalReviewENv6.pdf.

Global Affairs Canada. "Address by Minister Freeland to Open the Women Foreign Ministers' Meeting." Speeches. Gcnws, September 25, 2018. 2018c. www.canada.ca/en/global-affairs/news/2018/09/address-by-minister-freeland-to-open-the-women-foreign-ministers-meeting.html.

Global Affairs Canada. "Canada Hosts Conference on Human Rights and Corruption in the Americas." News Releases, March 19, 2018. 2018d. www.canada.ca/en/global-affairs/news/2018/03/canada-hosts-conference-on-human-rights-and-corruption-in-the-americas.html.

Global Affairs Canada. "Canada-Israel Free Trade Agreement: Trade and Gender." May 28, 2018. 2018e. www.international.gc.ca/trade-commerce/trade-agreements-accords-commerciaux/agr-acc/israel/fta-ale/text-texte/13.aspx?lang=eng.

Global Affairs Canada. "Canada-Chile Free Trade Agreement." 2019. 2019a. https://international.gc.ca/trade-commerce/trade-agreements-accords-commerciaux/agr-acc/chile-chili/index.aspx?lang=eng.

Global Affairs Canada. "Global Affairs Canada's Trade Policy and Negotiations Branch's Gender Pledge." March 11, 2019. 2019b. www.international.gc.ca/gac-amc/campaign-campagne/inclusive_trade/gender-genre.aspx?lang=eng.

Global Affairs Canada. "Global Affairs Canada: The Equality Fund: Transforming the Way We Support Women's Organizations and Movements Working to Advance Women's Rights and Gender Equality." Backgrounders. Gcnws, June 2, 2019. 2019c. www.canada.ca/en/global-affairs/news/2019/06/global-affairs-canada – the-equality-fund-transforming-the-way-we-support-womens-organizations-and-movements-working-to-advance-womens-rights-and-g.html.

Global Compact Network Canada. "Designing an Anti-Corruption Compliance Program: A Guide for Canadian Businesses." 2017. www.globalcompact.ca.

Haslam, Paul Alexander, Tanimoune, Nasser Ary and Razeq, Zarlasht M. "Do Canadian Mining Firms Behave Worse Than Other Companies? Quantitative Evidence from Latin America." *Canadian Journal of Political Science/Revue Canadienne de Science Politique*, 51(3), 2018: 521–551. https://doi.org/10.1017/S0008423918000185.

Haynes, Kathryn and Murray, Alan. "Sustainability as a Lens to Explore Gender Equality: A Missed Opportunity for Responsible Management." In Patricia M. Flynn, Kathryn Haynes and Maureen A. Kilgour (eds.), *Integrating Gender Equality into Management Education: Lessons Learned and Challenges Remaining* (For Responsibility in Management Education). Sheffield: Greenleaf Publishing, 2015.

Hill, Christina, Madden, Chris and Ezpeleta, Maria. "Gender and the Extractive Industries: Putting Gender on the Corporate Agenda." *Oxfam*, 2016. https://oxfamilibrary.openrepository.com/bitstream/handle/10546/620776/bp-gender-extractives-corporate-agenda-010516-en.pdf?sequence=1&isAllowed=y.

Imai, Shin, Gardner, Leah and Weinberger, Sarah. "The 'Canada Brand': Violence and Canadian Mining Companies in Latin America." *SSRN Scholarly Paper ID 2886584*. Rochester, NY: Social Science Research Network, 2017. https://papers.ssrn.com/abstract=2886584.

Kairos Canada. "Canadian Government Reneges on Promise to Create Independent Corporate Human Rights Watchdog." *KAIROS Canada*, April 8, 2019. www.kairoscanada.org/canadian-government-reneges-promise-create-independent-corporate-human-rights-watchdog.

Kamphof, Ries and Melissen, Jan. "SDGs, Foreign Ministries and the Art of Partnering with the Private Sector." *Global Policy*, 9(3), 2018: 327–335. https://doi.org/10.1111/1758-5899.12563.

Kantola, Johanna and Squires, Judith. "From State Feminism to Market Feminism?" *International Political Science Review*, 33(4), 2012: 382–400. https://doi.org/10.1177/0192512111432513.

Kenny, Charles. "A Gender Equality Toolbox: These Areas of Society Still Need Work: Here's How to Do It." *Opencanada.Org* (blog), March 13, 2018. www.opencanada.org.

Kilgour, Maureen A. "Corruption and Gender." In Deborah C. Poff and Alex C. Michalos (eds.), *Encyclopedia of Business and Professional Ethics*. Cham: Springer International Publishing, 2018: 1–6. https://doi.org/10.1007/978-3-319-23514-1_135-1.

Kourula, Arno, Moon, Jeremy, Salles-Djelic, Marie-Laure and Wickert, Christopher. "New Roles of Government in the Governance of Business Conduct: Implications for Management and Organizational Research." *Organization Studies*, 40(8), 2019: 1101–1123. https://doi.org/10.1177/0170840619852142.

Larouche-Maltais, Alexandre and MacLaren, Barbara. "Making Gender-Responsive Free Trade Agreements." *Conference Board of Canada*, 2019. www.conferenceboard.ca/temp/57fc239c-d5b4-42ec-8ac2-6af7c234c955/10077_GenderandTrade-RPT.pdf.

Maher, Rajiv, Valenzuela, Francisco and Böhm, Steffen. "The Enduring State: An Analysis of Governance-Making in Three Mining Conflicts." *Organization Studies*, 40(8), 2019: 1169–1191. https://doi.org/10.1177/0170840619847724.

Maquila Solidarity Network. "Civil Society, Labour Representatives Resign from Canadian Government's Corporate Accountability Multi-Stakeholder Body." July 12, 2019. www.maquilasolidarity.org/en/civil-society-labour-representatives-resign-canadian-government-s-corporate-accountability-multi.

Marques, José Carlos. "Private Regulatory Fragmentation as Public Policy: Governing Canada's Mining Industry." *Journal of Business Ethics*, 135(4), 2016: 617–630. https://doi.org/10.1007/s10551-014-2377-3.

Mawdsley, Emma. "'From Billions to Trillions': Financing the SDGs in a World 'beyond Aid'." *Dialogues in Human Geography*, 8(2), 2018: 191–195. https://doi.org/10.1177/2043820618780789.

McFarland, Janet. "NAFTA Must Include Gender Equality Protection, Trudeau Says: The Globe and Mail." *Globe and Mail*, September 11, 2017. www.theglobeandmail.com/news/national/nafta-must-include-gender-equality-protection-trudeau-says/article36227621/.

McLeod Group. "Gender Lens Investing: Canada's New Equality Fund." 2019. www.mcleodgroup.ca/2019/06/gender-lens-investing-canadas-new-equality-fund/.

Musindarwezo, Dinah. "The 2030 Agenda from a Feminist Perspective: No Meaningful Gains without Greater Accountability for Africa's Women." *Agenda*, 32(1), 2018: 25–35. https://doi.org/10.1080/10130950.2018.1427693.

Office of the Auditor General Canada. "Report 2: Canada's Preparedness to Implement the United Nations' Sustainable Development Goals." April 24, 2018. www.oag-bvg.gc.ca/internet/English/parl_cesd_201804_02_e_42993.html.

Parks, Rachel Bernice and Orozco, Diana Catalina Buitrago. "Closing the Gender Gap in Extractives: What Has Been Done and What Have We Learned?" *World Bank Group*, 2018/87. http://documents.worldbank.org/curated/en/187011536096997428/pdf/129731-BRI-PUBLIC-VC-LW87-OKR.pdf.

Percival, Valerie. "What a Real Feminist Foreign Policy Looks Like." *OpenCanada*, May 12, 2017. www.opencanada.org/features/what-real-feminist-foreign-policy-looks/.

Piscopo, Jennifer M. "States as Gender Equality Activists: The Evolution of Quota Laws in Latin America." *Latin American Politics and Society*, 57(3), 2015: 27–49. https://doi.org/10.1111/j.1548-2456.2015.00278.x.

Pittman, Sarah. "How Feminist Is Canada's New Foreign Aid Really?" *Centre for Feminist Foreign Policy* (blog), October 7, 2017. https://centreforfeministforeignpolicy.org/journal/2017/10/5/how-feminist-is-canadas-foreign-aid-really.

Rhodes, Francesca. "Tackling Inequalities in the Global Economy: Making Canada's Foreign Policy Work for Women." *Oxfam Canada*, 2017. www.oxfam.ca/wp-content/uploads/2017/11/tackling_inequalities_in_the_global_economy_report.pdf.

Ruggie, J. G. "The Social Construction of the UN Guiding Principles on Business and Human Rights." Corporate Responsibility Initiative Working Paper No. 67. 2017. Cambridge, MA: John F. Kennedy School of Government, Harvard University.

"SG-Financing-Strategy_Sep2018.Pdf." 2018. Accessed August 8, 2019. www.un.org/sustainabledevelopment/wp-content/uploads/2018/09/SG-Financing-Strategy_Sep2018.pdf.

Simons, Penelope. "Trudeau Government's Global Reputation at Risk Due to Poor Corporate Accountability." *The Globe and Mail*, June 5, 2019. www.theglobeandmail.com.

Siyanga, Lumba. "Funding Equality: Donor Trends and Women's Rights Organisations." *Gender and Development Network Briefings*, 2016. https://gadnetwork.org/gadn-news/2016/6/21/feminist-development-alternatives-pack-now-live.

Srdjan, Vucetic. "A Nation of Feminist Arms Dealers? Canada and Military Exports." *International Journal: Toronto*, 72(4), 2017: 503–519. http://dx.doi.org.uwinnipeg.idm.oclc.org/10.1177/0020702017740156.

Status of Women Canada. "Global Compact Network Canada." *Backgrounders: Women and Gender Equality*, March 8, 2018. www.canada.ca/en/status-women/news/2018/03/global-compact-network-canada.html.

Status of Women Canada. "Minister Monsef Announces Funding for Women's Economic Empowerment on International Women's Day." 2019a. www.newswire.ca/news-releases/minister-monsef-announces-funding-for-womens-economic-empowerment-on-international-womens-day-676256743.html.

Status of Women Canada. "Responsible Business Conduct Abroad: Questions and Answers." 2019b. www.international.gc.ca/trade-agreements-accords-commerciaux/topics-domaines/other-autre/faq.aspx?lang=eng.

Stephens, Hugh. "Canada's Progressive Trade Agenda and a Free Trade Agreement with China: Are They Incompatible?" *SSRN Scholarly Paper ID 3263714*. Rochester, NY: Social Science Research Network, 2018. https://papers.ssrn.com/abstract=3263714.

Swan, Michael. "Ombud's Much-Delayed Arrival Met with Anger." *Register*, 2019. www.catholicregister.org/item/29307-ombud-s-much-delayed-arrival-met-with-anger.

Transforming Our World: The 2030 Agenda for Sustainable Development. 2015. https://sustainabledevelopment.un.org/post2015/transformingourworld.

Trudeau, Justin. "(5) Justin Trudeau on Twitter:'I Am a Feminist: I'm Proud to Be a Feminist: #upfordebate'/Twitter." *Twitter*, September 25, 2015. https://twitter.com/justintrudeau/status/646103864454713344.

"UN Global Compact." 2019. www.unglobalcompact.org/.

UN Women. *Turning Promises Into Action: Gender Equality in the 2030 Agenda for Sustainable Development*. New York, NY: UN Women, 2018. Accessed May 12, 2019. www.unwomen.org/en/digital-library/publications/2018/2/gender-equality-in-the-2030-agenda-for-sustainable-development-2018.

Vucetic, Srdjan. "A Nation of Feminist Arms Dealers? Canada and Military Exports." *International Journal*, 72(4), 2017: 503–519. https://doi.org/10.1177/0020702017740156.

Ward, Bernie, Strongman, John, Eftimie, Adriana and Heller, Katherine. "Gender-Sensitive Approaches for the Extractive Industry in Peru: Improving the Impact on Women in Poverty and Their Families: Guide for Improving Practice." *67754: The World Bank*, 2011. http://documents.worldbank.org/curated/en/961001468058746060/Gender-sensitive-approaches-for-the-extractive-industry-in-Peru-improving-the-impact-on-women-in-poverty-and-their-families-guide-for-improving-practice.

Winkler, Inga T. and Williams, Carmel. "The Sustainable Development Goals and Human Rights: A Critical Early Review." *The International Journal of Human Rights*, 21(8), 2017: 1023–1028. https://doi.org/10.1080/13642987.2017.1348695.

Woodley, Thomas. "Liberals Lack the Political Will to Truly Push a Feminist Foreign Policy." *HuffPost Canada* (blog), March 8, 2019. www.huffingtonpost.ca/thomas-woodley/trudeau-feminist-foreign-policy_a_23686764/.

PART IV

Programs and partnerships in developing countries

13

SOCIAL INNOVATORS AS DRIVERS OF SOCIAL TRANSFORMATION IN MOROCCO

Majid Kaissar el Ghaib and Brahim Allali

Abstract

Like other developing economies, Morocco struggles against very compelling social and economic issues such as unemployment, food security, education, healthcare and human development. To cope with these structural issues, to lay the foundation for inclusive growth, and to achieve the United Nations (UN) Sustainable Development Goals (SDGs), social entrepreneurship offers very promising paths toward sustainable and inclusive solutions. Yet, it is critical first to create an environment conducive enough for social innovations to blossom and grow into successful inclusive businesses. In this chapter, two such businesses spun off from a social incubator, Enactus Morocco, are presented, and lessons stemming from such experiences are drawn and discussed.

Introduction

Today's world is faced with severe social, economic and environmental challenges. Poor and emerging countries are particularly hit by the externalities of economic transitions, deep social fractures and climate change threats.

Like other developing economies, Morocco does not create enough wealth to meet the pressing social challenges in terms of job creation, food security, education, healthcare and human development. To overcome these structural issues, to lay the foundation for inclusive growth and to achieve the UN Sustainable Development Goals (SDGs), Morocco can and should rely on a new generation of passionate and visionary social entrepreneurs to trigger and drive the needed social transformation of the country.

Indeed, social entrepreneurs are the biggest source of social innovation to date (Schöning, 2013). They are change agents who disrupt the status quo and "open up the space for solutions to take root, scale, and become the foundation of profound social transformation and a more peaceful and prosperous world" (Skoll Foundation, 2017).

Nevertheless, for a class of social innovators to emerge, it is paramount to invest in education, mentoring and stewardship of would-be social entrepreneurs, a role played nowadays in Morocco by some non-governmental organizations (NGOs) such as the Moroccan branch of Enactus in alignment with the UN SDGs, to address the country's major challenges.

This chapter presents some major social innovation practices in vogue in Morocco as well as the case of Enactus Morocco as a platform to prepare and launch high-impact innovative social projects. Two cases of incubated women social innovators are also presented and discussed in the light of the UN SDGs. These cases show that it is possible to set up a profitable business while positively impacting society.

Main challenges to social transformation in Morocco

Societal deficits in Morocco: current situation

Many efforts have been made to take Morocco to the level of an emerging economy. With the implementation of ambitious industrialization programs, access to renewable energies and the establishment of modern basic infrastructures, the country has given itself the means to achieve sustainable economic growth. Today, Morocco is an attractive country for foreign investment. The business environment, while still having some important areas for improvement, is quite conducive and can lead to the sought-after economic takeoff. However, given the constraints of population pressure, it would be difficult to create enough jobs for all the people entering the labor market. Moreover, many challenges remain in terms of human development, education, health and environmental protection to enable Morocco to make the transition to an emerging economy status.

In its 2018 report, Oxfam (2018) states that Morocco has the highest level of inequality in North Africa. On average, the standard of living of the richest 10 percent in Morocco is 12 times higher than that of the poorest 10 percent. Although the poverty rate was reduced threefold between 2001 and 2014, the number of poor and vulnerable people is still high, estimated respectively at 1.6 and 4.2 million inhabitants for a total population of about 35 million.

Education is also one of the major challenges facing Morocco. The World Economic Forum (WEF) ranks Morocco 119th out of 137 countries in the quality of primary education and 101st in vocational training and higher education. In terms of capacity for innovation, the country is ranked 83rd (WEF, 2018). For Oxfam (2018), education plays a key role in creating and reproducing inequalities. Despite undeniable improvements, one-third of the Moroccan

population is still illiterate, and nearly three quarters of young university gradu-
ates are unemployed.

In terms of health, the WEF ranks Morocco 81st out of 137 countries (WEF,
2018). Despite the efforts of the Moroccan government, the World Health
Organization (WHO) says that 40 percent of deaths are due to cancer and
metabolic diseases, 20 percent of the population is at least ten kilometers away
from a health facility and only six doctors are available per 10,000 inhabitants
(WHO, 2017).

Social inequalities and inadequacies in education and health contribute to the
weakness of the country's human development index, which ranks Morocco 123rd
out of 188 countries (Oxfam, 2018).

Finally, with regard to environmental challenges, Morocco remains fragile and
threatened by the risks of climate change and pollution. Desertification, water stress,
deforestation, air and water pollution and solid waste management are all issues that
threaten the environment in Morocco and its sustainable development.

Despite some initiatives such as the National Initiative for Human Development,
the Rural Drinking Water Supply Program, the National Construction Program
and the Global Rural Electrification Program, social disparities and environmental
challenges are still important and impede the country's development (El Ghaib and
Chaker, 2018).

Societal deficits in Morocco in relation to the SDGs

In Morocco, almost all the 17 SDGs defined in the UN 2030 Agenda are necessary to achieve an inclusive and sustainable future. However, given the most
compelling challenges of the country, priority should be given to the specific
SDGs given in Figure 13.1, as they can lead to a systemic change in the Moroccan society:

FIGURE 13.1 Most challenging SDGs in Morocco

Social innovation and social entrepreneurs

"Social innovation" as a new concept, and "social entrepreneurs" as change agents can play key roles in supporting state and private actors in solving societal issues that threaten growth and prosperity. They often go where governments and corporations do not dare to venture. However, they face many hurdles and impediments that must be removed to allow them to play their roles more effectively.

Social innovation: the concept

Defined by the European Commission as an innovation that is social both in its ends and in its means, this type of innovation represents new ideas (including products, services and business models) that simultaneously meet social needs (more effectively than alternatives) and create new social relationships or collaboration (European Commission, 2017). Mulgan et al. (2007) define social innovation as "innovative activities and services that are motivated by the goal of meeting a social need and that are predominantly developed and diffused through organizations whose primary purposes are social." The Young Foundation (2017) considers social innovation as "a new approach to tackling intractable or entrenched, or emergent social issues."

However, social innovation cannot happen without passionate and visionary social entrepreneurs (Schöning, 2013). Indeed, they are change agents who disrupt the status quo and "open up the space for solutions to take root, scale, and become the foundation of profound social transformation and a more peaceful and prosperous world" (Skoll Foundation, 2017).

Freed from traditional business thinking, social entrepreneurs are good at spotting innovation opportunities and transforming them into large-scale viable solutions. They rely heavily on design thinking as one of the most compelling processes for creating disruptive solutions for "extreme" social needs (Brown and Wyatt, 2010). Through an approach centered on the users and their needs, the work of social innovators is mainly based on the iterative revision of the overlapping "spaces" of inspiration, ideation and implementation. By working closely with users, design thinkers (Brown and Wyatt, 2010) and human-centered designers (IDEO, 2015) enable high-impact solutions to come from the bottom rather than being imposed from the top.

Impact scaling issues

However, social innovators are often faced with the classical "chasm" between ideation and successful scaling-up of the solution. Although this pattern is present within any typical innovation life cycle curve, it is particularly challenging in the social innovation area, which is dominated by "passionate and enthusiastic Social Entrepreneurs who burn for their solutions, [and who give] little attention . . . to the next steps" (Osburg, 2013).

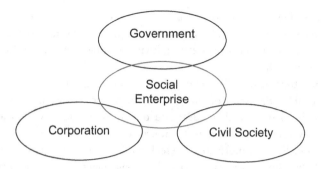

FIGURE 13.2 The social enterprise in the social ecosystem

Trapped between potentially revolutionary social innovations and the inability to readily transform them into scalable value solutions, social entrepreneurs occupy the empty space no one wants to enter, especially in ecosystems that do not foster creative entrepreneurial action for society (cf. Figure 13.2). Therefore, the need for structured working frameworks for social innovation is pressing. In Morocco where governance, institutional and cultural barriers are still important, such frameworks are even more essential for the advancement of social innovation (El Ghaib and Chaker, 2018).

Financing and partnerships issues

In setting the 2030 Agenda for Sustainable Development, the UN had recognized SDG #17 "Partnership for the goals" as one of the main goals to achieve. Indeed, "an unprecedented level of cooperation and collaboration among civil society, business, government, NGOs, foundations and others" is required for the achievement of sustainable development of our planet (Stibbe et al., 2018). In fact, this partnership goal came as a response to the limitations of traditional state-led, top-down development approaches used.

For social entrepreneurs to implement their solutions on a large scale, strong partnerships with governments and corporations are necessary. Social innovators, like all entrepreneurs, need strong financial support to scale their venture. It is not about charity or philanthropy; rather, it is about partnerships that set the foundations for the cocreation of a sustainable and more impactful value.

Enactus Morocco (EM): a social educator and changemaker

The Moroccan social innovation ecosystem

In analyzing the successes of, and challenges faced by, two social enterprises currently active across Morocco, it is important to understand the ecosystem facilitating their formation, acceleration and financing. The social innovation ecosystem in

Morocco is still in its embryotic stages. There are three layers of organizations within this ecosystem that can be grouped as inspirers, accelerators/incubators and funders. The inspirers are organizations that encourage young adults to pursue social entrepreneurship. Currently, the main inspirer is EM, which offers a platform for university students to collaborate and create social enterprises.

EM has enabled the two women entrepreneurs, whose case studies are presented in this chapter, to nurture their ideas and develop their businesses. It also acts as one of the key social incubators in Morocco, alongside the Moroccan Center for Innovation and Social Enterprise. These incubators provide training, mentoring and capacity building at the pre-seed and seeding stages of business development. The third and final level of the ecosystem is the funders, who finance the startups through various types of investment capital, including grant, equity and honor loans. Office Chérifien des Phosphates (OCP) Group and Caisse Centrale de Garantie are among the main funders. Because of the relative newness of the ecosystem, its structure is still new, and it lacks effectiveness in its ability to ensure the success of these blossoming social enterprises.

Enactus Morocco (EM)

EM is a nonprofit organization currently headed by Maha Echchefaa (cf. Figure 13.3). Maha is a woman social entrepreneur. She graduated from university as an IT engineer. Her passion for social entrepreneurship developed while volunteering in international and local NGOs to address Morocco's social challenges. She joined EM in 2015 and has been the Country Leader since 2018. EM was founded in 2003 as an affiliate of the international nonprofit organization Enactus (Enactus Morocco, 2018). EM was the foundation by which the two social enterprises came to fruition and has assisted in the development of over 20,000 students since its conception. Enactus' platform allows it to connect students and influence their business and leadership development through inspirational conferences and empowerment programs and also through a series of challenges and competitions as described in Figure 13.4.

FIGURE 13.3 Enactus Morocco – logo and country leader, (Maha Echchefaa)
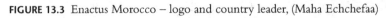

Idea challenges	Action challenges	Impact challenges	National Competition	World Cup
Pitching of +300 ideas	Pitching of 200 projects	Presentation of 120 projects	+1500 Participants	36 Countries
+500 Participants	1200 Participants	2000 Participants		3000 Participants

FIGURE 13.4 Successive phases of Enactus Morocco's yearly competitions

All companies founded through Enactus must adhere to the "Triple Bottom Line," which requires them to formulate their business models around economic wealth creation, human development and environmental protection. Since 2015, Enactus also requires businesses to follow the UN's SDGs. EM is currently connected to 119 universities in Morocco and in 2017 helped over 5,500 students create sustainable businesses. Fifty-five percent of these students are female. It launched its incubator, EMPACT, in 2015 with the help of the OCP Foundation. The incubation program assists the progress of high-impact startups through funding, mentoring and networking events, which further leverage these businesses.

Business model

Originally, EM was mainly financed through philanthropy and corporate donations but was struggling to raise the capital needed to scale up its business and impact more people. In 2013, it decided to shift its business model to one of creating shared value (CSV). The CSV concept (Porter and Kramer, 2011) was introduced to "enhance the competitiveness of a company while simultaneously advancing the economic and social conditions of communities in which it operates".

This has allowed EM to focus more on mentoring, training and financing. In shifting its business model, EM was able to increase its revenues in the course of three years from US$150,000 to US$1,200,000 and to provide the opportunity for teams to attain up to US$10,000 in grant money and US$25,000 in interest-free loans.

Social impact

The CSV model also expands EM's value proposition, allowing for larger social impact. The number of teams increased from 47 in 2014 to 119 in 2017. In 2017, EM implemented 256 projects allowing for the creation of more than 600 jobs and more than doubling the number of people impacted by the program from 80,000 to 195,000.

Illustrative cases

Go Energyless Solutions (GES)

GES is a social enterprise aiming to generalize the use of energy-saving products globally, starting with the North African region. Raowia Lamhar, women CEO and cofounder of GES, started this company during her student years at the university (cf. Figure 13.5). She joined the Enactus local team with the intent of tackling some key social issues related to environmental sustainability, job creation and waste reduction. GES designs, manufactures and markets sustainable products with a human-centric design process that also drives GES' business model.

"Fresh it," the first product GES developed is an all-natural, energyless refrigerator meant for rural areas of Morocco, where up to 45 percent of the population does not have access to electricity. GES' innovative, handcrafted clay-made refrigerator requires no electricity; holds up to eight kilograms of products and can keep produce, drinks and temperature-sensitive products, such as medicine, cool for up to 15 days. Such an innovation hugely contributed to reducing the percentage of food spoiled due to absence of refrigeration, which had been estimated at 80 percent.

Business model

The core of GES' business model is its value proposition to democratize access to energy-saving products globally. As Raowia describes, "Our business model is based on customers' needs, innovation and successful solutions." This is achieved by providing products like "Fresh it" in two versions to two key customer segments. A high-end version is marketed and sold to organic food and Lifestyle of Health and Sustainability (LOHAS) consumers for $50. A basic version is sold for $22 in rural communities to families with lower buying power and limited to no access to electricity.

FIGURE 13.5 Go Energyless Solutions – logo and CEO (Raowia Lamhar)

The revenue model is that of "the rich compensates for the poor," which allows GES to cover its production costs and provide "Fresh it" at an affordable price to rural consumers. To build trust and customer relationships with the people in the rural communities, GES employs local ambassadors to sell its products. For the LOHAS, GES currently sells its products online and looks forward to selling in larger quantities globally in stores. GES subcontracts the production of "Fresh it" to potters in Tameslouht, in the Marrakech region, thus contributing to creating stable and high-paying jobs for local potters.

Current impact

GES strives to revitalize the clay industry in Morocco by creating clay products yearlong. By the same token, it disruptively innovates in the manufacturing process and supply chain. It is noteworthy that about 62 percent of the potters in Morocco make only $300 per month during the summer and about half that amount during the winter. GES has been able to increase the income of its ten potters by about 30 percent while creating new jobs. Moreover, the 1,200 refrigerators GES has sold so far reduced toxicity problems in more than 4,800 cases, saving about 24,000 kilograms of food. Truly, by avoiding food waste and energy consumption for more than 500 families in rural Morocco, such an innovation reduced their cost of living by about 25 percent. As a social enterprise, GES has been able to fundraise $55,000 through EM's incubator.

SDGs

As a social enterprise, GES aims to tackle five main SDGs (See Figure 13.6). By creating sustainable products without energy waste and providing secure incomes to potters and local ambassadors, GES can disconnect economic growth from environmental deterioration. The employment of local potters also strengthens and protects the cultural and economic significance of pottery in Morocco, ensuring the livelihood of these people and the development of the craft. Raowia and her team's focus "has always been human centered, as [they] believe that only [their] beneficiaries, clients, employees, mentors and founders could shape the way [their] business is seen and lived," as Raowia likes to recall. Their products sustainably increase the standard

FIGURE 13.6 Go Energyless Solutions – social impact and related SDGs

of living for families in rural communities, while radically changing the food preservation tactics of consumers in developed economies.

Challenges

In the pursuit of social innovation, there are several challenges GES is struggling to overcome. The limited accessibility to the scattered rural population and the difficulty in convincing them to buy the products or trust the local ambassadors affect GES' ability to penetrate new regions. GES is approaching these challenges by setting a new model in rural areas, by providing easy payment options to buyers and reducing delivery costs.

GES also realized a commonality throughout the communities, as the people who are most trusted (as ambassadors) are typically well-educated, respected local people. This makes it easier for GES to identify the best candidates to approach as local ambassadors. As it started receiving more orders from abroad, specifically from France, GES decided to distribute its products cost-effectively in these areas in larger quantities so that it can address the new demand.

HydroBarley (HB)

HB is a social enterprise cofounded by Hanane Rifai, CEO and woman entrepreneur (cf. Figure 13.7). Hanane started her business while being a student at the university in Rabat. As an Enactus student, she was concerned with the high price of fodder in the village of Moulay-Driss-Aghbal in Rabat's outskirts, which was forcing families to withdraw their children from school to work in the pastures. It is noteworthy that up to 83 percent of Moroccan agricultural land is not irrigated (FAO, 2016), and small farmers are suffering from the global climate change effects that negatively impact pasture and water availability. This, in turn, leads to drastic variations in quality and increases in fodder prices. The goal of HB at its inception

FIGURE 13.7 HydroBarley – logo and CEO (Hanane Rifai)

was to create low-cost green fodder for livestock farmers, so that their children, freed from pasturing, could return to school. Hanane's goal in her own words "is to bring Morocco into the future of agriculture while supporting small farmers and their families." To do this, HB decided to develop barley fodder using hydroponic technology that reduces the space and water needed to grow fodder, thus, cutting costs and allowing them to sell it at an affordable price. The barley is produced on shelves that allow water to infiltrate through all the layers.

When a lack of funds was inhibiting HB's ability to expand into new regions, Hanane decided to open HB's value proposition to selling a variety of sheep fed on its green fodder allowing HB to increase its profit margins. Morocco's diverse range of climates makes fodder production in each region drastically different depending on the season and rainfall variation. Thus, the demand for fodder is highly inconsistent. To provide a steadier revenue flow for themselves, HB intends to launch a line of hydroponic equipment units for farmers to allow them to grow their own green fodder cost-effectively. Hence, farmers would be able to convert the small amount of land they have into vegetable plots and other higher-value crops to increase their income and improve their quality of life.

Business model

Based on its value proposition of providing low-cost green fodder to rural farmers, HB developed an innovative business model in terms of its customer relationships and cost structure. It developed personal relationships with farmers based on customized solutions to farmers' agricultural challenges. It also provided teaching and personalized follow-up counseling to ensure all the needs of the clients were being met and then assisted the farmers' children in returning to school.

By offering the tools and hydroponic production units to the farmers, they can lower the costs of producing the product itself. HB also offers support for farmers wishing to develop new techniques on their small plots or to monitor the status of their livestock through their veterinary partners. HB's revenue structure is flexible and dependent on the individualized sales it negotiates with the farmers. It is currently in the process of partnering with different cooperatives to help it distribute its product more easily and make it more broadly available to potential customers.

Current impact

Currently able to produce one ton of barley fodder per day, HB generated $27,000 in revenue in 2017. Through its hydroponic growing techniques, HB can reduce the amount of water used in fodder production by 1,500 times and protect biodiversity by reducing the superficies of lands typically used for fodder production by 4,000 times as compared to traditional production techniques. HB has ten permanent clients who use its hydroponic system and 170 clients purchasing barley fodder. As its client base has grown, HB has been able to add two full-time and one part-time employees, in addition to five interns paid proportionally to their contribution. Moving forward, Hanane has expressed, "Our objective is to reach 1000 clients throughout Morocco by building approximately 10 units of production with a total capacity of 10 tons of fodder per day by the end of 2021. Such an objective, if attained, will allow us to positively impact about 500 children by helping them go back to school and prepare themselves for a better future."

SDGs

HB's unique business model and product offering allows the company to address six SDGs (See Figure 13.8). Its innovative technology is a more sustainable solution to other forms of green fodder and gives HB the ability to combat climate change and the economic externalities that result from it and affect rural farming communities. HB-associated farmers have also been able to successfully send children back to school and increase the income levels of their families and their standards of living.

Challenges

Culturally, there are a couple of barriers at play for HB to overcome as the company progresses. Farmers, especially those whose agricultural practices have been passed down over several generations, tend to be averse to change and distrustful of new techniques. This is a barrier in each new market that HB attempts to enter, and its entrepreneurs must overcome this initial distrust in its products. To combat this, HB started feeding sheep with its own fodder to highlight the value of its product and offering a week's worth of free fodder for farmers to test with their livestock.

HB is also struggling to convince farmers to send their children back to school to show them how valuable such an investment is for the future of the family. HB has decided to offer a 50 percent discount to farmers with school-age children on the condition that they bring the children back to school. This cuts the opportunity costs of keeping the kids in the pastures and incentivizes the farmers to continue their children's education.

HB attempts to cope with the difficulties of creating products in responding to the diverse needs of its clients and in competing with the other existing products on the market. By deeply analyzing its customers' needs and developing new products, HB can provide tailor-made offerings to a large range of livestock. However, to attain this level of analysis and product diversification quickly, it requires more funding to allow HB to scale up its business and expand into new regions. Although

FIGURE 13.8 HydroBarley – social impact and related SDGs

HB has been able to use the ecosystem financial support in Morocco, it is still struggling to secure enough funds to increase production and thus cut the per-unit costs, which will allow higher profit margins and further development of its business.

Conclusion and lessons learned

The Moroccan economy does not create enough wealth to meet the pressing social challenges in terms of job creation, education, healthcare and human development. Even worse, the wealth created is not fairly redistributed. As a consequence, some segments of the population see their social and economic situation worsening year after year. Social innovation, as a new concept and social innovators, as a new generation of entrepreneurs, can be significant drivers of social transformation in Morocco.

However, for such a generation of entrepreneurs to blossom and develop, it is necessary to properly educate and mentor would-be social innovators within non-profit supporting entities to help them spot, structure and seize social opportunities. The purpose here is not to create social companies that need to be subsidized, but rather, to develop a new generation of socially inclusive and economically self-sustaining profitable businesses. Not only have the two illustrative cases presented in this chapter shown such a combination of profit-seeking and social inclusion is possible but they also provide some important and insightful lessons.

First, it is noteworthy that the SDGs have helped Moroccan supporting organizations such as EM adjust their value proposition to better address the country's major social challenges and put young would-be entrepreneurs on the sustainable path early on. Moreover, in terms of gender equality, women are very present in the new wave of Moroccan social entrepreneurs. Indeed, more than half of all EM-incubated businesses are women led. The two cases presented in this chapter are just samples of successful social enterprises created by women.

Second, both cases have shown that the right solutions to local people's needs should stem from their own environment and take into consideration their own economic, social and environmental constraints. The GES case arose from the need of rural people to preserve their products' freshness and that of local potters with dwindling income. GES came up with a solution that addresses both needs. The HB case aims at helping farmers cope with the increasing prices of fodders while keeping their children schooled. By the same token, it addresses other important issues such as water and land scarcity.

Third, both cases have shown how important it is to engage local partners in implementing and facilitating the solution. The GES case involves, in addition to targeted customers and potters, local ambassadors to recruit buyers, distribute products and collect payments. The HB case involves veterinarians to help farmers with their livestock as well as teachers to convince them to send their children back to school.

Fourth, the two social companies are wrestling with issues chiefly pertaining to financing their activities as well as their expansion. As they are operating in an environment set up and meant for traditional for-profit companies, they suffer from the absence of appropriate funding mechanisms. This appeals to creating new funding tools specifically meant for such social enterprises.

Fifth, due to their size and weak resources, both the scope and reach of such social companies are very limited. They are usually contained within the borders of a small area and, hence, cannot attain a big-enough scale to make a significant difference. Nevertheless, scaling up to the level of the current and future social needs of the Moroccan society remains the next challenge of EM and all social enterprises spun off from its incubator. This important challenge can be addressed with well-rounded partnerships with public and private stakeholders and with adequate financing.

References

Brown, T. and Wyatt, J. "Design Thinking for Social Innovation IDEO." *Stanford Social Innovation Review: Development Outreach*, 12(1), 2010: 229–231.

El Ghaib, M. K. and Chaker, F. "Social Innovation as a Driver of Large-Scale Social Impact in Africa: The Case of an NGO in Morocco." *5ème Conference Internationale sur la Responsabilité Sociale des Organisations*. Casablanca, 2018.

Enactus Morocco. "Notre Réseau (Our Network)." 2018. www.enactus-morocco.org/notre-reseau/.

European Commission. "Social Innovation." 2017. http://ec.europa.eu/growth/industry/innovation/policy/social_en.

FAO. "Morocco in the Face of Climate Change." 2016. www.fao.org/fileadmin/user_upload/FAO-countries/Maroc/docs/2017-CC-FAO-EN.pdf.

IDEO.org. "The Field Guide to Human Centered Design." 2015. https://d1r3w4d5z5a88i.cloudfront.net/assets/guide/Field%20Guide%20to%20Human-Centered%20Design_IDEOorg_English-0f60d33bce6b870e7d80f9cc1642c8e7.pdf

Mulgan, G., Tucker, S., Ali, R. and Sanders, B. "Social Innovation: What It Is, Why It Matters and How It Can Be Accelerated." Skoll Centre for Social Entrepreneurship, 2007.

Osburg, T. "Social Innovation to Drive Corporate Sustainability." *Social Innovation*, Springer, 2013: 13–22.

Oxfam International. *Reward Work, Not Wealth*. Oxford, UK, 2018.

Porter, M. E. and Kramer, M. R. "The Big Idea: Creating Shared Value." *Harvard Business Review*, 89(1), 2011: 2.

Schöning, M. "Social Entrepreneurs as Main Drivers of Social Innovation." *Social Innovation*, Springer, 2013: 111–118.

Skoll Foundation. "Skoll Foundation Approach." 2017. http://skoll.org/about/approach/.

Stibbe, D. T., Reid, S., Gilbert, J. "Maximising the Impact of Partnerships for the SDGs", The Partnering Initiative and UN DESA, New York, 2018.

World Economic Forum, WEF. "The Global Competitiveness Index." 2018. www3.weforum.org/docs/GCR2017-2018/03CountryProfiles/Standalone2-pagerprofiles/WEF_GCI_2017_2018_Profile_Morocco.pdf.

World Health Organization, WHO. "Global Health Observatory." 2017. www.who.int/gho/countries/mar/country_profiles/en/.

The Young Foundation. "Humanity at Work: MONDRAGON." A Social Innovation Ecosystem Case, 2017.

14

PARTNERING FOR SUSTAINABLE DEVELOPMENT IN NIGERIA – CHALLENGES AND OPPORTUNITIES OF MULTI-STAKEHOLDER PARTNERSHIPS

Ijeoma Nwagwu

Abstract

The enormity and complexity of current global challenges, plus the scale and scope of the environmental, economic and social transformation envisioned by the 2030 Agenda, make it clear that no single sector – government, business or civil society – can achieve this transformation alone. There is a need for diverse stakeholders from multiple sectors to mobilize knowledge, expertise and financial resources to achieve the Sustainable Development Goals (SDGs). This chapter presents the tremendous opportunity multi-stakeholder partnership holds in accelerating the attainment of the SDGs in Nigeria. Two illustrative cases, the Food and Beverage Recycling Alliance (FBRA) and the Committee Encouraging Corporate Philanthropy (CECP)-Nigeria, are discussed as models of multi-stakeholder partnership driving the attainment of the SDGs. Careful study of these organizations reveals the opportunities and obstacles inherent in partnerships for driving sustainable development.

Introduction

Attaining sustainable development depends largely on the ability to engage in innovative ways with stakeholders across different sectors of society. This is due to the enormity and complexity of the challenges to sustainable development facing our world today. UNESCO (2005) rightly stated "no institution, even at a global scale, can manage to achieve the goals of sustainable development on its own. Only united together, from North to South, East to West, can we be sure to build a viable world for us and for generations to come."

We are witnessing an unprecedented upsurge in problems across the globe including poverty, malnutrition, epidemic diseases, wars, environmental problems (climate change, nuclear pollution, biodiversity loss, etc.), discrimination and human rights abuse.

While globalization has many positive effects, it has led to the escalation of inequalities within and between countries. Two-thirds of the world's extremely poor are based in African countries. Facts show that if current trends persist, Africans will account for nine-tenths of the world's extreme poor by 2030. A report from the Brookings Institute, for instance, showed that at the end of May 2018, Nigeria had about 87 million people living in extreme poverty (Cuaresma et al., 2018; Kharas et al., 2018). Also, unemployment in the country was 18.8 percent in May 2018, while an estimated 27.9 percent of the population was multidimensionally poor – that is, deprived in several domains including health, education, living environment and access to basic amenities (PWC, 2018). Indeed, income inequality, measured by the Gini Coefficient,[1] stands at 48.1 percent (Ewubare and Okpani, 2018). In a nutshell, the marked economic growth achieved at the turn of the century, between 2000 and 2014, did not translate into tangible development outcomes for most of the people of Nigeria, and many people are, evidently, being left behind (Ajakaiye et al., 2015; PWC, 2018).

In the latest Commitment to Reducing Inequality Index[2] (CRI) report, Nigeria ranked at the bottom of the table among 157 countries. The report states: "Nigeria has the unenviable distinction of being at the bottom of the Index for the second year running. Its social spending (on health, education and social protection) is shamefully low, which is reflected in very poor social outcomes for its citizens. One in 10 children in Nigeria does not reach their fifth birthday, and more than 10 million children do not go to school. Sixty percent of these are girls."

The need for multi-stakeholder partnerships in advancing sustainable development is articulated in the preamble of the 2030 Agenda for Sustainable Development, which calls for revitalized global partnerships for sustainable development based on a spirit of strengthened global solidarity, focused in particular on the needs of the poorest and most vulnerable and with the participation of all countries, stakeholders and people (United Nations (UN), 2015). Sustainable Development Goal (SDG) #17 captures this focus where it seeks to "strengthen the means of implementation and revitalize the Global Partnership for Sustainable Development." SDG #17 consists of 19 targets divided into five topics: finance, technology, capacity building, trade and systemic issues. Some of the major targets covered include strengthening domestic resource mobilization and promoting the development, transfer, dissemination and diffusion of environmentally sound technologies to developing countries on favourable terms. There is also a stated commitment to enhance international support for implementing effective and targeted capacity building in developing countries to support national implementation of all the sustainable development goals (UN, 2015).

The challenge of extreme poverty in Nigeria motivates business efforts to contribute to sustainable development by investing in corporate social responsibility programmes, particularly in the areas of health (contributes on SDG #3), education (contributes on SDG #4) and youth empowerment. However, most of these efforts have been in silos, hence, limiting the scale and potential of their impact. In this context and the situation of many African countries, multi-stakeholder partnership is an approach that holds great promise.

Scope

This chapter examines the phenomenon of business, government and civil society partnerships in the pursuit of sustainable development. It explores the immense possibilities of multi-stakeholder partnerships in driving sustainable development, the challenges multi-stakeholder partnerships present and solutions to tackling these challenges.

This chapter is based on a theoretical examination of the literature on partnerships (collaborative governance and multi-sector partnerships in the field of public policy and the business management literature, which focuses on business-NGO relationships), sustainability, corporate social responsibility and sustainable development. The chapter also explores illustrative cases of corporate efforts at partnering for sustainable development through two collaborative action platforms – FBRA (Food and Beverage Recycling Alliance) and CECP-Nigeria (The Committee Encouraging Corporate Philanthropy).

FBRA is an alliance of companies sharing a mutual concern for the environment and a commitment to collaborate with all stakeholders to build a sustainable recycling economy for food and beverage packaging waste. Endorsed by the Association of Food, Beverage and Tobacco Employers (AFBTE), an influential industry group, the alliance aims to foster industry partnership and engagement. CECP-Nigeria is the organized private sector response to the disease of cancer. CECP-Nigeria focuses on mobilizing Nigerians and corporate organizations to unite in finding innovative ways of fulfilling unmet societal needs around cancer awareness, diagnosis and treatment.

Each of these organizations presents a platform on which to explore multi-stakeholder partnerships driving the attainment of the SDGs. Table 14.1 enumerates the SDGs each organization is advancing.

TABLE 14.1 Illustrative case organizations and the sustainable development goals they address

Organization	SDGs Addressed
FBRA (Food and Beverage Recycling Alliance)	Goal #17: Partnerships for the goals
	Goal #15: Life on land
	Goal #14: Life below water
	Goal #12: Responsible consumption and production
	Goal #8: Decent work and economic growth
	Goal #6: Clean water and sanitation
CECP-Nigeria (The Committee Encouraging Corporate Philanthropy)	Goal #17: Partnerships for the goals
	Goal #3: Good health and well-being

Understanding multi-stakeholder partnerships

Strategic alliances between government, businesses and civil society are a growing feature of both developed and emerging economies. Such multi-stakeholder partnerships are necessary because it is increasingly clear that no single sector in society can deliver the complexities of sustainable development alone. Multi-stakeholder partnerships involve alliances between parties drawn from government, business and civil society that strategically provide the expertise and resources of each to solve key sustainable development challenges. Such partnerships must be based on the principles of *shared risk, cost and mutual benefit* (UN, 2018; Brouwer et al., 2015).

The term "multi-stakeholder partnership" has gained much currency in development circles recently (Kassa, 2016). According to Van Huijstee et al. (2007), multi-stakeholder partnerships for sustainable development are collaborative arrangements in which actors from different sectors of society work together towards developmental goals. The Centre for Development Innovation defines multi-stakeholder partnership as "a process of interactive learning, empowerment and participatory governance that enables stakeholders with interconnected problems and ambitions, but often differing interests, to be collectively innovative and resilient when faced with the emerging risks, crises and opportunities of a complex and changing environment" (Brouwer et al., 2015).

Different stakeholders perceive and tend to approach economic, environmental and social issues in different ways. This diversity of approaches is often predicted to be a disadvantage and a clog in the wheel of multi-stakeholder collaboration. However, this divergence most often becomes an added advantage when the stakeholders agree to achieve a common objective by sharing expertise and resources together. Studies show that even very divergent stakeholders can come together, agree and achieve a common objective when they are convinced that their collaborative work is worthwhile and that the partnership can succeed (Gray, 1989; Malena, 2004).

The following section describes and discusses how FBRA and CECP-Nigeria are driving sustainable development through multi-stakeholder partnerships. Using a qualitative approach, data was gathered through desk review of documents, media and scholarly articles; in-depth interviews and surveys.

FBRA (Food and Beverage Recycling Alliance) driving environmental sustainability

Plastic pollution

Plastic pollution is one of the biggest issues threatening the sustainability of our planet. About 300 million tons of plastic are produced worldwide each year. From the 1950s up to 2018, an estimated 8.3 billion tons of plastic have been produced worldwide, of which an estimated 9 percent has been recycled and another 12 percent has been incinerated. This large amount of plastic waste unavoidably enters the environment, with studies suggesting that the bodies of 90 percent of seabirds contain plastic debris

(UN Environment, 2018). Recently there have been numerous advocacies on the need to beat down plastic pollution. The 2018 World Environment Day was tagged "Beat Plastic Pollution." In some areas there have been significant efforts to reduce the prominence of plastic pollution, through reducing plastic consumption and promoting plastic recycling. However, much still needs to be done in tackling the issue.

Tackling one of the biggest sustainability issues the world is facing today requires a collective approach from industry leaders, governments and civil society. The Food and Beverage Recycling Alliance (FBRA) case demonstrates how companies can work together in partnership to cocreate solutions to reduce the environmental impact of their packaging waste.

The FBRA journey

FBRA started off as a self-regulatory initiative that Coca-Cola Nigeria began in 2005 when it partnered with a private investor, Alkem Nigeria Limited, to set up a large-scale recovery and buyback scheme for PET (polyethylene terephthalate) bottles, which were recycled into synthetic fibre. This initiative was taken as part of Coca-Cola's effort to achieve one of its 2020 sustainability goals (Coca-Cola, 2017). Realizing that achieving its goal would require partnership efforts, Coca-Cola, with support from the National Environment Standards Regulation and Enforcement Agency (NESREA), eventually reached out to other leading beverage companies in the country. This led to the formation of a voluntary group in 2012, which currently includes the Nigerian Bottling Company (NBC), Nestle Nigeria Plc, Nigerian Breweries Plc, AB InBev, Diageo (Guinness Nigeria), Intercontinental Distillers Ltd., Seven-Up Bottling Company Plc, Tulip Cocoa and Coca Cola, all of which became the nucleus of the FBRA that was formed in 2015. FBRA was designed to serve as the Producer Responsibility Organisation (PRO) for the food and beverage sector.

FBRA partners

FBRA opens its doors to membership from players in the food and beverage industry dedicated to working as a team to implement programmes that will help preserve the environment, create jobs and entrepreneurship opportunities, ignite innovation for repurposing of packaging waste and avert reputational and regulatory risks for businesses.

Besides partnering with other food and beverage companies, FBRA also partners with enterprises sharing similar concerns for the environment (e.g., Wecyclers Nigeria and Recycle Points), local communities, consumers and government and nongovernmental organizations. FBRA currently partners with the Lagos State Government in a bid to clean up and prevent waste pollution from plastics and other food and beverage packaging on Lagos State's inland waterways, save aquatic life and avert other environmental problems associated with poor waste management. Lagos State being the commercial hub of Nigeria has witnessed tremendous pollution related to urbanization and industrialization. The industrialization level in the state has generated huge waste and raised concerns from a public health and environmental risk standpoint.

FBRA's mission and impact

The primary aim of FBRA is to facilitate industry compliance with the Extended Producer Responsibility (EPR) policy[3] of the Federal Government of Nigeria as well as drive nationwide coverage and sustainability of the packaging collection and recycling programme. FBRA's goal includes a social advocacy campaign for responsible packaging disposal habits and developing capacity for local collection and recycling organizations as well as building thought leadership to promote a circular economy in Nigeria. The alliance has completed the development of a viable collection and recycling plan with initial focus on the major food and beverage packaging materials that pose a significant challenge for the Nigerian national waste management system.

"We are looking at the entire packaging life cycle – from how bottles and cans are designed and made, to how they are recycled and re-purposed. We want to reduce the waste we generate as much as possible, encourage recycling, and our initiatives in this regard has been well tailored in achieving tangible results along with our partners," stated the FBRA Vice Chairman, Adekunle Olusuyi. The organization's mission is to recover and recycle food and beverage packaging waste and thereby create a sustainable recycling economy that will stimulate employment, innovation and wealth creation (FBRA, 2018). FBRA is also committed to ensure the success of the EPR policy. One of the key elements of the EPR policy is the requirement for sectoral collective action under the platform of a Producer Responsibility Organisation (PRO). This ensures that companies do not struggle in silos to recycle their packaging waste, as that would be overwhelming. Rather, they can pool resources as a sector to develop and fund a robust buyback scheme, attract investors to fund recycling infrastructure and invest in research and development of eco-friendly packaging as well as alternative uses for their packaging waste. The FBRA case demonstrates the fact that companies can compete for market share and still cooperate effectively for social good.

Efforts by the FBRA have so far recorded recycling of almost one billion bottles into fibre and over 1,800 in direct employment on an average income of six dollars per day (three times the national average) as well as the production of synthetic fibre for local industries and export (Adekoya, 2018).

The Committee Encouraging Corporate Philanthropy (CECP-Nigeria)

The CECP-Nigeria partnership model

The Committee Encouraging Corporate Philanthropy (CECP)-Nigeria provides a national institutional platform for promoting private-social partnership (PSP) in Nigeria. It is a private sector–led fundraising platform that was initiated by Mass Medical Mission a registered nonprofit organization associated with the Union for International Cancer Control (UICC). CECP is promoted by the Organized Private Sector (OPS) with the goal of creating a vibrant social sector through private-public-social (tripartite) partnership.

CECP unites diverse types of organizations and associations – sociocultural groups, religious organizations, professional associations, workplace affiliations – into a formidable movement for the common good. The fundamental belief of CECP is that without joint and concerted action, there are risks of tokenism, duplication of effort and lack of real progress (CECP Nigeria, 2018). CECP therefore labours to promote united and synergistic action in a common direction. The committee aims to make people truly philanthropic – giving because of a sincere interest in the wellbeing of others and for tackling major societal problems.

CECP-Nigeria's strategy is to take one core societal problem at a time and empower a nonprofit organization to deploy an effective solution that will resolve the problem. The flagship cause is the BIG WAR against Cancer. The BIG WAR is aimed at taking holistic preventive healthcare to the grassroots using Mobile Cancer Centres (MCC). The BIG WAR is powered by the National Cancer Prevention Programme (NCPP). Cancer, a noncommunicable disease that can be terminal if not detected early, is fast becoming a big health challenge globally and in Nigeria. According to the World Health Organization (WHO), cancer is the second leading cause of death globally (WHO, 2018). Late-stage presentation and inaccessible diagnosis and treatment are the major challenges to managing cancer. In 2017, only 26 percent of low-income countries reported having pathology services generally available in the public sector. Only one in five low- and middle-income countries have the necessary data to drive cancer policy (International Agency for Research on Cancer, 2018). Consequently, approximately 70 percent of deaths from cancer worldwide occur in low- and middle-income countries (WHO, 2018).

According to the Executive Secretary of the CECP, Dr Abia Nzelu, "the Committee is trying to get prevention to the grassroots. The problem we have about cancer is not about incidence, the number of people that have it, but the death rate. In Nigeria right now out of every 5 people that have it, one survives, four will die." Over 100,000 Nigerians are diagnosed with cancer annually, and about 80,000 die from the disease, averaging 240 Nigerians every day or 10 Nigerians every hour (Salako, 2018). It is feared that by 2020, cancer incidence for Nigerian males and females may rise to 90.7/100,000 and 100.9/100,000, respectively (CECP Nigeria, 2018). Further complicating the cancer problem is the fact that a majority of the medical centres in Nigeria lack the diagnostic capacity to quickly detect and treat cancer cases. This has forced several Nigerians to travel to nations like India and the United Kingdom in search of treatment. Also, the level of awareness of Nigerians about cancer prevention and early detection is very low, especially among rural women.

CECP-Nigeria: mission and impact

The scale of the cancer problem puts a huge burden on the government, which obviously cannot carry it alone. CECP-Nigeria therefore aims to synergize resources from all sectors in bringing cancer under control. To achieve this, CECP collaborates with different bodies to organize awareness and screening and treatment programmes. Speaking to its collaboration with CECP, the former governor of Lagos State, Akinwunmi Ambode, pledged "to mobilise philanthropists and corporate organizations towards establishing one comprehensive cancer centre in the state." The CECP has gone on to collaborate with the state to provide mobile cancer trucks to serve under-resourced communities, in an attempt to the bridge the gap in finance and institutional structures the government is unable to fill on its own.

The short-term goal of the CECP-Nigeria is to raise funds towards the acquisition of 37 Mobile Cancer Centres to take cancer prevention and holistic preventive healthcare to the grassroots in Nigeria. CECP works with the NCPP in partnership with state governments, corporations, hospitals and the general public to achieve its goal of establishing diverse levels of infrastructure for cancer care in Nigeria. CECP is taking strides to ensure that this goal is met. CECP has successfully raised funds for the pilot set of Mobile Cancer Centres. In addition, four fixed cancer prevention and health promotion centres have been established, strategically located in each of the four geopolitical regions of Nigeria.

Challenges of multi-stakeholder partnerships

Synergizing stakeholders from different sectors is often difficult and challenging (UNESCO, 2005). Numerous challenges emerge, including low trust, divergent visions, problems of communication across sectors, differing time frames, limited participation and inadequate organization among stakeholders (Kassa, 2016; Malena, 2004). These challenges affect organizations in diverse ways depending on their environment, partnership model and approach.

A major challenge that these organizations face is that they often find it difficult securing political buy-in and sustained engagement on the key issues and goals they address. In order to sustain a large-scale and long-term impact, there is a need to engage with government, policy makers and regulators. However, through relentless efforts, patience and commitment, these organizations are gradually scaling past this hurdle. For example, Coca-Cola after much negotiation eventually got the support of regulators to establish the FBRA. Also, recently FBRA signed a memorandum of understanding with the Lagos State Government for a three-year partnership. CECP-Nigeria has also been able to mobilize government support, which has helped to scale its impact and accelerate its progress. To secure political engagement and buy-in of authorities, there must be a relentless commitment to dialogue and communication. Goals, missions and plans must be properly set and communicated.

Another major factor that slows down progress and limits the impact of partnerships is the fact that it is often difficult to sustain long-term commitments from partners. For partnerships to succeed, to create and perpetuate the desired impact, the combined willingness, capability and resources of partners must be both synergized and sustained. However, since partnership is voluntary, and stakeholders are often not bound by stringent rules or formal agreements, they tend to not pull their weight and not consider the implications on overall goals. According to Tandon (1991), stakeholders may choose to join in or not to join in at a different stage or drop out at a subsequent stage. To avoid this, and ensure sustained and long-term commitment from partners, communication must be strengthened to ensure all parties are carried along on the goals, progress, prospects and needs. It is also important that conflicts and disagreements of any sort are dealt with quickly. Also, formal agreements and institutions – in this case CECP and FBRA – can be established to increase stakeholders' sense of commitment and responsibility.

The lack of a strong institutional capacity is another major challenge faced by the case organizations. Both case organizations are lean and loose with respect to their institutional constitution. They are currently limited in the institutional capacity, governance structure and resources necessary to scale their impact and effectively root out the problems they are addressing. Their capacity is relatively small for large-scale thought leadership and action in key areas. There is therefore a need for a strong and efficient governance structure and system in order to increase effectiveness and scale impact.

Conclusion

For multi-stakeholder partnerships to be effective, all the parties involved must sincerely acknowledge their individual vision, interests, strengths and weaknesses as well as power differentials in the relationship. Furthermore, there is a need to establish clear rules and constitutions that will guide operations. And to avoid any party shirking responsibility, it is important that each party's role is clearly negotiated. For example, in the memorandum of understanding signed between FBRA and the Lagos State Government, the roles and responsibility of each party are clearly spelt out as partners on an equal footing.

FBRA and CECP-Nigeria show the tremendous opportunities multi-stakeholder partnerships hold in realizing the SDGs. While FBRA is advancing environmental sustainability and economic prospects through multi-stakeholder partnerships (broadly touching on SDGs #17, #15, #14, #12, #8 and #6), CECP-Nigeria is strategically promoting good health and wellbeing by uniting resources from all sectors (touching on SDGs #17 and #3). FBRA particularly exemplifies the fact that businesses competing for market share can at the same time collaborate to create solutions to societal problems. Companies can draw from the FBRA example and form sectoral collaborations to tackle issues common to their sector. The CECP-Nigeria case also points to the fact that by synergizing resources from diverse groups, major gaps in social services that are difficult for the government to fulfil can be more easily addressed.

Both organizations examined demonstrate that more can be achieved through multi-stakeholder partnerships; solo efforts are often stressful and produce very little and often short-term results. To achieve the 2030 goals, businesses, governments and civil society must cease to work in silos and create more strategic and innovative alliances. Furthermore, to scale impacts, alliances must continually grow their networks and institutional capacity.

Notes

1 The Gini coefficient, introduced by Italian statistician Corrado Gini in 1912, is a statistical measure of distribution that is often used as a gauge of economic inequality, measuring income distribution in a population. The coefficient ranges from 0 (or 0%) to 1 (or 100%), with 0 representing perfect equality and 1 representing perfect inequality (Catalano et al., 2009).
2 The CRI index 2018 is a global ranking of governments based on what they are doing to tackle the gap between the rich and poor. The index is based on a new database of indicators, now covering 157 countries, which measures government action on social spending, tax and labour rights – three areas found to be critical to reducing the gap.
3 The Extended Producer Responsibility (EPR) is a deliberate policy to promote total life cycle environmental improvement of product systems by extending the responsibility of manufacturers to various parts of the entire life cycle of their product and especially to the take-back, recycle and final disposal of the product.

References

Adekoya, F. "Nigeria: Recycling Group, Lagos Government to Clean Waterways' Plastic, Packaging Waste." *The Guardian*, August 1, 2018. https://guardian.ng/business-services/recycling-group-lagos-government-to-clean-waterways-plastic-packaging-waste/.

Ajakaiye, O., Jerome, A., Nabena, D. and Alaba, O. "Understanding the Relationship between Growth and Employment in Nigeria." 2015/124. Helsinki: UNU-WIDER.

Brouwer, H., Woodhill, J., Hemmati, M., Verhoosel, K. and van Vugt, S. "The MSP Guide: How to Design and Facilitate Multi-Stakeholder Partnerships." Centre for Development Innovation, Wageningen University and Research, 2015.

Catalano, M. T., Leise, T. L. and Pfaff, T. J. "Measuring Resource Inequality: The Gini Coefficient." *Numeracy*, 2(2), 2009. http://dx.doi.org/10.5038/1936-4660.2.2.4.

Coca-Cola. "Goals and Progress." December 18, 2018. www.coca-colacompany.com/content/dam/journey/us/en/private/fileassets/pdf/2018/2017-Sustainability-Report-2020-Goals-Progress.pdf.

The Committee Encouraging Corporate Philanthropy, Nigeria. "About Us." November 19, 2018. www.cecpng.org/.

Cuaresma, J. C., Fengler, W., Kharas, H., Bekhtiar, K., Brottrager, M. and Hofer, M. "Will the Sustainable Development Goals be Fulfilled? Assessing Present and Future Global Poverty." *Palgrave Communications*, 4(29), 2018: 1–8.

Ewubare, D. B. and Okpani, A. O. "Poverty and Income Inequality in Nigeria (1980–2017)." *International Journal of Advanced Studies in Ecology, Development and Sustainability*, 5(1), 2018: 138–151.

Food, Beverage and Recycling Alliance. "FBRA Affirms Recycling Crucial to Environmental Preservation, Job and Wealth Creation." December 18, 2018. www.fbranigeria.ng/fbra-affirms-recycling-crucial-to-environmental-preservation-job-and-wealth-creation/.

Gray, B. *Collaborating: Finding Common Ground for Multiparty Problems* (Jossey Bass Business and Management Series). San Francisco, CA, USA: Jossey-Bass, 1989.

International Agency for Research on Cancer Global Initiative for Cancer Registry Development. "Cancer: Key Facts." September 12, 2018. https://www.who.int/news-room/fact-sheets/detail/cancer

Kassa, K. "Managing Multi-Stakeholder Partnership (MSP) in Higher Education: Challenges, Opportunities and Implications for Sustainable Development." *Proceedings of the 14th International Conference on Private Higher Education in Africa*, 2016: 311–319.

Kharas, H., Hamel, K. and Hofer, M. "The Start of a New Poverty Narrative." November 1, 2018. www.brookings.edu/blog/future-development/2018/06/19/the-start-of-a-new-poverty-narrative/.

Malena, C. "Strategic Partnership: Challenges and Best Practices in the Management and Governance of Multi-Stakeholder Partnerships Involving UN and Civil Society Actors." *Background Paper Prepared for the Multi-Stakeholder Workshop on Partnerships and UN-Civil Society Relations*. Pocantico Hills, NY, November 1, 2004.

PricewaterhouseCoopers Limited. "Structural Transformation and Jobless Growth in Nigeria." PWC Ltd., Nigeria, 2018.

Salako, A. "The Cancer Epidemic." *The Sun*, May 15, 2018. https://sunnewsonline.com/the-cancer-epidemic/.

Tandon, R. "Holding Together: Collaborations and Partnerships in the Real World." *IDR Reports*, 8(2). Boston, MA: Institute of Development Research, 1991: 1–28.

UNESCO. "World Summit on Information Society: Partnerships in Development Practice: Evidence from Multi-Stakeholder ICT4D Partnership Practice in Africa." UNESCO Publications for the World Summit on the Information Society, 2005.

United Nations. "Resolution Adopted by the General Assembly on 25 September 2015." *United Nations*, 2015. www.un.org/en/development/desa/population/migration/generalassembly/docs/globalcompact/A_RES_70_1_E.pdf.

United Nations. "Our Planet Is Drowning in Plastic Pollution." *United Nations Website*, 2018. www.unenvironment.org/interactive/beat-plastic-pollution/.

United Nations. "Partnering for Sustainable Development: Guidelines for Multi-Stakeholder Partnerships to Implement the 2030 Agenda in Asia and the Pacific." United Nations University Institute for the Advanced Study of Sustainability, Tokyo and Bangkok, 2018.

Van Huijstee, M. M., Francken, M. and Leroy, P. "Partnerships for Sustainable Development: A Review of Current Literature." *Environmental Science*, 4, 2007: 75–89.

World Health Organization. "Cancer." Accessed December 17, 2018. www.who.int/newsroom/fact-sheets/detail/cancer.

15

HELP ISN'T ALWAYS HELPFUL

Lessons from seeking inclusive education in rural Malawi

Patricia Winter and Brooke Blanks

Abstract

The chapter, "Help Isn't Always Helpful," is a description of experiences and lessons learned from a multiyear effort to provide culturally responsive, sustainable, and disabilities-focused technical assistance to teachers in rural primary schools in Malawi. The authors' understanding of what is and what is not effective evolved over the course of their engagement with local stakeholders, particularly the recipients of the technical assistance. The authors explore the cultural factors that affected their decision-making and reflect on participants' responses to interventions in order to draw lessons on the craft of developing locally appropriate development-assistance interventions across cultures.

Background

Malawi is affectionately named "the Warm Heart of Africa" and is the only country in the top ten poorest countries in the world that has never seen a civil war. In June 2018, Malawi was ranked as the third poorest country in the world (Martin, 2018), with a per capita gross domestic product of US$345 per year. While Malawi provides free primary education for all children from grade one to grade eight, there are still issues related to the identification and inclusion of children with disabilities into primary grade classrooms. The World Health Organization (WHO) and World Bank (2011) estimated that the vast majority of children with disabilities live in poverty-stricken countries like Malawi. At this time, there is little reliable data on the number of children and the educational needs of those with disabilities (Tataryn et al., 2017).

Information gathered by the Southern African Federation of the Disabled indicated that in 2008 there were over 69,000 school-aged children with learning impairments, including visual impairments and blindness, hearing impairments, physical impairments and learning difficulties across the five countries of Lesotho, Malawi, Namibia, South Africa and Swaziland. It is important to note that these data are quite dated but are the most up-to-date resource outlining the disabilities landscape among the countries that are listed. Lang (2008) cautions that statistics on children with disabilities "do not capture all learners enrolled in mainstream classes with impairments or learning difficulties such as intellectual disabilities, emotional and behavioral difficulties, specific learning disabilities, health impairments and language and communication difficulties" (p. 71).

These data highlight the critical importance of addressing the United Nations' (UN) Sustainable Development Goals (SDGs), especially the need for inclusive and equitable quality education (SDG #4). Within the goal areas, the UN has outlined specific targets for ensuring equitable education for all including Target 4.5, to eliminate gender disparities and ensure equal access to all levels of education and vocational training for the vulnerable, including persons with disabilities, indigenous peoples and children in vulnerable situations; Target 4a, to provide safe, nonviolent, inclusive and effective learning environments for all and Target 4c, to substantially increase the supply of qualified teachers, including through international cooperation for teacher training in developing countries (United Nations, Sustainable Development Goal 4, 2018).

Teacher preparation in special education is relatively new and not yet widely available in Malawi (Itimu and Kopetz, 2008). Policy efforts such as the Disability Act (2012), the National Policy Guidelines on Special Needs Education (2007), the National Education Strategic Plan (2008–2017), and the National Policy on the Equalization of Opportunities for Persons with Disabilities (2006) speak to an ongoing commitment to inclusive education and a focus on building an inclusive society. This progressive policy environment, peaceful social context and persistently significant poverty mean that Malawi is well positioned to receive international assistance for improving students' educational options and outcomes.

Indeed, millions of dollars in international aid have been invested in Malawian schools in an effort to improve student learning, particularly in literacy, but with unsatisfying results. Often, grant-funded resources are vast in scale but not accessible to teachers or not used by teachers due to lack of adequate training opportunities. The issues that were faced by the authors during the very small-scale engagement of this project are a microcosm indicative of issues faced by large-scale efforts, such as managing the delivery of materials in an environment that is difficult to navigate and a lack of meaningful professional development that is sensitive to the context of Malawian schools.

Education in rural Malawi

The work outlined in this chapter took place in a rural region of Malawi, between five and eight kilometers from the capital city of Lilongwe. Transportation to the backcountry is arduous during the dry season and nearly impossible during the rainy season. Malawi is a tropical country, and for approximately half the year, there is intense rainfall and flooding. Dirt roads to the backcountry are narrow and heavily rutted. These roads are the main arteries to the small rural villages and are often choked with traffic that includes large trucks hauling produce, bicycles, pedestrians, and livestock.

Each school zone is approximately five square kilometers and can serve up to 1,000 children. It is common for early primary-grade classrooms to house up to 200 children per room. Class sizes greatly decrease as children age and move up in grade level. The rural government is tribal in its social structure, and each village has a chief or headman who oversees the governance of the village. While the headman is in charge of governance, the school block buildings are the center of community activities beyond what happens during the school day.

Malawi has two primary languages, Chichewa and English. Children learn Chichewa until they reach grade three and then switch to English from grades three to eight. While children hear both English and Chichewa prior to entering grade three, the complete shift to English does create some challenges for the students as they learn to navigate the materials and a classroom environment in a relatively new language. Other challenges presented to the communities include the very heavy rainfall associated with the tropical climate, which leads to considerable food insecurity, as the rainy season precludes the ability to grow produce.

Malawi is also a tropical, disease-prone country, with significant numbers of residents diagnosed with malaria and little to no access to treatment. In 2008, the World Health Organization (WHO) estimated that there were approximately five

PHOTO 15.1 Rift valley ringed by the Mangochi escarpment (Winter, 2013).

million cases of malaria in Malawi, with the highest burden carried by those under five years of age (Mathanga et al., 2013). Symptoms of malaria include concomitant seizures and encephalitis resulting in severe and profound cognitive delays and impairment. If seizure activity is ongoing, it significantly impairs cognitive functioning in those diagnosed and ultimately leads to death. HIV infections are also very prevalent in the country with an estimated one million people living with HIV in 2016 (UNAIDS, 2018), which included an increase of 4,300 children who were newly infected in 2016.

Year one: call to mission

For many years, the authors' home institution in the United States had an ongoing study abroad project in Malawi. This project was linked closely to one primary school in particular and was the location of a collaborative project between stakeholders in the community, the school administration, and the educators from Radford University. This project was typical of exchange programs in that the time on site was limited by the university schedule, student resources, and the alignment of the Malawian school year with Radford's school year. This relationship has been favorable and ongoing and has netted opportunities for students from a variety of backgrounds to experience educational practices in a third world country and to share insights from their learning as US-trained educators.

In 2012, this relationship sparked the interest of special educator and chapter co-author, Brooke Blanks, who became curious about the incidences of disabilities within the schools of Malawi. Blanks's interest was not necessarily focused on the study abroad program but rather encapsulated a desire to understand, on a much larger scale, the numbers and types of disabilities that were most represented within the schools. Blanks was also interested in understanding how children with disabilities were identified and the techniques and strategies employed by Malawian educators to meet emergent needs as they unfolded within the educational environment.

Prior to arrival in the country, Blanks contacted Landirani Trust, now African Vision Malawi (AVM), a boots-on-the-ground nongovernmental organization (NGO), based in the United Kingdom (UK), and asked for access to the schools that were being served by the organization. The vision of AVM "is to see a healthy, educated, and self-sufficient community in Malawi" (African Vision Malawi, 2018). AVM is committed to sustainable practices that emerge from the communities it serves. Efforts focus on the establishment of essential working relationships within the tribal structures that are typical of rural Malawian life.

AVM hires Malawians to work in local communities and mobilize their resources by providing care through maternal health programs and birthing centers, medical care for community members, especially burn and wound care, and varied assistance to a large catchment of rural schools. Assistance provided includes procurement and installation of solar panels, installation of safe water containment structures, the drilling of boreholes (wells), procurement of supplies and local labor to build and repair school block buildings and provision of literacy and educational resources as well as the transfer of sustainable living and agricultural practices.

While in Malawi, Blanks spent time surveying the incidences of disabilities by spending two weeks traveling with the Education Director from AVM to local village schools in the rural areas supported by the NGO. She interviewed teachers and administrators to attempt to determine how children with disabilities are identified, the number of children with disabilities in the schools, and how the identified students were being served. Results suggested limited capacity for the identification of such children and a limited ability to serve children with disabilities in the region.

Blanks then met with the Assistant to the Deputy Director of the Malawi Ministry of Special Needs Education (MMSNE). Discussions focused on the overall inadequacies present in the current culture of professional development for educators. The major finding from this initial conversation was that the MMSNE had created a "Disability Toolkit" to help Malawian teachers identify students with disabilities in their classrooms.

The issue with implementation was that little training had been provided on how to use the instrument effectively. At the request of school administrators, Blanks created and implemented a series of professional development workshops for 18 primary schools in two rural school zones. These workshops focused on setting goals for sensitization and identification of children with disabilities. One year after the workshop, the participating schools reported a 200 percent increase in the number of students identified with disabilities. This initial success set the stage for work in year two.

PHOTO 15.2 Rural school block building M'bangombe primary school (Winter, 2012a).

Year two: interprofessional collaboration

In 2013, Blanks, enlisted two higher education faculty colleagues to return to Malawi. One of the colleagues was from literacy education and the other was this chapter's co-author, Patricia Winter, from the music therapy program. The goals of this visit were 1) to leverage the local cultural and musical traditions as agents of social change to address traditional beliefs about disability and 2) to increase teachers' use of research-based practices in early literacy education. Both the music therapy and literacy practices were steeped in Western traditions and stemmed from the collaborators' practices that were situated in training programs and clinical settings in the United States.

In Western contexts there is a value on educational practices that focus on creativity and that are steeped in the ideals of Bloom's taxonomy (1956), which emphasizes creativity, student-to-student collaboration, and the generation of novel ideas to problems encountered in educational and real-world settings. Malawian schools focus on educational practices that are largely prescriptive and that rely heavily on rote memorization due to a lack of educational resources and the exceptionally large numbers of students in each classroom.

Music therapy

Music therapy is an arts-based healthcare profession that requires, at a minimum, a bachelor's degree in music therapy with a six-month internship. Advanced-level practice can be conducted post master's degree, and there is doctoral-level training in music therapy. Music therapists in the United States become certified to practice through a national exam from the Certification Board for Music Therapists. Music therapists typically follow a consensus model of practice in which the therapist and client establish a contract for services in a clinical setting, which can include hospitals, psychiatric and forensic institutions, hospices, medical settings, private homes and schools.

US-trained music therapists are required to learn to play the guitar, piano, and percussion instruments and to sing. Most music therapy training programs are housed in Western Classical music programs and while cultural competence is critical to the development of music therapists, that competency includes a focus on the cultures one might encounter in healthcare settings in the United States. There are four main methods used in music therapy, including listening to music, recreating music, improvising music, and composing music.

Within the profession of music therapy are a number of orientations to practice. One particularly fitting orientation can be found in the practice of Community Music Therapy (CoMT). The tenets of this orientation include 1) mobilization of personal strengths and social, cultural, and material resources; 2) attention to the ecological contexts of participants; 3) the acknowledgment that lay and local knowledge is central to the process and that the music therapist is not the sole expert; and 4) a focus on ethics and human rights (Stige and Aarø, 2012). CoMT is not bound by location and is not tied to a clinical setting. Rather it happens within the contexts that make the most sense for the communities that are being served and the locations that are most meaningful to that community.

As a practicing music therapist in the United States, Winter works in a clinical setting where clients come to a room that is outfitted with a piano, a guitar, a variety of percussion instruments such as hand drums and frame drums, and other auxiliary percussion such as maracas and jingle bells. Clients contract for services, which happen at a prescribed time of day and week and last for a prescribed amount of time such as 50 minutes for 15 weeks. Music therapists are bound to maintain client confidentiality and the mandates of the Healthcare Insurance Portability and Accountability Act (HIPAA), which assures that client information is only shared with parties that have a right to that information.

This type of service delivery is very difficult in a place such as Malawi where the community is central to the survival of each individual and where the ideals of confidentiality become reconfigured by the environment. Malawians have a collectivist culture in which they are often in very close physical contact and where their daily lives unfold in settings where there are no windows or doors. Therefore, the overarching tenets of CoMT were a more fitting framework for the community-based Malawian context. The role of the music therapist, then, was to understand the sociocultural role of music within the classrooms and communities in order to create points of accessibility for schoolchildren with disabilities.

Year two: workshops and discoveries

In May 2013, the authors returned to Malawi for three weeks. Given this very truncated period of time, it was determined that the work should proceed with great care. Therefore, the best course of action was to provide sustainable and culturally responsive professional development that teachers could implement in their own classrooms over time. The authors were committed to the idea that Malawian educators are the experts in their classrooms and that we were bringing tips, techniques, and strategies that may enhance their existing teaching practices.

In service to this effort, the authors spent several days observing and interviewing educators to become familiarized with the local context. These observations were an access point to the music and rituals of Malawian culture, educational practices across the primary school grades, and an opportunity to continue to build upon Blanks's established relationships with educators and administrators at the schools.

The authors were joined by a new NGO, the CharChar Trust, that provided books for teachers to use in their classrooms. The authors decided to develop and implement a series of workshops on best practices in literacy education to support teachers in using these new books effectively. This decision did not come as a request from the teachers and was not predicated on suggestions from the teachers.

Several workshops were organized based on perceptions of need and only included strategies that have been effective for Western teachers/therapists. These strategies included opening and closing rituals involving music, evidence-based

PHOTO 15.3 Grade 8 children writing practice exams (Winter, 2012b).

literacy strategies validated in Western classrooms, and information about how educators could continue to identify children with disabilities in their classrooms.

At the end of the workshops all teachers were asked to set goals for incorporating
these strategies into their practices. When the authors returned one year later, there
was no evidence that teachers were using the strategies. Reports from our NGO
partners who visited the classrooms throughout the school year and self-reports
from the teachers suggested the same. One issue that became evident was an overall
culture of protecting material resources, as resources were limited and difficult to
obtain. The NGO that supplied the reading materials took great care in creating
a child-friendly curriculum with books for different reading levels, crayons, pen-
cils, erasers, and posters. However, those materials were largely untouched during
the year as they were too precious to "ruin." This preservationist attitude kept the
resources out of the classroom and locked away in a storage area to be used only for
very special occasions and only by teachers or upper-grade-level students.

Year three: disruptions to collaboration

In 2014, the research team comprised co-authors Blanks and Winter and a graduate student from the Special Education Teacher Training Program at Radford University. The literacy specialist was committed to a study abroad program in Malawi and returned to those duties rather than accompanying Blanks and Winter on this trip. At this time, Malawi was in the midst of a volatile presidential election, which resulted in significant disruptions to our access to the schools and prevented us from being able to implement any professional development. Limited time at the schools was spent in observing classroom teaching practices and meeting with administrators.

The team also visited a private and a public teacher training college in order to learn more about the educational requirements for teachers. During this visit it was decided, without teacher input, that the team needed a more sustained presence throughout the school year. To this end, the researchers decided to work with a partner to establish a technology pathway for ongoing professional development and to collect data on teachers' experiences.

Year four: distance education

In 2015, Blanks and Winter recorded several 20- to 30-minute videos demonstrating strategies selected by the authors. The videos included ideas for further development of classroom music experiences and continued curricular recommendations capitalizing on the tenets of Universal Design for Learning (UDL) with a focus on the primary school curriculum established by the Malawian government.

The emphasis of UDL is to develop flexible learning environments that can accommodate individual learning differences (www.cast.org). In order to address the needs of all students, an educator should provide multiple means of engagement, representation, and action and expression. Blanks and Winter learned that it was difficult to identify Malawian children with disabilities when there were over 200 children in the room. While efforts to identify children were of utmost importance, it was also important to consider how to adapt the learning environment to meet the needs of all children.

UDL is a common practice in the educational practices in the United States and is in line with SDG Target 4.1 that seeks to ensure that all girls and boys complete free, equitable, and quality '. . . education that leads to relevant and effective learning outcomes. UDL approaches also create an environment in which people with disabilities, indigenous peoples, and children in vulnerable situations have greater access to the educational offerings within the classroom and across grade levels (SDG #4.5)

To create the videos at a professional quality level, Blanks and Winter partnered with the Communication Department at Radford and recruited undergraduate and graduate music therapy students to help model the music experiences. This endeavor was rife with challenges, as the attempts to use the internet to deliver the videos failed. Ultimately our NGO contact downloaded the video in the United Kingdom, burned it onto a CD, and hand delivered it to the village schools to be played on a laptop. The outcome from the videos was a teacher-generated list requesting future professional development trainings in math education and opportunities for more formal music education initiatives. The authors did not visit Malawi in 2015 due to personal circumstances that arose for one of them.

Year five: opportunities and limitations

In 2016, the CharChar Trust contacted Blanks to ask for assistance with validating their materials as a research-based instructional intervention for Malawian students and for help in creating professional development opportunities for teachers who would be coached and sustained by NGO staff in Malawi. The researchers and the NGO fell into a pattern of informal conversations in which Blanks shared information about best practices for inclusive literacy instruction in the context of US public schools and brainstormed with the NGO staff member about how those practices may or may not work for Malawian teachers. This relationship was most accurately characterized as informal consulting and problem solving. Outcome data for this phase have not yet been evaluated.

In spite of the ongoing long-distance relationship with both NGOs, neither author has been able to return to Malawi. Ongoing work in country is prohibitively expensive, and sustained engagement is difficult when faced with competing obligations of professional work in the United States. The authors hope that collaboration can continue on some level and that a mechanism can be established to maintain an ongoing relationship that reflects the in vivo experiences of Malawian educators and the local schoolchildren with and without identified disabilities.

Reflections on the Malawi experience

The authors have been challenged to put into words all that was learned from several years of work in Malawi. The experience was unlike anything that Blanks and Winter could have imagined. Below are reflections outlining what the authors learned from this extraordinary endeavor.

Reflection 1

Malawian teachers are open to professional development. They put forth great efforts to learn new strategies that might help them to become more effective teachers for all their students. Teachers walked several miles to attend last-minute professional development sessions, watched videos that may or may not have been useful, and displayed enthusiasm for information that they could actually use with their students in the contexts of their own classrooms. This bodes exceptionally well for SDG Target 4c to substantially increase the supply of qualified teachers through the inclusion of opportunities for teacher training that include international collaboration.

Reflection 2

Changes in Malawi are only sustainable when they come from Malawians themselves. Across five years, the only intervention that demonstrated sustainable changes in teacher practice was showing the teachers how to use the identification tool developed for and by the Malawi Ministry of Special Needs Education. Unlike the other attempted interventions, this topic of professional development was requested by Malawians and was a tool that had already been a part of their school culture. Everything else offered by the authors, across several years, was based on our Western perceptions of teachers' needs and included strategies and techniques that we introduced into the Malawian context. None of these efforts created sustained changes in the teachers' knowledge or practice. Therefore, if international collaboration is a target for the UN's mission, then the collaborators must honor the expertise that is present within the communities that are being served. Collaborators must also look to the educators to define what constitutes a vulnerable population, what issues are most pressing for the students and communities, and to determine what practices are culturally sensitive and that contribute to safe, effective, and inclusive learning environments for all (SDG #4a).

Reflection 3

Similar to Reflection 2, Malawians know where they need help, and they know what kinds of help they can use. The constraints of working from a distance during years four and five taught the authors a great deal about working effectively. In year five, Blanks was able to respond to specific questions and needs that came directly from Malawians themselves, and only then was there a meaningful exchange of information that may lead to sustained changes in practice.

The authors' early hypothesis was that the lack of change in teacher practice was due to interference or competing demands from large-scale projects that are typically funded by international aid organizations. Yet, small-scale efforts have also not resulted in significant changes in teacher practice or student outcomes. As the authors reflect on this experience, they have come to believe that sustainable changes in inclusive teacher practice will only result from efforts that emerge from within the Malawian school system. The only lasting changes are those that emerged from Malawian teachers' requests for help and that relied exclusively on Malawian tools. This lesson is essential to the continued efforts of the UN in addressing the SDGs. It is of critical importance for all stakeholders to be involved and invested in any and all initiatives that unfold within these communities.

Final thoughts

Western educational and music therapy practices have originated from, and are viable in, Western contexts. While the authors were sensitive to the environment and spent time in observation of educational practices, an opportunity was missed to collaborate with the Malawian educators. The authors wished to deconstruct their roles as experts, yet those roles remained firmly in place when they found themselves working in a context that was foreign to a Western mode of practice. The role of expert was in some ways a compensatory strategy for the unique environment and the extensive and overwhelming tasks that Blanks and Winter had hoped to accomplish.

The authors now recognize that Malawians know what changes are possible within their local contexts. This simple yet powerful idea is critically important when thinking about sustainable changes in cultures and communities vastly different from our own. When the authors listened to Malawian requests for help, they were able to provide actual help. When the authors assumed that they knew what was best, based on their Western observational lenses and experiences, they failed to connect with the teachers in meaningful ways. Going forward, it is imperative to recognize that changes happen slowly and that small and incremental steps should never be viewed as a limitation, but rather a cause for celebration! Finally, it should be understood that an outsider's definition of help isn't always helpful.

References

African Vision Malawi. *Our Vision*. September 4, 2018. www.africanvision.org.uk/.

Bloom, B. *Taxonomy of Educational Objectives: The Classification of Educational Goals*, 1st ed. New York: Longmans, Green, 1956.

CAST. *Universal Design for Learning Guidelines Version 2.2*, September 4, 2018. http://udl guidelines.cast.org.

Itimu, A. N. and Koptez, P. B. Malawi's Special Needs Education (SNE): Perspectives and Comparisons of Practice and Progress. *Journal of Research in Special Educational Needs*, 8(3), 2008: 153–160. Doi: 10.1111/j.1471-3802.2008.00113.x.

Lang, R. *Disability Policy Audit in Namibia, Swaziland, Malawi and Mozambique: Final Report*. Prepared by the Southern African Federation of the Disabled, University College, London, 2008.

Martin, W. "Ranked: The 28 Poorest Countries in the World: Where People Live on Less Than $1,000 Per Year." *Business Insider*, 2018. www.businessinsider.com/poorest-countries-in-the-world-2018-5.

Mathanga, D. P., Walker, E. D., Wilson, M. L., Ali, D., Taylor, T. E. and Laufer, M. K. "Malaria Control in Malawi: Current Status and Directions for the Future." *Acta Tropica*, 121, 2013: 212–217.

Stige, B. and Aarø, L. E. *Invitation to Community Music Therapy*. New York, NY: Routledge University Press, 2012.

Tataryn, M., Polack, S., Chokotho, L., Mulwafu, W., Kayange, P., Banks, L. M. and Kuper, H. "Childhood Disability in Malawi: A Population-Based Assessment Using the Key Informant Method." *BMC Pediatrics*, 17(1), 2017: 198.

UNAIDS. "Country: Malawi, 2018." www.unaids.org/en/regionscountries/countries/malawi.

United Nations. "Sustainable Development Goals Knowledge Platform, 2018." https://sustainable development.un.org/topics/sustainabledevelopmentgoals.

The World Bank. "World Bank Development Indicators, Malawi, 2015." http://databank. worldbank.org/data/reports.aspx?source=2&country=MWI.

Winter, P. "Rural school block building M'bangombe Primary School." *Personal photograph*, 2012a.

Winter, P. "Grade 8 children writing practice exams." *Personal photograph*, 2012b.

Winter, P. "Rift valley ringed by the Mangochi escarpment." *Personal photograph*, 2013.

CONCLUSION

Tay Keong Tan, Milenko Gudić and Patricia M. Flynn

The 2030 Agenda

When the United Nations (UN) General Assembly adopted the intergovernmental agreement and declaration, "Transforming Our World: The 2030 Agenda for Sustainable Development" (the 2030 Agenda), the Sustainable Development Goals (SDGs) were brought to the forefront of the global development agenda. These goals, although they remain nonbinding and aspirational for the nations of the world, present a unifying worldwide agenda, applicable to all countries, despite national and regional differences (UN General Assembly, 2015). Building upon the progress made by the Millennium Development Goals (MDGs) from 2000 to 2015, and operationalized into 169 specific, measurable and time-bound objectives and some 232 indicators, the SDGs focus the world's attention on the most serious challenges facing humanity over the 15-year time frame, 2016–2030. Jeffrey Sachs, Professor of Health Policy and Management at Columbia University, postulated that the world is entering a new "Age of Sustainable Development," an epoch in which the nations of the world will collaborate and contribute to address the most intractable problems of persistent extreme poverty, social exclusion, economic injustice, poor governance, and environmental degradation (Sachs, 2015).

Yet, at the inception of the 2030 Agenda in September 2015, humanity's very survival was said to be gravely at risk, as monitored by the Doomsday Clock, which represents in a countdown the likelihood of a man-made global catastrophe that would destroy human civilization as we know it. Maintained since 1947 by the members of the Bulletin of the Atomic Scientists, in early 2020 the Doomsday Clock was just 100 seconds to midnight (which signifies the closeness to man-made global catastrophe, like climate change and nuclear war), the closest it has been since 1953 (Bulletin of the Atomic Scientists, 2017).

At the same time, atmospheric chemist and Nobel laureate Paul Crutzen and other experts have argued (since 2000) for the term "Anthropocene Age" to denote this geological timescale as the "new age of Man." This is because humanity has caused severe climate change, mass extinctions of plant and animal species, polluted oceans and the atmosphere and permanent alteration of Earth's ecosystems. This new epoch follows the Holocene Age, designated by the International Union of Geological Sciences as the geological epoch of the planet since the last major ice age. The Holocene Age was characterized by the past 12,000 years of stable climate during which all human civilizations developed.

In October 2018, the UN Intergovernmental Panel on Climate Change (IPCC) released its report calling for urgent climate action tied to the global targets set by the Paris Climate Accord in 2016 to keep temperatures no higher than 1.5°C above the pre-industrial average (IPCC, 2018.) In this report, climate scientists reviewed over 6,000 published works and concluded that we have only a dozen years before such temperatures will exceed 1.5°C above the pre-industrial level. Beyond this threshold, they warned that the planet would experience heightened risks of droughts; floods; sea-level rise from ice melts; extreme weather patterns and the ensuing food scarcity, water stress and climate-related poverty for hundreds of millions of people around the world. They insist that humanity must transform the world economy within the next few years, or face global damage at the price tag of $54 trillion (ibid).

While there is hope for political resolve and concerted action by multiple stake-holders worldwide to bring about real change and advance the Global Goals, these trends portend a new urgency for the work of advancing sustainable development. The lackluster early results in pursuit of the Paris Agreement do not inspire opti-mism in the world's delivery on the promises of the 2030 Agenda for Sustainable Development. Jeffrey Sach's "Age of Sustainable Development" is far from assured.

It is in this global context that we assess the work by entrepreneurs, community leaders and civic activists, many of them unsung heroes working in the trenches, who have developed and implemented significant strategies and solutions to tackle enduring sustainability challenges. These individuals emerged from unlikely places, from corporate boardrooms and community meeting places to public offices and factory floors. Often, a single person or a small group of people will serve as the dauntless driving force behind innovative programs and courageous experiments that make all the difference to the most deprived social groups and the most intrac-table problems. Somehow, these individuals were able to turn abstract goals and principles of sustainability into concrete programs and effective action. The follow-ing sections focus on the lessons learned from each of them.

Lessons learned

1. Expect obstacles and pitfalls

The challenges associated with the struggles for attainment of these Global Goals are as diverse and complex as the variety of human societies, national conditions and natural ecosystems across the globe. Despite decades of economic growth and technological advances, our world is plagued by poverty, hunger, disease, conflicts and inequality, and many societies are under the strains of environmental changes and governance failure.

As Glen Martin argues in Chapter 3, there are inherent contradictions between the structure of the contemporary international order based on sovereign nation-states and the concerns for global collective action and burden sharing embodied in the Global Goals. Martin highlights the presence of big-power dominance, imperialism and militarism in today's world. As powerful countries often ignore international law, reneging on treaties they signed and showing scant regard for international norms, the 2030 Agenda will be hampered by many wars that are currently devastating our world and its environment. Noteworthy is the fact that the nations of the world spend some $1.5 trillion annually on militarism worldwide. Imagine if instead these resources were used to address global sustainability.

There are also concerns that the 2030 Agenda is a nonbinding intergovernmental agreement that leaves it to national governments to decide on their implementation and obligation to fulfill its mandate regarding problems within its borders. Some states may neglect their commitments to advance the SDGs, reflective of the checkered record in the protection of universal human rights as required by the Universal Declaration of Human Rights (1948). The dependence on the national governments of countries to achieve the SDGs within their own jurisdiction may burden the poorest and least capable countries that tend to have the largest development-related problems and tasks.

In the light of these structural and systemic issues, the advancement of the SDGs highlighted throughout this book is *not* usually the result of a powerful government or big multinational corporation. Instead, progress tends to come from individuals and small groups of people, who work with severe resource constraints and are often hampered (rather than helped) by powerful local administrations and political interests. This is evident, for example, in Nuwan's case study (Chapter 6) of the novel waste recycling program in Sri Lanka's plantations, where the activists had to overcome resistance from plantation officials and local community members. These activists have to convince stakeholder groups, including the community, plantation companies, waste collectors and recyclers and local governments, of the benefits of waste management programs.

El Jadidi et al.'s Chapter 10 on women's struggle for representation on corporate boards in Africa demonstrates that equality (like women's rights) is not readily handed over to female executives and leaders. Rather, these individuals overcome entrenched organizational obstacles and cultural biases to claim these rights. These obstacles and opposition require creative solutions and pragmatic programs to overcome them in order to realize the sustainability projects to advance a more economically vibrant, socially inclusive, and environmentally sustainable future.

2. Use adaption and experimentation

As the stories and case studies from the trenches of practice reveal, favorable results and desired outcomes are far from guaranteed, while sacrifice and obstacles are often inevitable. The global-scale challenges call for the SDGs to be translated beyond bold concepts and aspirational targets into concrete programs and feasible plans that are substantively valuable, locally acceptable and operationally implementable. The path forward usually requires difficult learning, experimentation and adaptation by multiple stakeholders.

In the global capitalist economic system, vast numbers of poor people are low-wage laborers with very few social safety nets. The companies and the global supply chain are structured to distribute the largest benefits to capital owners and investors. Corporations and business enterprises are expected to pursue self-interested profit maximization for their investors, while they externalize the costs of production and consumption onto society, the natural world or other persons. Hence, out-of-the-box thinking and novel solutions are often needed to counter powerful forces in a culture characterized by short-term profits, perpetual growth and low cost and expedient forms of production and consumption.

Toward this end, Isabel Rimanoczy, the protagonist in Margaret A. Goralski's case study in Chapter 2, has constantly experimented with new ways to promote a Sustainability Mindset to infuse values of sustainability in people's everyday lives. These values and principles "are good for themselves, but are also good for the earth and the people around them," but they are very hard to institute and sustain over time. Despite having built a strong global network of like-minded academics in the UN Principles of Responsible Management Education Working Group on the Sustainability Mindset and LEAP!, Rimanoczy has to continue to final novel ways to seek funding and institutional support to sustain her work.

She invented and experimented with multiple modes and media in her advocacy for the Sustainability Mindset. These range from writing books and articles on the "being dimension" of human development and presenting at global conferences to the use of LEAP Café, Storytelling Circles and a virtual fast-track course on sustainability for academics around the world. These demonstrate an indomitable spirit that persists in the face of the odds.

In Chapter 11, Zayer et al.'s study on the renaissance of gender research in the field of marketing is fueled by the emerging global political and social conversations on gender issues. The paths taken by academics and researchers to promote greater attention to and recognition of gender issues in marketing are multifaceted and innovative. These individuals adopted perspectives and frameworks that range from dominance and oppression, commodification, gender violence, neocolonialism and intersectionality to the capabilities approach. This is particularly important because the SDGs have been criticized for being weak in recognizing gender equality as a multidimensional concept. The UN targets for SDG #5 on gender equality do not include provisions on ending discrimination, violence against gender expression and denials of sexual and reproductive rights based on a person's sexual orientation (Gupta and Vegelin, 2016). These important fundamental human rights are crucial to social inclusion.

In Chapter 1 ("Struggles and Successes of Transformative Learning for the SDGs: A Case Study"), Cottafava et al. discuss the struggles and successes of a project in transformative learning for the advancement of the SDGs at the University of Torino (UniTo).

Experimental components of the program Education for Sustainable Development included experiential learning approaches such as team gaming, multi-stakeholder simulations in problem solving and negotiations and the use of project-cycle management and visual thinking tools. The program also experiments with public speaking and with interviews that were publicized on social media networks (Facebook, Twitter and Instagram) and the YouTube channel of the Green Office of UniTo.

Workable solutions inevitably involve trade-offs and compromises that address the concerns of diverse groups. These champions forge paths forward – advocating ideas, mobilizing support and exercising leadership – in diverse nations, organizations and communities. In their struggle, they develop plans and solutions that inevitably involve adaptation, sacrifice, trade-offs and compromises that address the concerns of competing groups.

3. Forge productive partnerships and local participation

Another lesson from the early successes, productive failures and personal practices in seeking sustainability and social responsibility is the importance of partnerships. A critically important characteristic exemplified by these global champions is the willingness to work with other stakeholders to advance the cause. In Chapter 15, the poignant lessons by Blanks and Winter from their years of outreach to the rural schools in Malawi underscore the important of stakeholder participation in defining the kind and mode of interventions. Western educational and music therapy practices that have worked well, and are viable in Western school contexts, may not be sustainably practiced in the poorest schools in the developing world. This remains true despite the best intentions and valiant efforts of foreign technical assistance professionals.

Social inclusion is not only good for sustainability projects; it is also an important tenet of good leadership and team performance. Sander et al. in Chapter 4 advocate for specific measures to address unconscious biases and to foster an inclusive working environment, which social entrepreneurs could take to heart. Inclusive leadership strengthens organizations at the forefront of sustainable development, by unleashing the advantages of diversity of skills and perspectives that are so critical for partnerships that work.

In the case study of creative industries in rural Serbia in Chapter 8, Hristina Mikić documents events such as the Creative Economy Forums and Rural Creative Industries Fair that bring new partnerships of mutual benefit to creative entrepreneurs, working with NGO members, government bodies, touristic organizations and other businesspeople. In some of these projects, international partnerships and local community involvement make the difference between success and failure. Work on advancing social goals, environmental objectives and economic development must be brought down to local realities if they are to succeed in changing the world for the stakeholders.

In the chapter on social innovators in Morocco (Chapter 13), El Ghaib and Allali present several compelling case studies that represent "a new generation of socially inclusive and economically self-sustaining to profitable businesses" – all initiated and incubated by women social innovators. In each of the cases (Enactus Morocco, Amendy Foods, HydroBarley and Go Energyless Solutions), the entrepreneurs sought and cultivated important partnerships with public and private stakeholders and secured adequate funding and resources to help scale and sustain their projects.

Vázquez-Maguirre writes in Chapter 9 about three successful social enterprises in indigenous rural communities in Mexico, Peru and Guatemala. These ventures were driven by partnerships and locally centered participatory processes that made all the difference to the empowerment and mobilization of indigenous women. Participatory processes and support from partners helped the indigenous women overcome obstacles in the male-dominated culture in each community. Such support enabled these women to incubate productive entities, secure access to decent job opportunities, undertake business training and skills development and institute governance practices based on local values. Participation and partnership gave dignity and self-respect to the indigenous women and made them realize their potential as social entrepreneurs and community leaders.

Finally, the analysis of Canada's feminist foreign policy (Chapter 12) by Kilgour demonstrates that Canada's feminist international aid policy and Canadian MNCs can play powerful and enduring roles in addressing gender issues through their development assistance and commercial activities in Latin American countries. Her review of Canada's SDG initiatives in support of gender equality provides insights into ways by which national governments can work constructively with businesses to embed sustainability practices, especially the socially inclusive policies in promoting gender equality and the empowerment of women issues, in foreign policy and international business practices.

4. Leverage on new and innovative technologies

Wynn and Jones's discussion of ICT4D in Chapter 7 highlights the enabling and connecting power of the information and communications technology (ICT) industry. ICT can be a key enabler of change in social entrepreneurship programs and one that can help create significant business opportunities. Wynn and Jones note that ICT services are spreading quickly around the world, in the "near-ubiquity of mobile, spread of broadband, more big/open/real-time data, use of field sensors/embedded computing, more social media, more crowd-sourcing models, more cloud, more smartphones, and 3D printing." ICT can be an important means for people to transcend the constraints of geography and political boundaries at greater speeds and lower costs.

New technology, especially with the recent advances of new energy and green technology, can directly foster positive impacts on the environment by reducing pollution and improving the conservation of nonrenewable resources. New technologies have the potential to increase the rate of diffusion of a wide range of sustainability practices across an economy. Acceleration of the uptake of these technologies may be the key to achieving many of the SDGs by their target date of 2030.

In the midst of a large and growing digital divide between technologically advanced countries and technologically lagging economies, the transfer of innovative applications alone may benefit some enterprises, but it may obscure the endemic problem of a widening global digital divide and an emerging "AI arms race." Developing countries need systematic assistance and sustained developmental aid to strengthen their education systems, business enterprises and governance to enable them to reap the benefits of green technologies, underscored by the Global Goals Industry, innovation and infrastructure (SDG #9), sustainable cities and com- munities (SDG #11) and partnerships for the goals (SDG #17).

Hristina Mikić's study of the Creative Economy Group Foundation in Pirot, Serbia (Chapter 8) shows that creative use of digital platforms can enable rural craftspersons and entrepreneurs to connect with new clients and better market their products in cost-efficient ways. In Chapter 5 on community renewable energy (CRE), Deanna Grant-Smith and Judith Marie Herbst provide a powerful case study on Australia's Hepburn Wind project, demonstrating how new energy tech- nologies can fuel promising community renewable energy from the bottom-up. The authors highlight the importance of "deep consultation and ongoing com- munication with affected stakeholders" to safeguard the reputation of the project. Stakeholder management strategies to build trust and confidence are shown to be critical to the successful implementation of new and innovative technologies. This Wind project is a grassroots initiative that leverages the advancement of green tech- nology for an affordable, reliable, sustainable, decentralized and clean energy supply. This is particularly relevant to SDG #7 on affordable and clean energy.

Final remarks

These lessons from ongoing struggles and early successes – including productive failures and emerging practices – are precious nuggets that can be identified, ana- lyzed and promulgated for interdisciplinary learning by, and for the inspiration of individuals, organizations, communities and nations worldwide. The book also seeks to inform and enrich the curricula in universities, training institutions and schools to prepare future generations of citizens, leaders and activists with the ethos and values of advancing global sustainability in personal lives and in professional practices.

References

Bulletin of the Atomic Scientists. "The Doomsday Clock: A Timeline of Conflict, Culture, and Change." May 2017. Accessed February 24, 2020. http://thebulletin.org/timeline.

Gupta, J. and Vegelin, C. "Sustainable Development Goals and Inclusive Development." *Inter- national Environmental Agreements: Politics, Law and Economics*, 16, 2016: 433–448. https:// doi.org/10.1007/s10784-016-9323-z.

Intergovernmental Panel on Climate Change. *Special Report: Global Warming of 1.5°C*. Geneva, Switzerland: United Nations, October 2018. Accessed January 18, 2019. www. ipcc.ch/sr15/chapter/summary-for-policy-makers/.

Sachs, J. *The Age of Sustainable Development*. New York, NY: Columbia University Press. 2015.

UN General Assembly. *Transforming Our World: The 2030 Agenda for Sustainable Development*. New York: United Nations, October 2015.

INDEX